MANHATTAN GMAT

The Official Guide Companion for Sentence Correction

GMAT Strategy Supplement

This book provides detailed, step-by-step approaches to all 158
Sentence Correction problems in *The Official Guide for GMAT
Review, 13th Edition.*

The Official Guide Companion for Sentence Correction GMAT Strategy Guide, First Edition

10-digit International Standard Book Number: 1-937707-41-5
13-digit International Standard Book Number: 978-1-937707-41-5
eISBN: 978-1-937707-42-2

Layout Design: Dan McNaney and Cathy Huang
Cover Design: Evyn Williams and Dan McNaney
Cover Photography: Alli Ugosoli

INSTRUCTIONAL GUIDE SERIES

0 GMAT Roadmap
(ISBN: 978-1-935707-69-1)

1 Fractions, Decimals, & Percents
(ISBN: 978-1-935707-63-9)

2 Algebra
(ISBN: 978-1-935707-62-2)

3 Word Problems
(ISBN: 978-1-935707-68-4)

4 Geometry
(ISBN: 978-1-935707-64-6)

5 Number Properties
(ISBN: 978-1-935707-65-3)

6 Critical Reasoning
(ISBN: 978-1-935707-61-5)

7 Reading Comprehension
(ISBN: 978-1-935707-66-0)

8 Sentence Correction
(ISBN: 978-1-935707-67-7)

9 Integrated Reasoning & Essay
(ISBN: 978-1-935707-83-7)

SUPPLEMENTAL GUIDE SERIES

Math GMAT Supplement Guides

Foundations of GMAT Math
(ISBN: 978-1-935707-59-2)

Advanced GMAT Quant
(ISBN: 978-1-935707-15-8)

The Official Guide Companion
(ISBN: 978-0-984178-01-8)

Verbal GMAT Supplement Guides

Foundations of GMAT Verbal
(ISBN: 978-1-935707-01-9)

**The Official Guide Companion
for Sentence Correction**
(ISBN: 978-1-937707-41-5)

MANHATTAN
PREP

December 3rd, 2013

Dear Student,

Thank you for picking up a copy of *The Official Guide Companion for Sentence Correction*. I hope this book provides just the guidance you need to get the most out of your GMAT studies.

As with most accomplishments, there were many people involved in the creation of the book you are holding. First and foremost is Zeke Vanderhoek, the founder of Manhattan Prep. Zeke was a lone tutor in New York when he started the company in 2000. Now, 13 years later, the company has instructors and offices nationwide and contributes to the studies and successes of thousands of students each year.

Our Manhattan Prep Strategy Guides are based on the continuing experiences of our instructors and students. For this volume, we are particularly indebted to our instructors Kim Cabot, Whitney Garner, Dave Mahler, Emily Sledge, Ryan Starr, and Tommy Wallach for their hard work editing the explanations. Very special thanks to Liz Ghini and Stacey Koprince, our lead content developers and the primary authors and editors of this book. Dan McNaney and Cathy Huang provided their design expertise to make the books as user-friendly as possible, and Liz Krisher made sure all the moving pieces came together at just the right time. Beyond providing additions and edits for this book, Chris Ryan and Noah Teitelbaum continue to be the driving force behind all of our curriculum efforts. Their leadership is invaluable. Finally, thank you to all of the Manhattan Prep students who have provided input and feedback over the years. This book wouldn't be half of what it is without your voice.

At Manhattan Prep, we continually aspire to provide the best instructors and resources possible. We hope that you will find our commitment manifest in this book. If you have any questions or comments, please email me at dgonzalez@manhattanprep.com. I'll look forward to reading your comments, and I'll be sure to pass them along to our curriculum team.

Thanks again, and best of luck preparing for the GMAT!

Sincerely,

Dan Gonzalez
President
Manhattan Prep

HOW TO ACCESS YOUR ONLINE RESOURCES

If you...

⊙ **are a registered Manhattan GMAT student**

and have received this book as part of your course materials, you have AUTOMATIC access to ALL of our online resources. This includes all practice exams, Question Banks, and online updates to this book. To access these resources, follow the instructions in the Welcome Guide provided to you at the start of your program. Do NOT follow the instructions below.

⊙ **purchased this book from the Manhattan GMAT online store or at one of our centers**

1. Go to www.manhattangmat.com/practicecenter.cfm.

2. Log in using the username and password used when your account was set up.

⊙ **purchased this book at a retail location**

1. Create an account with Manhattan GMAT at the website: www.manhattangmat.com/createaccount.cfm.

2. Go to: www.manhattangmat.com/access.cfm.

3. Follow the instructions on the screen.

Your one year of online access begins on the day that you register your book at the above URL.

You only need to register your product ONCE at the above URL. To use your online resources any time AFTER you have completed the registration process, log in to the following URL: www.manhattangmat.com/practicecenter.cfm.

Please note that online access is nontransferable. This means that only NEW and UNREGISTERED copies of the book will grant you online access. Previously used books will NOT provide any online resources.

⊙ **purchased an eBook version of this book**

1. Create an account with Manhattan GMAT at the website: www.manhattangmat.com/createaccount.cfm.

2. Email a copy of your purchase receipt to gmat@manhattanprep.com to activate your resources. Please be sure to use the same email address to create an account that you used to purchase the eBook.

For any technical issues, email techsupport@manhattanprep.com or call 800-576-4628.

Please refer to the following page for a description of the online resources that come with this book.

YOUR ONLINE RESOURCES

Your purchase includes ONLINE ACCESS to the following:

⊛ 6 Computer-Adaptive Online Practice Exams

The 6 full-length computer-adaptive practice exams included with the purchase of this book are delivered online using Manhattan Prep's proprietary computer-adaptive test engine. The exams adapt to your ability level by drawing from a bank of more than 1,200 unique questions of varying difficulty levels written by Manhattan Prep's expert instructors, all of whom have scored in the 99th percentile on the Official GMAT. At the end of each exam you will receive a score, an analysis of your results, and the opportunity to review detailed explanations for each question. You may choose to take the exams timed or untimed.

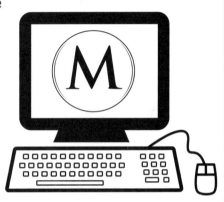

The content presented in this book is updated periodically to ensure that it reflects the GMAT's most current trends and is as accurate as possible. You may view any known errors or minor changes upon registering for online access.

Important Note: The 6 computer adaptive online exams included with the purchase of this book are the SAME exams that you receive upon purchasing ANY book in the Manhattan Prep Complete Strategy Guide Set.

⊛ *OG Archer* Official Guide Tracker

The OG Archer is an online interface for answering OG problems and measuring your performance. Time yourself on individual questions, mark the problems you guessed on, and note those you'd like to do again later. Then, view performance statistics and review answer explanations written by Manhattan Prep Instructors.

⊛ Online Updates to the Contents in this Book

The content presented in this book is updated periodically to ensure that it reflects the GMAT's most current trends. You may view all updates, including any known errors or changes, upon registering for online access.

TABLE *of* CONTENTS

Chapter *of* 1

The Official Guide Companion for Sentence Correction

Introduction

In This Chapter...

Introduction

Do read this chapter first! Yes, we know that introduction chapters are usually boring, but we've stripped this down to the absolute necessities, we promise.

You want to succeed. We want you to succeed. This chapter will help you to do so!

What This Dook Does and Doesn't Do

This guide provides in-depth explanations for all 158 Sentence Correction questions from *The Official Guide for GMAT Review, 13th Edition (OG13)*.

While the explanations discuss grammar, this isn't actually a grammar book. We've already published one of those: our *Sentence Correction GMAT Strategy Guide*. This book does include a pretty extensive glossary at the end but, if you want more, jump over to *Sentence Correction*.

In this book, the questions are organized into four broad difficulty buckets: Easier, Moderate, Harder, and Devilish. We based these ratings primarily on data collected from student responses to the questions. These ratings don't correspond to any particular GMAT score; they reflect *relative* difficulty levels among the questions.

How do you approach these questions? Well:

If you've already done a lot of *OG13* questions…	Dive right into the explanations!
If you're not sure where to start…	Start with some lower-numbered questions, which are often easier or moderate questions. Move to higher-numbered problems as you feel ready.
If you learn new things from explanations even when you answer the question correctly…	Then don't jump to higher-numbered questions yet!

How an Explanation Works

Question # and a brief description

Lists the correct answer as well as the errors in the four incorrect answers.

Describes the first clues that a top SC test-taker would spot

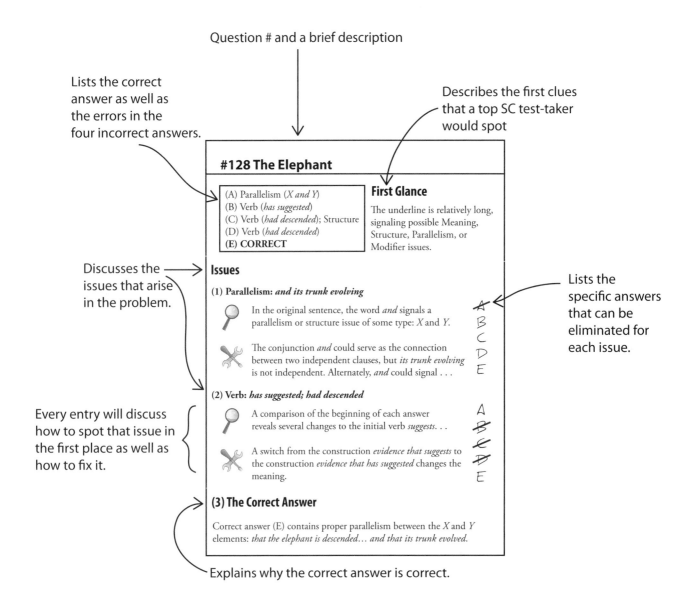

#128 The Elephant

(A) Parallelism (*X and Y*)
(B) Verb (*has suggested*)
(C) Verb (*had descended*); Structure
(D) Verb (*had descended*)
(E) CORRECT

First Glance

The underline is relatively long, signaling possible Meaning, Structure, Parallelism, or Modifier issues.

Discusses the issues that arise in the problem.

Issues

(1) Parallelism: *and its trunk evolving*

In the original sentence, the word *and* signals a parallelism or structure issue of some type: *X* and *Y*.

The conjunction *and* could serve as the connection between two independent clauses, but *its trunk evolving* is not independent. Alternately, *and* could signal . . .

(2) Verb: *has suggested; had descended*

A comparison of the beginning of each answer reveals several changes to the initial verb *suggests*. . .

A switch from the construction *evidence that suggests* to the construction *evidence that has suggested* changes the meaning.

Lists the specific answers that can be eliminated for each issue.

Every entry will discuss how to spot that issue in the first place as well as how to fix it.

(3) The Correct Answer

Correct answer (E) contains proper parallelism between the *X* and *Y* elements: *that the elephant is descended… and that its trunk evolved.*

Explains why the correct answer is correct.

MANHATTAN
PREP

How to Do an SC Problem

Overall, the main goal when starting any test question is the same: *find a starting point*. On GMAT Sentence Correction questions, you use that starting point to cross off wrong answers:

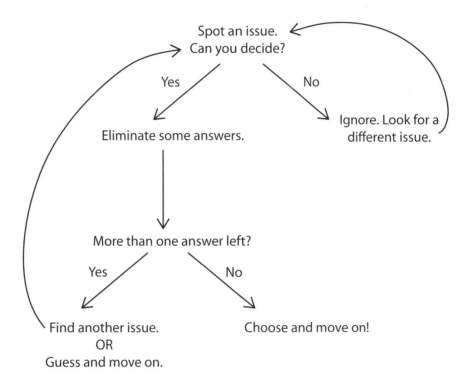

That doesn't look too terrible, does it? Unfortunately, it can get more complicated. In Sentence Correction, there are multiple possible locations for that starting point. How do you actually find these Issues that need to be addressed? In addition, how do you know when to guess and move on?

Your "default" SC process will answer all of these questions.

Step 1: Take Your **First Glance**

Step 2: **Read** the Sentence

Step 3: **Compare** the Answers

Step 4: **Decide** and Move On

As you learn this process below, keep two overarching principles in mind:

> **1. Whenever you find an issue that you know how to handle, tackle it immediately!**
>
> **2. If you spot a difference that you *don't* know how to handle, ignore it.**

Step 1: Take Your First Glance (3–5 seconds)

To start, take a First Glance at the problem to spot any clues that will give you some quick hints about potential issues.

Here's an example:

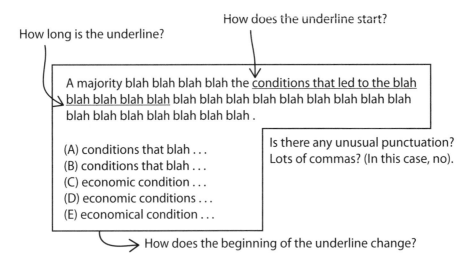

Do any of those clues tell you what to think about when you read the sentence?

For example:

> *First Glance:*
>
> The first word of the underline, *conditions*, varies in the answers. Sometimes it's singular (*condition*) and sometimes it's plural. I should look for singular / plural issues (either subject–verb or pronouns) when reading the sentence.

You'll learn how to perform a First Glance as you use this book.

Step 2: Read the Sentence

After the First Glance, read the original sentence, keeping in mind any clues you might have spotted during the First Glance. Read until you spot something or you reach the period, whichever comes first.

As always, whenever you spot something that you know how to handle, tackle it!

Here's the full example sentence:

> A majority of analysts believe that the <u>conditions that led to the economic depression has also caused</u> the value of the local currency to drop relative to the currencies of other countries.

As you're reading, you might think:

Read the Original Sentence:

Hmm. *Conditions* is a plural subject. Let's see. The verb is *has caused*. *Conditions has caused* … This is wrong!

Because you found an outright error in the original sentence, you now know that answer (A) is wrong (this answer always repeats the original underline). Cross it off immediately.

Next, scan the remaining answers and cross off any that repeat this same error. This step is so important that we're going to repeat it:

Any time you find an error, cross off *all* answers that contain that same error!

Here are the five answers; check the subject–verb pairs:

(A) conditions that led to the economic depression has also caused

(B) conditions *that led to the economical depression* had also caused

(C) *economic* condition *that led to the depression* have also caused

(D) *economic* conditions *that led to the depression* have also caused

(E) *economical* condition *that led to the depression* will be causing

In your mind, gray out or try to ignore the pieces that you don't want. Just concentrate on what you need.

Keep track of your answers on your scrap paper. Answer (A) is already wrong. Answer (C) pairs a singular subject with a plural verb. Cross both off.

Okay, what next? You need to find another issue to tackle.

A
B
C
D
E

Possibility #1: If you spotted anything else while considering your starting point, address that issue next.

Possibility #2: Return to the original sentence and continue reading until you find a second issue or reach the end of the sentence.

Possibility #3: Compare the answer choices. (We'll talk more about this below.)

While tackling the subject–verb issue, you might have noticed that those verbs changed tenses as well. Should the sentence be in past perfect, present perfect, or future? If you know, tackle that next.

Step 3: Compare the Answers

At some point, you'll go to the answers. The crucial strategy here is to *compare the answer choices against each other.* Don't just read each choice by itself!

Here's the example problem again:

A majority of analysts believe that the <u>conditions that led to the economic depression has also caused</u> the value of the local currency to drop relative to the currencies of other countries.

(A) conditions that led to the economic depression has also caused

(B) conditions that led to the economical depression had also caused

(C) economic condition that led to the depression have also caused

(D) economic conditions that led to the depression have also caused

(E) economical condition that led to the depression will be causing

You've already eliminated (A) and (C) for bad subject–verb agreement. Let's say that you spot the difference in verb tense, but you're not sure how to tackle that. Ignore that issue—don't spend another second on it—and look for something else.

Compare the remaining answers vertically. What other differences do you spot?

The word *economic* changes form—sometimes, the answer uses *economical* instead. Also, the word moves around; sometimes, it is before the noun *depression* and other times, it's before the word *condition(s)*.

The location of the word is a red herring (something designed to throw you off the trail of the answer). It's acceptable to talk about the *economic conditions* or the *economic depression*.

The form of the word, however, is a major issue. The two words don't mean the same thing!

Economic refers to the economy; an *economic condition* is a monetary or business condition. *Economical*, on the other hand, typically means "in a frugal or cost-effective manner." *Economical condition*, then, means the *condition* itself is *cost-effective*—which is illogical. Answers (B) and (E) are incorrect.

MANHATTAN
PREP

Step 4: Choose an Answer and Move On

At some point, one of two things will happen: you'll get down to one answer or you'll get stuck. If you know the answer, pick it. The answer to the above question is (D).

If you get stuck at any point along the way, you can try once or twice to unstick yourself (using the techniques discussed in the next section). After that, though, pick an answer and move on.

> Do *not* agonize back and forth between the final two answers.
> Compare once, then pick and move on!

Expect to average roughly 1 minute 20 seconds to 1 minute 30 seconds on Sentence Correction. If you're approaching the 2-minute mark and you're stuck, stop being stubborn! Choose an answer and start your next question.

Why Ignoring Is Often a Wise Thing to Do

In the example above, notice that you got all the way to the answer without having to decide which verb tense was right (*had caused* versus *have caused* versus *will be causing*). That's not unusual. Many wrong answers are wrong for more than one reason, and, when the clock is ticking, you need to find just one reason to cross off an answer. On the test itself, go for the easiest material first and avoid the difficult fights as much as possible.

When you're studying, after you're done with the test or problem set, go back and review everything that was going on in each problem. Then ask yourself whether there is a better path to the answer, given what you know now.

How to Handle Harder Questions

What happens when you don't spot a starting point in the original sentence—or you don't even understand what the original sentence means? What about when the splits, or differences among the answers, are not very easy to compare? For example, a modifier might appear at the beginning of one answer choice but at the end of another.

When this happens, be flexible. If you can't understand the meaning itself, read it again—but, this time, try to break it into more manageable parts. Try to find a subject and a verb and picture just that action or activity. Ignore any modifiers. Once you have the basic idea, add any other subjects or verbs into the picture, and, finally, add in the modifiers.

If the most confusing portion is the underlined portion, try substituting a different answer choice into the sentence. If that still doesn't work, guess and move on.

If you do understand the sentence but you're struggling to find a starting point, try these two tactics:

1. Compare the beginning word of each answer choice. Also compare the ending word of each choice. Do those differences give you any clues about what the sentence might be testing?

2. Compare answer (A), which you've already read, to answer (B). Concentrate only on differences between the two and ask yourself what those differences could possibly be testing.

When the answer choices are changing so much that they're difficult to compare, you're going to start looking at chunks of the sentence. (We call a string of words that goes together, such as a modifier, a chunk.) Let's say that a modifier is jumping around in the answers. Find the equivalent modifier chunk in each choice and see where it attaches to the main sentence.

Here's an example:

(A) Manufactured in Germany, engineers in Japan designed the car.

(B) Manufactured in Germany, Japanese engineers had designed the car.

(C) Japanese engineers, manufactured in Germany, designed the car.

(D) Japanese engineers designed the car and manufactured in Germany.

(E) Japanese engineers designed the car, which was manufactured in Germany.

The modifier *manufactured in Germany* moves around in the sentence. Furthermore, in one case, the modifier is no longer a modifier—it has become part of the core of the sentence. (If you missed that, look at the answers again. Can you find it?)

Because *manufactured in Germany* was a modifier at first, start by examining the choices in that context. Logically, the *car* was *manufactured in Germany*, so the modifier has to be placed to make this clear.

In answers (A) and (B), the sentence implies that the *engineers* were *manufactured in Germany*. That's illogical, so cross off (A) and (B).

What happens in (C)? The modifier is closer to the word *car*. Is it close enough? Nope. It's even closer to the noun *engineers*; plus, the verb *designed* separates the modifier from the word *car*. The modifier is still talking about the *engineers*. Eliminate (C).

Skip answer (D) for the moment (this is the one in which the modifier turned into part of the sentence core). Answer (E) properly places the modifier right next to the word *car*. Answer (E) is okay on this modifier issue, so leave it in.

Back to (D). In this choice, the word *manufactured* is now one of the main verbs: *the engineers designed and manufactured*. This sentence, then, doesn't violate the modifier rule. You'll need another starting point to decide between (D) and (E).

After you've done some work in the book, come back to this one and see whether you can articulate why the correct answer is (E).

Good luck and happy studying!

Chapter 2
of

The Official Guide Companion
for Sentence Correction

Diagnostic Test
Explanations

In This Chapter...

Diagnostic Test Explanations

#35 Mesopotamian Cities

(A)   Comparison (*Unlike X, Y*); Meaning; Parallelism (*X and Y*)
(B)   Comparison (*Unlike X, Y*); Meaning
(C)   Comparison (*Unlike X, Y*); Meaning; Parallelism (*X and Y*)
(D)   **CORRECT**
(E)   Comparison (*Unlike X, Y*); Parallelism (*X and Y*)

First Glance

The long underline contains two commas and a colon. Look for Structure, Modifier, and Meaning issues. The only word before the underline is the Comparison marker *unlike*.

Issues

(1) Comparison: *Unlike X, Y*

 The sentence contains a comparison marker: *unlike X, Y.* Check the *X* and *Y* portions in the five answers for a logical and parallel comparison.

 Answers (A) and (B) compare the *buildings* in one area to *the plan for cities* in another area. *Buildings* and a *plan* are not logically comparable. Answer (C) compares the *arrangement of buildings* in one area to the *cities* of another. Again, the *arrangement* and the *cities* are not logically comparable. Finally, answer (E) compares the *cities* to the *plan*. Only answer (D) offers a logical comparison: the *cities* of one area and the *cities* of another. Eliminate answers (A), (B), (C), and (E) for illogical comparisons.

(2) Meaning

 This issue is hard to spot. The original sentence talks about the *buildings in Mesopotamian cities, which were arranged haphazardly*. What was arranged haphazardly: the *buildings* or the *cities*?

 It's possible to arrange *buildings* or *cities* haphazardly; both meanings pass the common-sense test. A "comma *which*" modifier is supposed to refer to the closest main noun and, ideally, the closest noun. In this case, *buildings* is the main noun and *cities* is the closest noun, so it is impossible to tell which were arranged haphazardly. Eliminate answers (A), (B), and (C) for introducing an ambiguous meaning.

(3) Parallelism: *X and Y*

The sentence contains a parallel structure after the colon:

  (A) *with houses laid out, and houses and walls were built*
  (B) *houses were laid out, and houses and walls were built*
  (C) *houses laid out, and houses and walls were built*
  (D) *houses were laid out, and houses and walls were built*
  (E) *houses that were laid out, and houses and walls were built*

 Answers (B) and (D) offer a parallel subject–verb structure: *houses were laid* and *houses were built*. Answers (A) and (C) don't contain a verb for the *X* portion of the parallel structure. Answer (E) appears to contain a verb, but it is not a main verb—*that were laid out* is a modifier. Eliminate answers (A), (C), and (E) for a lack of parallelism.

The Correct Answer

Correct answer (D) properly compares *cities* to *cities*, makes clear that the *buildings* were arranged haphazardly, and employs a parallel *X and Y* structure for the portion after the colon.

#36 US Forest Service

  (A) Idiom (*for every X, Y*); Pronoun (*it*); Verb (*would not*)
  (B) **CORRECT**
  (C) Structure; Idiom (*for every X, Y*);
  (D) Structure; Idiom (*for every X, Y*); Pronoun (*it*)
  (E) Structure; Idiom (*for every X, Y*); Meaning (*would not*)

First Glance

Most of the sentence is underlined. Look for Big 4 issues: Structure, Meaning, Modifiers, or Parallelism.

Issues

(1) Idiom: *for every X, Y*
  Pronoun: *it*

 The original sentence introduces a two-part idiom: *for every dollar spent* on something, *it saves seven dollars* on other things. As with any two-part idiom, the *X* and *Y* portions need to be parallel. Further, to which noun does *it* refer?

 There is no referent for the pronoun *it*. Eliminate answers (A) and (D).

Next, *every dollar* and *it* are not parallel; the original sentence lacks parallelism in the *X* and *Y* portions of the idiom. Check the remaining answers:

(A) *for every dollar spent,*   *it saves seven dollars*
(B) *for every dollar spent,*   *seven dollars are saved*
(C) *for every dollar spent,*   *saves seven dollars*
(D) *for every dollar spent,*   *that it saves seven dollars*
(E) *for every dollar spent,*   *that seven dollars are saved*

Answer (B) offers a parallel structure: *every dollar* matches *seven dollars* and *spent* matches *saved*. Eliminate answers (A), (C), (D), and (E) for lack of parallelism.

(2) Verb / Meaning: *would not*

 The original sentence says that the action *saves seven dollars that would not be spent*. This meaning is illogical; the money is saved now, so it's already clear that it won't be spent either hypothetically or in the future.

 The intended meaning is that the money saved *would* otherwise *have been spent* in the past. Eliminate answer (A) for bad verb tense.

Answer (E) reverses the meaning: *seven dollars are saved that would not have been spent*. This is illogical because that money actually *would have been spent* if it had not been *saved*. Eliminate answer (E) for illogical meaning.

(3) Structure

 The first three answers begin with the word *that*; the other two move the word *that* to later in the sentence.

 Answers (A) and (B) correctly use the complex sentence structure Subject–Verb-That-Subject–Verb. This structure needs to contain a clause both before and after the word *that*: She believed that despite his gruff demeanor, he was friendly.

Answer (C) omits a subject for the second clause: *New data show that (for every dollar spent) saves seven dollars.* Eliminate answer (C).

Answers (D) and (E) move the word *that*: *new data show (for every dollar spent), that*. In the Subject–Verb-That-Subject–Verb structure, it's strongly preferable to place the word *that* as close as possible to the first verb (ideally immediately after). An alternate placement, particularly after a comma, introduces ambiguity: She believed despite his gruff demeanor, that he was friendly. Is the word *that* part of the sentence core, or it is introducing a separate modifier? Eliminate answers (D) and (E).

The Correct Answer

Correct answer (B) removes the faulty pronoun *it* and uses the parallel structure *for every dollar spent, seven dollars are saved*.

#37 Argentine Pampas

(A)	Meaning
(B)	**CORRECT**
(C)	Comparison (*Like X, Y*)
(D)	Comparison (*Like X, Y*); Structure
(E)	Comparison (*Like X, Y*); Structure

First Glance

The underline starts just after a comma, but there are no other good clues. Be prepared for anything.

Issues

(1) Meaning

The original sentence structure is problematic enough to result in an ambiguous meaning:

Like the fields and pastures, the sandpipers vanishing is a result of X and of Y.

What is the subject of the sentence? The singular verb *is* implies that the gerund *vanishing* should be the subject: *The vanishing is a result.* If this is the case, though, then *sandpipers* should be a possessive noun: *the sandpipers' vanishing.* Alternately, maybe *sandpipers* is the subject? The sentence contains the comparison *like X, Y.* The *X* portion is *fields and pastures,* so the *Y* portion should be comparable. *Fields and pastures* are comparable to *sandpipers* (all are things), not the action *vanishing*—but if the subject is *sandpipers,* then the singular verb *is* doesn't match. Eliminate answer (A).

A̶
B
C
D
E

(2) Comparison: *Like X, Y*

The meaning issue above highlights the comparison *like X, Y.* Check the comparison structure in the remaining answers:

(B)	*Like the fields and pastures,*	*the bird*
(C)	*Like the fields and pastures,*	*that the birds*
(D)	*Like the fields and pastures,*	*sandpipers' vanishing*
(E)	*Like the fields and pastures,*	*the sandpipers' vanishing*

Answer (B) compares *fields and pastures* to *the birds.* All are regular nouns (in this case, things) and all can be described as *vanishing,* so this is acceptable. Answer (C) compares the *fields and pastures* to a clause: *that the birds are vanishing.* This is not okay. Answers (D) and (E) compare the *fields and pastures* to the action of *vanishing*; even though *vanishing* is a noun, it's not acceptable to compare a thing to an action. Eliminate answers (C), (D), and (E).

A
B
C̶
D̶
E̶

MANHATTAN
PREP

(3) Structure

While examining the comparison issue, you might spot a sructure issue in answers (D) and (E). The portion before the first comma is not an independent clause, so the portion after the comma has to be. However, both answers (D) and (E) have the following structure: *In the US, sandpipers' vanishing, a result of X and Y.*

These two options contain a subject (*vanishing*) but no verb. A sentence without a verb is a fragment; eliminate answers (D) and (E).

The Correct Answer

Correct answer (B) clears up the original errors by comparing *fields and pastures* to *birds* and making clear that all three are *vanishing.*

#38 Dolphin Cognition

(A) Structure (*indicate*); Parallelism (*X and Y*)
(B) Structure (*indicate*); Parallelism (*X and Y*);
Idiom (*considered as*)
(C) Structure (*indicate*); Parallelism (*X and Y*)
(D) Idiom (*ability of*); Idiom (*considered as*)
(E) **CORRECT**

First Glance

The underline contains two hyphens; make sure to compare those portions when you get to the answers.

Issues

(1) Structure: *indicate*

The original sentence contains the structure *studies indicate dolphins as capable.* The other answers offer varying structures:

(B) *studies indicate dolphins' ability*
(C) *studies indicate dolphins to be capable*
(D) *studies indicate that dolphins have the ability*
(E) *studies indicate that dolphins are capable*

When a subject is *indicating* an entire clause of information, *indicate* should be followed by *that*: the *studies indicate that* something is true of the dolphins. Eliminate answers (A), (B), and (C) for failing to start the clause with *that*.

(2) Parallelism: *X and Y*

 The word *and* appears just after the second hyphen. *X and Y* is a parallelism clue; what is parallel to what?

 In the original sentence, the *X* portion is *of recognizing* and the *Y* portion is *to grasp*. One is a prepositional phrase; the other is an infinitive verb. Eliminate answer (A) for lack of parallelism.

Answer (C) also contains *of recognizing* and *to grasp*. Answer (B) reverses the two (*to recognize* and *of grasping*), but they're still not parallel. Eliminate answers (A), (B), and (C).

(3) Idiom: *considered as; ability of*

 Between the two hyphens, some choices say that the *ability is considered a sign*, while others say that the *ability is considered as a sign*. Are both acceptable?

While both *X is considered Y* and *X is considered as Y* can be correct constructions, they are used differently. The first is used when someone believes that *X* is essentially the same thing as *Y*: *The ability is a sign.*

X is considered as Y, on the other hand, is used when making a choice: Jin considered Alan as a study partner, but ultimately decided to work with Mario instead. In the given problem, nobody is trying to make a choice with respect to *the sign*. Rather, the sentence is saying that the *ability* is itself *a sign*, so the first form of the idiom should be used. Eliminate answers (B) and (D).

Answer (D) contains another idiom error. Some answer choices use the idiom *capable of* and others use the form *ability to*; both of those are correct. Answer (D), though, uses the incorrect idiom *ability of*, giving you a second reason to knock out answer (D).

The Correct Answer

Correct answer (E) fixes the original structure error: *Studies indicate that dolphins are capable.* It also uses proper parallelism: *of recognizing* and *of grasping*.

MANHATTAN
PREP

#39 Earliest Writing

(A)	Parallelism (*X, Y, and Z*)
(B)	**CORRECT**
(C)	Parallelism (*X, Y, and Z*)
(D)	Parallelism (*X, and Y*)
(E)	Verb (*was*); Idiom (*as*); Parallelism (*X, and Y*)

First Glance

The underline is pretty short; a quick glance at the answers shows that the structure changes pretty significantly. Keep an eye out for Structure, Meaning, Parallelism, or Modifier issues.

Issues

(1) Parallelism: *X, Y, and Z; X, and Y*

 The sentence contains a parallel construction:

(A)	*writing **was** not a rendering,*	*but **was to begin** a system, and **merged***
(B)	*writing **was** not a rendering,*	*but **began** as a system, and **merged***
(C)	*writing **was** not a rendering,*	*but **beginning** from a system, and **merged***
(D)	*writing **was** not a rendering,*	*but **it was** begun from a system, **and merged***
(E)	*writing **was** not a rendering,*	*but **it was** likely that it began a system, **and merged***

 The structure of the first three answers requires three parallel verbs: *the writing was not X, but [the writing was] Y, and [the writing] merged with Z*. The middle verb should be in the simple past tense to match the first and third verbs. Only answer (B) offers this. Eliminate answers (A) and (C).

The last two answer choices change the structure; the new clause (*it was*) chops out the first item (*was not*) and reduces the sentence to a two-item list. In such a list, no comma is needed between the two items (she sang and danced every day), but this sentence does contain a comma before the final item, *and merged*. Because of this comma, it's not acceptable to turn the original three-item list into a two-item list. Eliminate answers (D) and (E).

A̶
B
C̶
D̶
E̶

(2) Verb: *was*
   Idiom: *as*

 You might spot a couple of issues in answer (E) when examining this portion of the parallel construction: *it was likely that it began a system*.

 First, the likelihood is today, not in the past. The sentence should say *it is likely*, not *was*. Second, the writing *began as a system*. The word *as* is necessary in this idiom, but the construction is missing the word *as*. Eliminate answer (E).

A
B
C
D
E̶

The Correct Answer

Correct answer (B) fixes the original parallelism error by matching *was, began, and merged*.

#40 Richard Stallman

(A)	**CORRECT**
(B)	Parallelism (*X and Y*)
(C)	Structure
(D)	Structure
(E)	Parallelism (*X, Y, and Z*)

First Glance

The underline contains a comma and ends with the word *and*; look for Parallelism or Modifier issues.

Issues

(1) Parallelism: *X and Y; X, Y, and Z*

The sentence contains a parallel structure:

(A)	*an observation, **first made***	*and **now included***
(B)	*an observation, **first made***	*and **it is now included***
(C)	*an observation, **first made***	*and **now included***
(D)	*an observation, **first made**,*	*it is now included*
(E)	*an observation, first made,*	*and **is now included***

Answer (B) fails the Parallelism test: *laws, which (X) was an observation and (Y) it is now included.* The *X* portion begins with a verb while the *Y* portion begins with a subject. In answer (E), the parallel structure is *one of Kirchoff's laws that was (X) an observation, (Y) first made in 1845, and (Z) is now included.* The verb *was* applies to all three items in the list, so the *Z* portion, which has its own verb (*is*), is not parallel. Eliminate answers (B) and (E).

Answer (D) changes the structure by removing the parallelism marker *and*, so it's a Structure issue, rather than a Parallelism issue (see below).

(2) Structure

When examining the parallelism issue above, you may notice that answer (D) changes the structure of the sentence: *Stallman testified that a colleague had managed to win a patent for one of Kirchoff's laws, an observation first made in 1845, it is now included in every textbook.*

The portion before the first comma is an independent clause; so is the portion after the second comma. Connecting two independent clauses with only a comma is a run-on sentence: *The honey badger is a mammal, it is a carnivore.*

Do any answer choices make this same error? Yes! Answer (C) is also a run-on: *Stallman testified that a colleague had managed to win a patent, it was an observation first made in 1845.* Eliminate answers (C) and (D) for bad sentence structure.

The Correct Answer

Correct answer (A) properly employs the parallel *X and Y* construction and does not contain any structural errors.

#41 Indus Valley

(A) Subject–Verb (*indicate*); Pronoun (*their*); Structure
(B) Subject–Verb (*indicate*); Meaning / Modifier (*using*)
(C) Pronoun (*their*); Meaning / Modifier (*using*)
(D) Structure; Pronoun (*their*)
(E) **CORRECT**

First Glance

The underline starts with a verb; glance at the beginning of each answer choice. Subject–Verb Agreement must be one issue.

Issues

(1) Subject–Verb: *indicate*

 The sentence is seriously complex. Break it down:

(modifier)
at the Indus Valley site of Harappa in eastern Pakistan

Excavators ⤢ say the discovery , indicate   (parallelism!)

of inscribed shards dating to circa 2800–2600 B.C.
(modifier)

| their development . . . , | occurred earlier |
| the use . . . , |
| and |
| the standardization |

 Check it out! The sentence contains a subject–verb mismatch. The *discovery* is singular and *indicate* is plural. Eliminate answers (A) and (B).

A̶
B̶
C
D
E

(2) Pronoun: *their*

 In the list of three parallel items, the first is introduced by the pronoun *their*. It's possible to have just one of the items begin with a pronoun, so parallelism isn't necessarily an issue, but do check the antecedent for the pronoun.

 Their development of a writing system should refer to some group of people. The only people in the sentence, though, are the excavators; the other nouns refer to locations. Eliminate answers (A) and (C) for failing to provide a noun that matches with the pronoun *their*.

(3) Structure

 When separating out the core structure from the modifiers, you might spot another issue with the original sentence: *Excavators say the discovery indicate[s] their development occurred earlier.*

 Does the *discovery indicate the development*, by itself? Or does the *discovery indicate* some more complex fact about the *development*? In this case, the sentence discusses a more complex situation (a clause): *the discovery indicates* that *the development occurred earlier*. This is a Subject–Verb-THAT-Subject–Verb structure! It's not acceptable to omit the word *that*. Eliminate answers (A) and (D) for bad structure.

(4) Meaning / Modifier: *using*

 Answers (A), (D), and (E) contain an *X, Y, and Z* list: *development, use, and standardization.* Answers (B) and (C), though, change the second list element (*use*) into a "comma -ing" modifier: *using inscribed seals impressed into clay for marking ownership.*

 The *using* modifier refers to the clause to which it is attached: *the development of a writing system occurred decades earlier.* The writing system was developed using seals for marking ownership? That doesn't make sense. Rather, a *writing system* was developed and, separately, *seals* were used to *mark ownership* of something. Eliminate answers (B) and (C) for an illogical meaning.

The Correct Answer

Correct answer (E) fixes the original subject–verb mismatch by using the singular *indicates* to match the singular *discovery*. It also removes the faulty pronoun *their* and employs correct sentence structure.

MANHATTAN
PREP

#42 Supreme Court

(A)	Meaning; Pronoun (*they; their*)
(B)	Meaning
(C)	Meaning
(D)	**CORRECT**
(E)	Meaning; Verb (*be*)

First Glance

The underline begins with a preposition (*with*); keep an eye out for Modifier, Meaning, and Structure issues.

Issues

(1) Meaning
    Pronoun: *they; their*

The modifier structure in the original sentence results in an ambiguous meaning: *universities can collect fees even with students' objections to particular activities.*

Even with objections does not mean the same thing as *even if students object.* The construction in answer (A) could be read to mean that the fees are collected along with objections or in conjunction with the objections. Further, later in the sentence, a pronoun ambiguity exists: *the groups they give money to will be chosen without regard to their views.* Two instances of a similar pronoun (*they, their*) in one sentence should refer to the same noun, but *they* refers to *universities* and *their* refers to *groups.* Eliminate answer (A) and check the meaning of the remaining answers.

Answer (B) doesn't fix the problem. First, *they* must refer to *universities* (because the plural noun *students* doesn't exist in the sentence), but the *universities* aren't the ones *objecting*; the *students* are. Second, a parallel structure exists: *universities can collect fees even if X (they have objections) and Y (the groups are chosen).* This meaning is illogical: the universities don't collect the fees *even if the groups are chosen* in a certain way. Rather, the schools are allowed to collect the fees *as long as the groups are chosen* in a certain way. Eliminate answer (B). Also eliminate answer (C) because it contains the same pronoun (*they*) error.

Answer (E) messes up the meaning. *Even though* and *even if* do not mean the same thing. She likes to sing even though she's not very good. The action after *even though* is true and always applies. She studies every night even if she's tired. The action after *even if* only happens sometimes. In the given sentence, it's illogical to imply that all students will definitely object to an activity. Rather, the idea is that *even if* some students object, the university can still collect the fees. Eliminate answer (E).

A̶
B̶
E̶
D
E̶

(2) Verb: *be*

 The verb tense for the final action changes from choice to choice: *the groups will be, are, have to be, be.*

 For most of the answers, the first portion of the scenario is stated in present tense (*if they have objections,* or *if they object*). It's appropriate, then, to use a present-tense verb for the second portion of the scenario as well, so answers (B), (C), and (D) are okay. It's not acceptable to use the subjunctive, *be*; the sentence requires a regular clause at this point. Eliminate answer (E).

The future tense, in answer (A), is debatable; the ruling has already taken place in the past, so future doesn't seem appropriate. There are circumstances in which future tense could be used, though, so avoid crossing this off for incorrect verb tense unless you're stuck and have to make your best guess.

The Correct Answer

Correct answer (D) is the only one that presents a clear and unambiguous meaning: *universities can collect fees even from students who object, so long as the groups are chosen* in a certain way.

#43 Women in Law School

(A) Subject–Verb (*proportion have*)
(B) Subject–Verb (*proportion have*); Modifier (*women*)
(C) **CORRECT**
(D) Meaning; Modifier (*women*)
(E) Meaning

First Glance

The underline begins just after a comma; watch out for Structure, Modifier, or Parallelism issues.

Issues

(1) Subject–Verb: *proportion have*

 The underlined portion is an independent clause; mentally chop out the modifiers and check the subject and verb: *the proportion* *of judges and partners at major law firms who are women have not risen.*

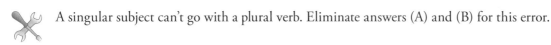 A singular subject can't go with a plural verb. Eliminate answers (A) and (B) for this error.

(2) Modifier: *women*

The word *women* moves around in the answer choices. Three choices use the phrasing *who are women* while the other two use *women judges and partners*.

The word *women* is a noun. It's acceptable to say *who are women*, but in the phrase *women judges and partners*, the word *women* is incorrectly acting as an adjective. The correct adjective form for designating gender is *female*, as in *female judges and partners*. Eliminate answers (B) and (D).

(3) Meaning

The original sentence contains the structure *despite* a certain fact, a particular outcome has not occurred. Answers (D) and (E) insert an additional word at the beginning of the answer: *despite* a certain fact, *yet* a particular outcome has not occurred.

Despite and *yet* both indicate contrast and are both used to connect two halves of a sentence. It's redundant to use both words; only one is needed. Eliminate answers (D) and (E).

The Correct Answer

Correct answer (C) fixes the original subject–verb error, correctly uses *women* as a noun, and does not introduce any redundancy.

#44 Erie Canal

(A) Parallelism (*Seldom X, but Y*)
(B) **CORRECT**
(C) Structure; Meaning (*and; or; but*)
(D) Meaning / Modifier (*which*); Meaning (*and*)
(E) Structure

First Glance

The long underline starts right away and contains a couple of commas; keep an eye out for Modifier, Parallelism, Meaning, or Structure issues.

Issues

(1) Parallelism: *Seldom X, but Y*

The original sentence begins with a modifier:

> *Seldom more than 40 feet wide, but it ran 363 miles, the Erie Canal connected the Hudson River to the Great Lakes.*

Everything before *the Erie Canal connected* is a modifier. The structure *seldom X, but Y* needs to contain parallel elements, but the phrase *more than 40 feet wide* is not parallel to the clause *it ran 363 miles*. Eliminate answer (A) for faulty parallelism.

(2) Structure
Meaning / Modifier: (*which*)

Any sentence has to contain an independent clause. In the original sentence, part of the independent clause is underlined, so check the answers to see whether they contain an independent clause:

> (A) *Seldom more than X, but Y, the Erie Canal connected*
> (B) *Seldom more than X but Y, the Erie Canal connected*
> (C) *It was seldom more than X, and Y, but the Erie Canal, connecting*
> (D) *The Erie Canal was seldom more than X, and it ran Y, which connected*
> (E) *The Erie Canal, seldom more than X, but Y, connecting*

Answers (A) and (B) both contain an independent clause: *the Erie Canal connected*. Answers (C), (D), and (E) change the structure significantly, introducing an independent clause at the beginning of the sentence. In answer (C), the construction ... , *but the Erie Canal* also introduces what should be an independent clause, but no verb exists for the subject *Erie Canal*. Eliminate answer (C).

Answers (D) and (E) both pull the subject, *Erie Canal*, to the beginning of the sentence. Answer (D) does provide a verb for the subject, but answer (E) does not. Eliminate answer (E).

While answer (D) does correctly provide a verb, the new structure creates a different error. The *which connected* modifier should refer to the closest preceding main noun. In answer (D), that could be either *New York* or *the wilderness*; in either case, the meaning is wrong, as *the Erie Canal connected* the two bodies of water. Eliminate answer (D).

(3) Meaning: *and*; *or*; *but*

In various answers, the words *and* and *but* seem to interchange. These are conjunctions, but they have different meanings.

Examine this difference:

> (A), (B), (E): *seldom more than X but Y*
> (C), (D): *seldom more than X and Y*

The word *but* indicates contrast. The word *and* does not. Logically, the sentence should contain a contrast here: the Canal isn't very big at any one point, *but* it is very long. Eliminate answers (C) and (D).

MANHATTAN
PREP

The Correct Answer

Correct answer (B) fixes the initial parallelism error: the description *more than 40 feet wide* is parallel to the description *running 363 miles*. How? Even though they look different, both descriptions function as adjectives in the sentence, describing the noun *Erie Canal*.

#45 Supreme Court

(A)   Idiom (*declared X as Y*); Structure
(B)   Idiom (*declared X as Y*); Structure
(C)   **CORRECT**
(D)   Modifier / Meaning (*ruling*)
(E)   Structure; Idiom (*declared X as Y*)

First Glance

The long underline ends in a comma followed by the word *and*. Look for Structure, Parallelism, or Modifier issues.

Issues

(1) Idiom: *declared X as Y*

 The original sentence contains an idiomatically incorrect expression: *declared a minimum wage as unconstitutional*.

 When assigning a characteristic to something, the correct idiom is *declare X Y*: She declared the spaghetti wonderful. Eliminate answers (A), (B), and (E) for incorrectly inserting the word *as* into the idiom.

Note: It is acceptable to invert the idiom, as the correct answer does; this is typically done when the *X* portion is long and complex:

She declared wonderful the spaghetti made by her mother using her grandmother's recipe.

(2) Structure
   Modifier / Meaning: *ruling*

 Answers (D) and (E) significantly change the sentence structure, so examine the core of each choice:

      (A), (B): *The Supreme Court declared X, and ruling that*
      (C): *The Supreme Court declared X, ruling that*
      (D): *A minimum wage was declared X, ruling that*
      (E): *When the Court declared a minimum wage X, ruling that*

 Answers (A), (B), and (C) all begin with an independent clause. Answers (A) and (B) then use the construction *and ruling that*. Either the portion following *and* should be an independent clause (it isn't) or the word *and* should not be there. Eliminate answers (A) and (B).

Answer (E) doesn't contain an independent clause at all! *When the Court declared* is a subordinate clause and *ruling that* is a modifier. Eliminate answer (E) because it's a sentence fragment.

Answer (D) does contain an acceptable independent clause, but the sentence structure introduces a meaning error. A "comma -ing" modifier refers to the subject and verb of the main clause. In answer (D), the sentence implies that *the minimum wage* was responsible for *ruling* something. This is illogical; *the Supreme Court* was responsible for *ruling* something. Eliminate answer (D).

The Correct Answer

Answer (C) employs the correct, though inverted, idiom: *The Court declared unconstitutional a minimum wage for women and children.* This choice also removes the word *and*; as a result, the "comma -ing" *ruling* modifier is correctly constructed.

#46 Blind from Birth

(A) **CORRECT**
(B) Verb / Meaning (*saw*); Modifier (*frequent*)
(C) Modifier (*gesturing*)
(D) Verb / Meaning (*having seen*); Modifier (*frequent; gesturing*)
(E) Verb / Meaning (*having seen*; *to make*)

First Glance

The very long underline points to possible Structure, Meaning, Modifier, or Parallelism issues.

Sentence Structure

The sentence is unbelievably long and convoluted.

First Read: Original Sentence	Thoughts
Researchers have found that	Complex structure. They're about to tell me what the researchers found.
individuals who have been blind from birth,	Certain people…
and who thus have never seen anyone gesture,	Um…
nevertheless make hand motions when speaking	Where is this sentence going? Go back and find the basics: *Researchers have found that certain individuals make hand motions.* Okay, all that *who* stuff in the middle was just a very complex modifier structure. Back to the sentence.
just as frequently and in virtually the same way as sighted people do,	Crazy! Okay, *just as frequently* is a modifier. These people *make hand motions* often and *in the same way as* others do.

MANHATTAN
PREP

and that they will gesture	This doesn't really seem to follow that last piece. The word *and* is a parallelism marker; what is this parallel to? The word *that* is a pretty good clue… searching… oh, way up at the beginning: *Researchers have found that*. Okay, maybe the structure is *researchers have found that X and that Y?*
even when conversing with another blind person.	Yet another modifier. Yep, I think the overall structure is that the *researchers have found that* two things are true: *X and Y.*
	I don't see anything grammatically wrong with the original, so I'm going to compare it to answer (B) to see what differences I can find.

Issues

(1) Verb / Meaning: *saw; having seen; to make*

The verb tenses change. Here's the first split:

(A), (C): who **have been** *blind, and who thus* **have never seen**
(B): who **have been** *blind, and who thus* **never saw**
(D), (E): who **have been** *blind, and thus* **never having seen**

At the most basic level, parallelism only requires the same kind of word (such as a verb); it doesn't necessarily require identical verb tenses. In that sense, each of the choices is parallel. Meaning, however, does come into play. *Thus* indicates something that happens as a result of the first event: people *have been blind from birth* and so, after birth, *have not seen anyone gesture.*

It's inappropriate, then, to pair the present perfect *have been blind* with the past tense *thus never saw.* Similarly, the structure *never having seen* refers to something that occurred before the first action, not after. Eliminate answers (B), (D), and (E) for an illogical time sequence.

Check for other possible verb issues elsewhere:

(A), (B): *found that individuals* **make** *motions, and that they* **will** *gesture*
(C), (D): *found that individuals* **made** *motions, as well as* **gesturing**
(E): *found that individuals* **to make** *motions, and* **to gesture**

Individuals needs to be followed by a conjugated verb (such as *make*), not an infinitive (*to make*). Eliminate answer (E). Answers (C) and (D) change the structure, turning the last part into a "comma -ing" modifier. Technically, the verbs are fine, but there is a modifier issue. See below.

A
B̶
C
D̶
E̶

(2) Modifier: *gesturing*

What is the difference between these two structures?

(A), (B): *Researchers have found that individuals make motions when speaking, and that they will gesture.*
(C), (D): *Researchers have found that individuals make motions when speaking, as well as gesturing.*

In general, a "comma -ing" modifier refers to the main subject and verb to which the modifier is attached: *Researchers have found that individuals make motions.* The answers contain a complication, though—another "-ing" word, *speaking*.

Is *gesturing* parallel to *speaking*? Or is it a modifier referring back to the subject–verb structure at the beginning? This ambiguity is bad. Answers (A) and (B) offer a more clear structure. Eliminate answers (C) and (D) for introducing ambiguity in meaning.

(3) Modifier: *frequent*

Some answers use the word *frequent*; others use the word *frequently*.

Frequent can be a verb or an adjective. *Frequently* is an adverb. The modifier *just as frequently* refers to the verb *making hand motions*, so use the adverb form. Eliminate answers (B) and (D) for using the incorrect form of the word.

The Correct Answer

Correct answer (A) employs logical verb tenses throughout, as well as a clear structure for a very complex sentence.

#47 Embryonic Cells

(A)	Idiom (*ability of*)
(B)	**CORRECT**
(C)	Comparison (*Like X, Y*)
(D)	Comparison (*Like X, Y*)
(E)	Idiom (*ability of*); Comparison (*Like X, Y*)

First Glance

The first glance doesn't yield any obvious clues; be ready for anything!

Issues

(1) Idiom: *ability of*

The original sentence contains the structure the *ability of developing*.

The correct idiom is *ability* + infinitive, or *ability to develop*. Eliminate answers (A) and (E) for using an incorrect idiom.

(2) Comparison: *Like X, Y*

 The sentence begins with a comparison marker: *like embryonic germ cells*. The *Y* portion, *embryonic stem cells*, is underlined, so check it in the answers.

 Answers (A) and (B) both make an appropriate comparison. Answer (C), though, compares the *germ cells* to the subject *there* (*there is the ability*). Answers (D) and (E) both compare *germ cells* to *the ability*. Eliminate answers (C), (D), and (E) for making an illogical comparison.

The Correct Answer

Correct answer (B) fixes the initial idiom error and makes a logical comparison.

#48 New Missile Critics

(A) Parallelism (*more X than Y*)	
(B) **CORRECT**	
(C) Parallelism (*more X than Y*)	
(D) Parallelism (*more X than Y*)	
(E) Parallelism (*more X than Y*)	

First Glance

The beginning of the underline contains a split between *for manipulating* and *to manipulate*. This split might have to do with Structure, Parallelism, or Idiom issues.

Issues

(1) Parallelism: *more X than Y*

 The underlined region contains a comparison structure:

(A)	*more a tool* **for manipulating**	*than* **to fulfill**
(B)	*more a tool* **for manipulating**	*than* **for fulfilling**
(C)	*more a tool* **to manipulate**	*rather than* **that it fulfills**
(D)	*more a tool* **to manipulate**	*rather than* **fulfilling**
(E)	*more a tool* **to manipulate**	*than* **for fulfilling**

 Only answer (B) offers a parallel construction for the *X* and *Y* portions. Eliminate answers (A), (C), (D), and (E) for faulty parallelism.

Note that some answers change the comparison structure slightly: *more X rather than Y* (as opposed to *more X than Y*). This structure is acceptable (although the word *rather* does not add anything to the sentence).

The Correct Answer

Correct answer (B) offers a fully parallel comparison: *for manipulating* and *for fulfilling*.

#49 Stella Adler

(A) Modifier (*who trained; including*)	
(B) Modifier (*who include*)	
(C) **CORRECT**	
(D) Modifier (*one; including*)	
(E) Modifier (*one*)	

First Glance

The underline is long and starts just after a comma. Keep an eye out for Structure, Meaning, Modifier, or Parallelism issues.

Issues

(1) Modifier: *one*

 (Note: In this explanation, we're breaking our usual practice of starting with the first error in the original sentence; we explain why below.) The original sentence contains a classic opening modifier structure: *As an actress, Stella Adler was.* Such opening modifiers must refer to the subject right after the comma. Because the underline starts right after the comma, immediately check the answers to ensure that the correct subject follows.

 Answers (A), (B), and (C) correctly use *Stella Adler* as the subject. In answers (D) and (E), though, the subject is *one*, not *Stella*. Eliminate answers (D) and (E).

(2) Modifier: *who trained*

 Now that you've spotted one modifier issue, check the answers for other similar issues. The sentence structure changes significantly among the answers:

> (A) *Adler was an artist in the theater, who trained*
> (B) *Adler, an artist in the theater, trained*
> (C) *Adler was an artist in the theater, training*
> (D) *one artist in the theater was Adler, who trained*
> (E) *one artist in the theater, Adler, trained*

 Two choices contain modifiers beginning with a comma followed by the word *who*. These noun modifiers must refer to the closest preceding main noun. The construction is correct in answer (D), but not in answer (A). Eliminate answer (A).

Answers (B) and (E) turn the modifier into the main verb: *Adler trained.* This is acceptable.

(3) Modifier: *including; who include*

Keep going on the modifier issue!

    (A) *who trained generations of actors* **including** *Brando*
    (B) *trained generations of actors* **who include** *Brando*
    (C) *training generations of actors* **whose ranks included** *Brando*
    (D) *who trained generations of actors* **including** *Brando*
    (E) *trained generations of actors* **whose ranks included** *Brando*

Including is an exception to most words ending in "-ing"; it can be placed much more flexibly and still be correct. In the construction *generations of actors including*, the word *including* could refer either to *generations* or to *actors*. This (mild) ambiguity is okay, although you'd prefer something better, if possible. Put question marks next to answers (A) and (D).

In answer (B), the construction *who include* has two problems. First, it could refer to either *generations* or *actors* (earning this answer a question mark). Second, *include* is in the present tense but the sentence to this point has been in the past tense. While it's possible that the actors are still alive, it's better to continue within the same time frame already established: *Adler trained* them in the past, so they were *included* in this group in the past. Answer (B) gets a second question mark, almost certainly indicating that it is wrong.

Answers (C) and (E) use a more wordy construction—*whose ranks included*—but that extra word conveys a huge advantage. People have *ranks* and *generations* don't, so these two answers make very clear that the *actors' ranks included Brando and De Niro*. The earlier ambiguity is removed. Further, unlike (B), answers (C) and (E) also continue the past time frame.

A ?
B ??
C
D ?
E

The Correct Answer

Answers (A), (D), and (E) contain clear errors. Answer (B) has two questionable constructions. Answer (C) is better than answer (B) in both respects, so choose answer (C) over answer (B). (See the Modifier issue, above, for more detail.)

#50 SDMI

(A) **CORRECT**
(B) Parallelism (*X and Y*); Meaning
(C) Idiom (*for*); Pronoun (*it*); Meaning
(D) Meaning
(E) Pronoun (*it*); Meaning; Parallelism (*X and Y*)

First Glance

The long answers begin with *of distributing*, *for distributing*, or *to distribute*, so Parallelism, Structure, or Idiom issues are likely.

Issues

(1) Parallelism: *X and Y*
   Pronoun: *it*

 The sentence contains multiple instances of the parallelism marker *and*. Check them!

 The first instance, *songs and recordings*, is identical in all five answer choices. The second instance, based on the original sentence, is:

   (A) *that will* **protect** *and* **foil**
   (B) *to* **protect** *and* **foiling**
   (C) *it* **protects** *and* **foils**
   (D) *they will* **protect** *and* **foil**
   (E) *it will* **protect** *and* **foiling**

Answers (B) and (E) are not parallel; eliminate them. While examining the Parallelism issue, you might spot a pronoun split: answers (C) and (E) use the singular pronoun *it*, while answer (D) uses the plural pronoun *they*. The pronoun refers to the plural noun *associations*, so answers (C) and (E) are incorrect; eliminate them.

(2) Meaning
   Idiom: *for*

 While examining the parallelism issue above, you might also spot a Meaning issue:

   (A) *hope to create a way of X that will protect*
   (B) *hope to create a way of X and to protect*
   (C) *hope to create a way for X while it protects*
   (D) *hope to create a way to X while they will protect*
   (E) *hope to create a way to X and it will protect*

 The structure in answer (A) creates a substantially different meaning than the structure in answer (B). In answer (A), the *associations hope to create* one thing *that will* then accomplish something else. In answer (B), the *associations hope* to do two separate things: *create a standardized way and*, separately, *protect copyright*

holders. Answers (B) and (E) both use *and* instead of *that* to join the two concepts, losing the connection that the first thing will lead to the second. The *while* construction in answers (C) and (D) also introduces the same meaning error: the *associations* are doing two different things at the same time. Eliminate answers (B), (C), (D), and (E).

While examining this issue, you might spot another difference: *a standardized way of distributing, for distributing,* or *to distribute. Way of distributing* and *way to distribute* are both acceptable idioms, but *way for distributing* is incorrect. Eliminate answer (C).

The Correct Answer

Correct answer (A) offers a properly parallel construction and a clear connection in meaning: the *standardized way of* doing something *will protect* one group *and foil* another.

#51 Ramjets and Scramjets

(A)	Comparison (*Whereas X, Y*)
(B)	Comparison (*Whereas X, Y*)
(C)	Comparison (*Whereas X, Y*); Idiom (*ability is because*)
(D)	Idiom (*ability of*); Meaning
(E)	**CORRECT**

First Glance

The underline contains two commas, and a third one shows up just before the underline starts. Keep an eye out for Modifier, Parallelism, Meaning, or Structure issues.

Issues

(1) Comparison: *Whereas X, Y*

The sentence makes a comparison, which requires parallelism:

(A)	*Whereas a ramjet,*	*high speeds*
(B)	*Whereas a ramjet,*	*that high speeds*
(C)	*Whereas a ramjet,*	*the ability*
(D)	*Whereas a ramjet,*	*scramjets*
(E)	*Whereas a ramjet,*	*scramjets*

Fill in the blank: Whereas a ramjet (has a certain characteristic), _____. The *Y* portion of the comparison should fill that blank following the comma. The *X* portion is a *ramjet*, so the *Y* portion should be something that can logically be compared to a ramjet, such as a *scramjet* (or *scramjets*). Eliminate answers (A), (B), and (C).

(2) Idiom: *ability is because; ability of*

 Answer (C) uses the structure *the ability of scramjets is because*. Answer (D) says the *scramjets have the ability of attaining* something.

 It would be possible to say that *the ability of scramjets to achieve high speeds is due to* (or *a result of*) some characteristic, but it's not acceptable to say the *ability is because* of something. Similarly, it is correct to say *ability to attain* something, but it is incorrect to say *ability of attaining* something. Eliminate answers (C) and (D).

(3) Meaning

 Answer (D) contains a very subtle meaning change. This one is hard to spot: *scramjets have the ability (to attain) high speeds when reducing airflow compression.*

 Scramjets can attain these high speeds because of the way that they reduce airflow compression. The other answer choices convey this meaning. Answer (D), however, indicates that scramjets can only attain high speeds when they are reducing airflow compression. Otherwise, they don't attain these high speeds. This meaning, though, doesn't make sense when paired with the first part of the comparison: *whereas a ramjet generally cannot achieve high speeds* unless it has a certain advantage, *scramjets* can achieve high speeds all the time.

The Correct Answer

Correct answer (E) properly compares ramjets to scramjets, and avoids any idiom errors.

#52 Melting Sea Ice

(A) Comparison / Parallelism (*like X, so Y*)
(B) Comparison / Parallelism (*like X, so Y*)
(C) Comparison (*just X, so Y*)
(D) Parallelism
(E) **CORRECT**

First Glance

The underline begins with *like*, indicating possible Comparison or Parallelism issues.

Issues

(1) Comparison / Parallelism: *just X, so Y; like X, so Y*

 Examine the structure surrounding *like*. In all cases, the *Y* portion is identical: *so ice does not increase*. What is the *X* portion?

(A) *just like* a glass that will not overflow
(B) *just like* ice cubes that do not cause
(C) *just* a glass will not overflow
(D) *just as* ice cubes that do not cause
(E) *just as* ice cubes do not cause

 The given structure is testing the comparison idiom. The construction *just X, so Y* is definitely wrong; either *just like* or *just as* is needed. Because *X* and *Y* are both clauses, the correct comparison should use *as*. The *like* options are incorrect. Eliminate answers (A), (B), and (C).

In addition, the *X* and *Y* portions have to be parallel. The *Y* portion is a regular clause: *sea ice does not increase volume*. The *X* portion should be both structurally and logically parallel. Answers (A), (B), and (D) are not structurally parallel: *a glass that* or *ice cubes that* is not a regular clause with subject and verb. Answer (C) is not logically parallel; the subject of each clause should be the thing causing the potential overflow (*ice cubes, sea ice*). Eliminate answers (A), (B), (C), and (D) for faulty parallelism.

The Correct Answer

Correct answer (E) is the only one to offer a structurally and logically parallel comparison: *melting ice cubes do not cause a glass to overflow* in the same way that *melting sea ice does not increase* [the ocean's] *volume*. Answer (E) also corrects the original idiom error by using the appropriate comparison structure *just as X, so Y*.

Chapter *of* 3

The Official Guide Companion
for Sentence Correction

Sentence Correction
Explanations

In This Chapter...

Sentence Correction Explanations

#1 Two Swiss Psychologists

(A) Structure

(B) Structure; Idiom (*failed in controlling*); Comparison (*such X like Y*)

(C) Structure

(D) Verb (*fail*); Idiom (*failed in controlling*); Comparison (*such X like Y*)

(E) CORRECT

First Glance

The medium-length underline contains two commas, signaling likely Structure, Modifier, or Meaning issues.

Issues

(1) Structure

 Like many GMAT sentences, this one begins with an opening modifier, followed by the subject of the sentence, *two psychologists*, and then another modifier, *declaring that*. What verb goes with the subject?

 Although the modifier *declaring that … size* is not incorrect because it could potentially modify *psychologists*, a modifier cannot contain the sentence's main verb, so it can't help with the missing verb problem. The next and final chunk of the sentence, *none could be taken seriously*, is a complete clause on its own and does not contain a verb for *psychologists*. Answer (A) is just a sentence fragment.

Answer (B) is similar. It adds an *and* to the final clause, but the sentence still has no main verb to go with the subject *psychologists*. Eliminate answers (A) and (B).

Answers (C), (D), and (E) fix the missing verb problem by changing the modifier *declaring* into a main verb form: *declared*. Answer (C) creates another missing verb problem, though: *most of the studies* is also a subject that needs a verb but answer (C) replaces the verb *failed* with the modifier *having failed*. Eliminate answer (C).

(2) Verb: *fail*

 Scan the answers and note that there are three variations in verb tense: *had failed*, *failed*, and *fail*. When did the studies fail?

 The full clause states that *since the studies fail / failed / had failed, none could be taken seriously*. The verb form *could be* is either indicating a past tense or a polite statement or request (Could you please do this for me?). In this sentence, *could be* is indicating a past time frame, so *fail* shouldn't be in the present tense. Eliminate answer (D).

Answers (A), (B), and (E) all use acceptable past tenses; answer (C) changes the structure (see the discussion of Structure for more).

A
B
C
~~D~~
E

(3) Idiom: *failed in controlling*

The answers contain a split between *failed in controlling* in answers (B) and (D) and *failed to control* in answers (A), (C), and (E). Are both versions acceptable?

Try some simpler examples. She failed to control her temper. She failed in controlling her temper. The first example is the correct idiom; the second is incorrect. If some action is what failed to happen, use the infinitive form (in this case, *to control*) rather than the gerund form as the object of a preposition (in this case, *in controlling*). Eliminate answers (B) and (D).

(4) Comparison: *such X like Y*

Towards the end of the underlined section, there is a split between *such variables as social class* and *such variables like social class.*

The word *like* means "similar to." This sentence is trying to introduce examples of something; the correct idiom for introducing examples is *such as*. Eliminate answers (B) and (D).

The Correct Answer

Correct answer (E) contains a subject and a verb for both *psychologists* and *most of the studies*. It also uses the correct idiom, *such as*, to provide an example.

#2 Manufacturers Rate Batteries

(A) Meaning / Pronoun (*they*);
    Parallelism (*higher X, longer Y*)
(B) Parallelism (*higher X, longer Y*)
(C) CORRECT
(D) Parallelism (*higher X, longer Y*)
(E) Parallelism (*higher X, longer Y*)

First Glance

The answers appear to vary significantly, signaling likely Structure, Meaning, Modifier, or Parallelism issues.

Issues

(1) Meaning / Pronoun: *they*

The pronoun *they* must be referring to *manufacturers* (before the semicolon) because batteries cannot rate things. The second half, then, says: *if manufacturers rate* [batteries] *higher*, then the battery will last longer.

The manufacturers could make longer-lasting batteries, but answer (A) implies that simply changing the rating given to a battery will cause it to last longer. That doesn't make any sense; the actual battery would have to first last longer in order to deserve the higher rating. Eliminate answer (A).

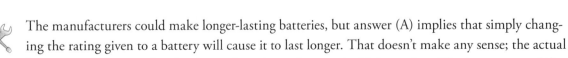

(2) Parallelism: *higher X, longer Y*

The sentence contains a cause-effect structure that needs to be parallel.

(A) *if they rate X higher*   *the longer the Y*
(B) *rating X higher*   *it is that much longer the Y*
(C) *the higher the X*   *the longer the Y*
(D) *the higher the X*   *it is that much longer that the Y*
(E) *when the X is higher*   *the longer it is the Y*

Answers (A), (B), (D), and (E) are all wrong; not one offers a parallel structure for *X* and *Y*. Eliminate answers (A), (B), (D), and (E).

The Correct Answer

Answer (C) offers the only parallel option: *the higher the X, the longer the Y.*

#3 Surge in Sales

(A) Subject–Verb (*have raised*)
(B) Meaning / Idiom (*hopes for*)
(C) Verb (*had raised*); Meaning / Idiom (*hopes for*)
(D) CORRECT
(E) Meaning / Idiom (*hopes for*)

First Glance

The very short underline makes it worthwhile to study the differences in the answers before reading the sentence. The answers start with a verb that changes from plural to singular, indicating a subject–verb issue.

Issues

(1) Subject–Verb: *have raised*

The original sentence says *a surge have raised hopes. Surge* is singular and *have raised* is plural.

Answer (A) is incorrect because of bad subject–verb agreement. The remaining answers contain singular verbs that match with the singular noun *surge*. Eliminate answer (A).

Note that the simple past tense verb form, *raised*, and the past perfect verb form, *had raised*, can be plural or singular, as in *they had raised* or *it has raised*.

(2) Verb: *had raised*

Scan the answers and note that there are three variations in verb tense: *raised*, *had raised*, and *has raised*. When were the hopes raised?

The economists say (present tense) something today, so the surge might be in the present or past. Simple past or present perfect are both acceptable, but the past perfect *had raised* in answer (C) is problematic. Past perfect requires either another verb in simple past or a past time marker, but neither exists in this sentence. Eliminate answer (C).

(3) Meaning / Idiom: *hopes for*

Towards the middle of the underlined section, there is a split between *hopes that*, in answers (A) and (D), and *hopes for*, in answers (B), (C), and (E).

Although *hopes for* and *hopes that* can both be correct idioms, check that each is used correctly.

Hopes for should be followed by a noun, whereas *hopes that* should be followed by a clause. For example, both of these sentences are idiomatically correct:

> She hopes for a reconciliation.

> She hopes that a reconciliation will occur.

But these two sentences are not idiomatically correct::

> She hopes for a reconciliation will occur.

> She hopes that a reconciliation.

In all of the answer choices, the portion after *hopes for* or *hopes that* is a clause. Answers (A) and (D) correctly use *hopes that*. Answers (B), (C), and (E) incorrectly use *hopes for*; eliminate these answers.

Although some might not like the use of the expression *there being* in answer (B), it means "the existence of" and is not, in and of itself, a grammatically incorrect expression.

The Correct Answer

In correct answer (D), *has raised* agrees in number with the subject and works with the present tense *economists say* and *recovery is*. Answer (D) also uses the correct idiom *hopes for*.

#4 Duke Ellington

(A) Parallelism (*not only X, but Y*)

(B) CORRECT

(C) Parallelism (*not only X, but also Y*);
Meaning (*in finishing*)

(D) Parallelism (*not only X, but Y*);
Meaning (*for finishing*)

(E) Parallelism (*not only X, but Y*); Meaning (*finishing*)

First Glance

The dash immediately before the underlined text sets that part of the sentence off for special emphasis. Since the entire underline is after the dash, the part before likely just provides context.

Issues

(1) Parallelism: *not only X, but also Y; not only X, but Y*

 The underline begins *someone not only who*. *Not only* can introduce the idiom *not only X, but also Y* (or the less common but acceptable *not only X, but Y*). Check for both proper idiom construction and parallelism between the *X* and the *Y* portions.

(A) *someone not only* **who could arrange**   *but* **mirroring**

(B) *someone who could not only* **arrange**   *but also* **mirror**

(C) *someone who not only* **could arrange**   *but also* **to mirror**

(D) *someone who could not only* **arrange**   *but* **mirroring**

(E) *someone not only* **who could arrange**   *but* **mirror**

 All five choices use either *not only X, but also Y* or *not only X, but Y*. All are correct in this respect. Next, check for parallelism. Note that the words before *not only* should apply to both the *X* and the *Y* portions of the sentence. For example, answer (A) says *someone who could arrange* and *someone mirroring*. The second modifier isn't parallel to the first and also creates an ungrammatical structure. Answers (C), (D), and (E) are also not parallel and create ungrammatical structures. Eliminate answers (A), (C), (D) and (E).

(2) Meaning: *in finishing; for finishing; finishing*

 The original sentence indicates that Duke Ellington looked for someone with two specific traits so that the person would be able to carry on his work: *someone who could not only X, but also Y in order to [accomplish] Z.* Answers (A) and (B) both contain the *in order to* language, but the other three answers offer different variations:

(C) *mirror his writing style* **in finishing** *the many pieces*

(D) *mirror his writing style* **for finishing** *the many pieces*

(E) *mirror his writing style,* **finishing** *the many pieces*

In answer (C), *in finishing* could be an acceptable construction in general but it doesn't convey the same meaning as *in order to*: Ellington specifically looked for the two traits *in order to* have a certain result. In answer (D), the words *style for finishing* seem to be describing the style of the writer: the writer's existing or preferred style is to finish the many pieces Ellington hadn't finished. That's illogical. Finally, answer (E) offers extra information—this person would also happen to finish Ellington's pieces. Again, the sentence loses the original intention: someone with these two traits would be chosen in order to finish the works. Eliminate answers (C), (D), and (E).

The Correct Answer

Correct answer (B) is the only option that makes *X* and *Y* parallel in the construction *not only X, but also Y.*

#5 Concentrated Migration

(A) Comparison (*X is more as Y*); Verb (*is*)
(B) Comparison (*X is more as Y*); Verb (*is*)
(C) Idiom (*it is none that*); Verb (*is*)
(D) Idiom (*it is none that*)
(E) **CORRECT**

First Glance

The relatively short underline ends with a split between *as* and *than*. This sentence is likely testing Comparison issues.

Issues

(1) Comparison: *X is more as Y*

 Comparing vertically, answers (A) and (B) say *more concentrated as* and answers (C), (D), and (E) say *more concentrated than*. Which is correct?

 The correct comparison structure is *X more than Y*. The word *as* would have to be used in the construction *X as much as Y*. Eliminate answers (A) and (B).

(2) Verb: *is*

 The main clause uses two tenses: *none is* (present) *more concentrated as the wave that brought* (past).

 The present tense *is* cannot correctly describe an action that occurred in the past. The *wave that brought 12 million immigrants* occurred in the past, so this event *was more concentrated*. Eliminate answer (A).

Answers (B) and (C) also use *is* to discuss an action that occurred in the past; eliminate both.

MANHATTAN
PREP

Answer (D) does change *is concentrated* to the past tense *was concentrated*, but adds in an extra construction: *it is none*. Examine that construction more closely (see the next page).

(3) Idiom: *it is none that*

While examining the verb tense issue, you might have noticed in answers (B), (C), and (D) some changing idiomatic expressions: *it may be that* and *it is none that*.

The construction in answer (B) is okay: It may be that she hasn't taken the GMAT yet. *It may be* is an acceptable idiomatic expression.

It is none that in answers (C) and (D) is not a valid idiomatic expression. Eliminate answers (C) and (D).

The Correct Answer

Correct answer (E) fixes the original error by changing the present tense *is* to the past tense *was*. Further, answer (E) employs an acceptable idiomatic structure: *X was more than Y*.

#6 Diabetes

(A) CORRECT
(B) Subject–Verb (*rank*); Modifier (*only*)
(C) Meaning (*has the rank of*); Modifier (*only*)
(D) Subject–Verb (*are*)
(E) Subject–Verb (*have*); Modifier (*only*)

First Glance

The underline starts with the singular verb *ranks*. Other answers begin with plural verbs, so Subject–Verb Agreement must be at issue.

Issues

(1) Subject–Verb: *rank; are; have*

The verb at the beginning of each answer choice flips back and forth between singular and plural.

The subject is *diabetes*. The phrase *together with its serious complications* is a modifier, not part of the main subject. Although the word *diabetes* ends in an *s*, the singular pronoun *its* in the modifier indicates that *diabetes* is a singular word.

Answer (B) uses the plural verb *rank*, answer (D) uses the plural verb *are,* and answer (E) uses the plural verb *have*. Eliminate all three.

(2) Modifier: *only*

The word *only* moves around in the answers.

Only is an adverb; it modifies some other word or set of words in the sentence. In answers (A) and (D), *only* modifies the prepositional phrase following it: *only by heart disease and cancer*. In answers (B), (C), and (E), *only* modifies the verb following it: *only surpassed*. Both variations might sound fine, but *only surpassed* is incorrect. Consider these two examples:

> She works only between 8pm and 11pm.

> She only works between 8pm and 11pm.

In the first option, if she is going to work, she will only do so between the hours of 8pm and 11pm. She may also do other things during those hours, such as eating and sleeping. The word "only" limits the hours that she works.

In the second option, between 8pm and 11pm, she does nothing else but work. She doesn't eat, she doesn't sleep … she does nothing except work. The word "only" limits the activity described by the verb.

The meaning of the given sentence matches the first example: *Diabetes is surpassed only by* the two given diseases and no others. The word *only* should modify the two diseases. Eliminate answers (B), (C), and (E).

(3) Meaning: *has the rank of*

Choice (C) contains a very subtle Meaning issue: *Diabetes has the rank of the nation's third leading cause of death.*

In answer (C), the language *has the rank of* indicates merely that diabetes has the same *rank* as the nation's third leading cause of death, but the sentence does not actually say what is ranked as the third leading cause of death. Surely diabetes itself would be ranked third, if it has the same rank as whatever is ranked third? The meaning is illogical. Eliminate answer (C).

The Correct Answer

Correct answer (A) pairs the singular subject *diabetes*, with the singular verb *ranks*. This answer also logically presents *diabetes* as the *third leading cause of death* and correctly uses *only* to modify *heart disease and cancer*.

#7 Compound Insect Eye

(A) Subject–Verb (*help*)
(B) Pronoun (*they*)
(C) Pronoun (*they*); Structure
(D) Subject–Verb (*help*); Structure
(E) CORRECT

First Glance

The underline is fairly long; it contains a comma, and a second comma appears just before the underline starts. Keep an eye out for Modifier, Meaning, and Structure issues.

Issues

(1) Subject–Verb: *help*

 The very complex sentence structure obscures a subject–verb issue in the original sentence:

(A) *The intricate structure ... , having ... , help explain*

 The subject *structure* is singular, but the verb *help* is plural. Answer (D) also makes this same error. The other three answers correctly switch to the singular verb *helps*. Eliminate answers (A) and (D).

(2) Pronoun: *they*

 The last word in the answer choices switches back and forth between *it* and *they*. Find the antecedent.

 Scientists have assumed that _____ evolved independently of the vertebrate eye. Logically, that blank should contain *the insect eye*; the *insect eye* is different from the *vertebrate eye* because the *insect eye* consists of a bunch of *miniature eyes*. *Eye* is singular, so the pronoun *they* is incorrect. Eliminate answers (B) and (C).

(3) Structure

 Two of the answers contain a non-preferred structure. It's not always wrong (and, in fact, this structure is found in the correct answer of at least one official problem), but it is wrong most of the time on the GMAT. Here's the structure:

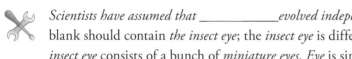

helps explain scientists' assuming that

As a general rule, the test writers don't like using a possessive noun (*scientists'*) right before a gerund (*assuming*, an -ing word acting as a noun). If a regular noun form of that gerund exists, the writers would prefer that form (e.g., *helps explain scientists' assumption that*). Other correct forms are also possible, as seen in this problem: *helps explain why scientists have assumed that*. Answers (C) and (D) earn question marks for this structure; don't choose them unless nothing better exists among the other answers.

MANHATTAN
PREP

The Correct Answer

Correct answer (E) fixes the original error by changing the plural verb *help* to the singular *helps*.

#8 Pharaoh Menkaure

(A) Meaning / Modifier; Pronoun (*its*);
     Idiom (*such X so that Y*)
(B) Meaning / Modifier; Pronoun (*its*); Parallelism (*X and Y*)
(C) Meaning / Modifier; Parallelism (*X and Y*)
(D) Idiom (*because of moisture raising*); Parallelism (*X and Y*)
(E) **CORRECT**

First Glance

The relatively long underline begins with a split between *due to* and *because of*. Watch out for Meaning, Modifier, and Idiom issues.

Issues

(1) Meaning / Modifier
   Idiom: *because of moisture raising*

 The answers contain a split between *due to* and *because of*.

 Due to X modifies a noun. Consider this example: His success was due to hard work. In this sentence, "due to hard work" modifies "success," meaning that his hard work resulted in success.

In the original sentence, the *moisture* resulted in *cleaning and repair*. This is true indirectly, but really the moisture caused a series of events: The humidity increased, causing the salt to crystallize, and as a result of that, the chambers were closed for cleaning and repair. The *moisture* didn't result directly in *cleaning and repair*. Look for a choice that offers a more clear causal sequence. Eliminate answers (A) and (B) for faulty meaning.

Answers (C), (D), and (E) all use *because*—one step in the right direction. Answer (C) still maintains a muddled meaning, though: *The chambers were closed because tourists were exhaling moisture.* Again, this is true only indirectly. Eliminate answer (C).

In answer (D), *because of moisture raising* is not a preferred idiomatic construction. A better idiomatic structure would be *because moisture raised*.

(2) Pronoun: *its*

 Two answers use the singular *its*; three answers use the plural *them*.

 The sentence indicates that *the chambers inside the pyramid were closed* because of problems; this doesn't necessarily mean that the entire pyramid was closed or affected by the humidity issues.

The pronoun, then, should refer to the plural *chambers*, not the singular *pyramid*. Eliminate answers (A) and (B).

(3) Idiom: *such X so that Y*

 The original sentence contains the construction *raised its humidity to such levels so that salt was crystallizing*.

 Such X so that Y is not a correct idiom. One correct idiom is *such X that Y*. Eliminate answer (A).

(4) Parallelism: *X and Y*

 The word *and* appears immediately after the underline ends, signaling an *X and Y* parallel structure. The *Y* portion is *fungus was growing*. Which *X* structures are parallel?

> (A) *the stone was crystallizing*
> (B) *the stone would crystallize*
> (C) *the stone would crystallize*
> (D) *to make the salt crystallize*
> (E) *the stone was crystallizing*

 Answers (A) and (E) are both parallel. In answers (B) and (C), the *would* structure doesn't make sense; the salt must already have crystallized, just as the fungus already grew, because *the chambers were closed* as a result. Answer (D) uses a completely different structure for the *X* portion; it is not parallel to the *Y* portion. Eliminate answers (B), (C), and (D).

The Correct Answer

Correct answer (E) conveys a clear causal sequence: *The chambers were closed because moisture had raised the humidity to such levels that* two bad effects occurred.

#9 Rice Production

(A) Pronoun (*those*)
(B) CORRECT
(C) Comparison (*X less than Y*)
(D) Comparison (*X less than Y*)
(E) Comparison (*X less than Y*); Pronoun (*that*)

First Glance

The underline is so short that it is worth comparing the answer choices before reading the original sentence. Notice the split between the comparison markers *less than* and *fewer than*.

Issues

(1) Pronoun: *those; that*
   Comparison: *X less than Y*

The original sentence uses the pronoun *those* to refer to the *41 million tons of rice*. Answer (E) changes the plural *those* to the singular *that*, which refers back to *production*.

Replace the pronoun with the noun. The original sentence reads *Lack of rain reduced production to 41 million tons, 25 percent less than the tons of the 1978 harvest.* Nothing can be *25 percent less than* a number of *tons*, because *tons* is a countable noun; if the comparison were between the two numbers of *tons*, the sentence would have to use *fewer than*. Eliminate answer (A) and note that the *fewer than / less than* split is definitely at issue.

Answer (E) does use *fewer than*, but it also changes the pronoun to *that*. Now, the sentence reads: *Lack of rain reduced production to 41 million tons, 25 percent fewer than the production of the 1978 harvest.* *Production* is not a countable noun; it needs the comparison marker *less than*. Further, *production* and *harvest* are synonyms, so *production of the harvest* is redundant. Eliminate answer (E).

Check the remaining answers for *X less than Y* or *X fewer than Y* issues. The comparison must be correctly constructed, and the *X* and *Y* portions must be properly parallel.

(B) *reduced* **rice production** *to 41 million tons,*   *25 percent less than* **the 1978 harvest**
(C) *reduced* **rice production** *to 41 million tons,*   *25 percent less than 1978*
(D) *reduced* **rice production** *to 41 million tons,*   *25 percent fewer than 1978*

Less than can be used to compare numerical quantities while *fewer than* is used to compare countable nouns. Answer (C) compares the amount produced during the 1979 harvest to the year 1978; this comparison is illogical. Answer (D) incorrectly uses *fewer than* to refer to the *production*. *Production* is not a countable noun. Eliminate answers (C) and (D).

The *less than* versus *fewer than* issue is tricky in this problem because the sentence includes the number *41 million tons*. It's certainly possible to compare the number of tons in 1979 to the number in 1978. However, this sentence also uses *25 percent*. Try this out in a simple sentence: M is *25 percent less than* N. M is *25 percent fewer than* N. The first version is correct.

The Correct Answer

Correct answer (B) is a logical comparison between the amount produced during the 1979 harvest and the amount produced during the 1978 harvest. It also uses *less than*, a correct comparison for the uncountable noun *production*.

MANHATTAN
PREP

#10 Big Bang Theory

> (A) **CORRECT**
> (B) Meaning / Verb (*had begun*)
> (C) Modifier (*that has expanded*)
> (D) Idiom / Structure (*holds that*);
>   Modifier (*that is expanding*)
> (E) Idiom / Structure (*holds that*);
>   Meaning / Verb (*to have begun*)

First Glance

The last word before the underline is a verb, *holds*, and answers (A), (B), and (C) start with *that* whereas answers (D) and (E) do not, suggesting a Structure issue.

Issues

(1) Idiom / Structure: *holds that*

 The last word before the underline is the verb *holds*. Answers (A), (B), and (C) all start with a *that*, whereas answers (D) and (E) do not.

 This sentence is another example of the Subject–Verb-THAT-Subject–Verb sentence structure. Because the verb *holds* is followed by a clause, the word *that* is needed. Cross off answers (D) and (E) for omitting the word *that*.

(2) Meaning / Verb: *had begun*; *to have begun*

 The original sentence has two verbs in different tenses bound together by an *and* in the second clause. Check the options that use *and* for Meaning or Parallelism issues:

(A) *universe* **began**	*and* **has been expanding**
(B) *universe* **had begun**	*and* **had been expanding**
(E) *universe* **to have begun**	*and* **has been expanding**

 In answer (A), the verbs *began* and *has been expanding* are correctly used because it is logical to say that first the universe *began* (in the past) and that it *has been expanding* ever since then.

In answer (B), *had begun* (past perfect) is incorrect because there isn't another simple past event or past time marker in the sentence. Similarly, since the intended meaning is that the universe is still expanding, *had been expanding* is also incorrect because it implies that the universe is no longer expanding. Eliminate answer (B).

In answer (E), *to have begun* is confusing. Is this a verb tense? An infinitive? Whatever it is, it's connected to *has been expanding* by the word *and*, so parallelism is required. Something that starts with an infinitive cannot be parallel to a conjugated verb tense. Eliminate answer (E).

An entirely different structure is used in answers (C) and (D). The word *and* has turned into *that*, so examine these two choices for modifier issues (see below).

MANHATTAN
PREP

(3) Modifier: *that has expanded; that is expanding*

Answers (C) and (D) change the original parallel *X and Y* structure:

> (C) *the beginning was an explosive instant that has expanded*
> (D) *the beginning to have been an explosive instant that is expanding*

The two noun modifiers, *that has expanded* and *that is expanding,* logically describe *the universe.* However, the closest main noun is the explosive *instant*—the moment the universe began. An instant can't expand; this is nonsensical. Eliminate answers (C) and (D).

The Correct Answer

Correct answer (A) has two verbs that work logically together: *The universe began and has been expanding ever since.* In addition, the sentence correctly uses the Subject–Verb-That-Subject–Verb structure.

#11 Brontes and Brownings

(A) Comparison (*like X, Y*)
(B) Comparison (*as X, Y*)
(C) Comparison (*like X, Y*); Pronoun (*that*)
(D) Comparison (*as X, Y*); Pronoun (*it*)
(E) CORRECT

First Glance

The relatively short underline starts with a split between *like* and *as*. This problem is likely a comparison issue.

Issues

(1) Comparison: *like X, Y; as X, Y*

The original sentence uses the comparison *like X, Y;* the word *like* is a comparison marker. Comparisons require parallelism between the *X* and *Y* portions:

(A) *Like* the idolization,	*Joyce and Woolf*
(B) *As* the idolization,	*Joyce and Woolf*
(C) *Like* that,	*Joyce and Woolf*
(D) *As* it is,	*Joyce and Woolf are*
(E) *Like* the Brontës and Brownings,	*Joyce and Woolf*

Since James Joyce and Virginia Woolf are people (they are famous 18th-century writers), they should be compared to other people. Answers (A) and (B) compare them to *idolization;* answer (C) compares them to something *that* can be *accorded to the Brontës and Brownings* (who are famous 19th-century writers). Although it isn't clear exactly what *that* refers to, *that* cannot refer to people. Likewise, answer (D) compares *Joyce and*

MANHATTAN
PREP

Woolf to *it*, another pronoun that can't refer to people. In contrast, answer (E) correctly compares the two sets of writers. Eliminate answers (A), (B), (C) and (D).

The comparison structures also test another issue: *like* versus *as*. The comparison *as X, Y*, used in answers (B) and (D), is used to compare clauses. However, in answer (B), *the Brontës' and the Brownings' idolization* does not contain a verb; it is not a clause, so *as* cannot be used for the comparison. Eliminate answer (B).

(2) Pronoun: *that, it*

 As mentioned earlier, answers (C) and (D) each contain a pronoun. Answer (C) uses *that* and answer (D) uses *it*.

 Because the comparison structure requires parallelism, the word *that* in answer (C) appears to refer to Joyce and Woolf. Logically, though, *that* really refers to *veneration*. Answer (D) presents a similar problem with the pronoun *it*. Eliminate answers (C) and (D) for pronoun ambiguity.

The Correct Answer

Correct answer (E) properly compares people to people and uses the comparison structure *like X, Y* to compare nouns.

#12 Carnivorous Mammals

(A) Verb (*kept*)
(B) CORRECT
(C) Verb (*has kept*)
(D) Verb (*has been keeping*)
(E) Verb (*kept*)

First Glance

The short underline features different forms of the verb *keep*. This problem must be testing verbs.

Issues

(1) Verb: *kept; has kept; has been keeping*

 The changing verb tense at the end of the short underline is a big clue. When did the heat exchange network keep the brain from getting too hot?

 In order to decide which verb tense or tenses are correct, you need to understand the meaning of the sentence. *Mammals can endure* the high body heat *because they have* a special characteristic.

Note that *can* and *have* are in the present tense. Unless there is a meaning-based reason to switch tenses (and here there isn't), *keep* should also be in the present tense. The *mammals have* a special characteristic that allows them (now, in the present) to stay cool. Eliminate answers (A), (C), (D), and (E).

The Correct Answer

Correct answer (B) uses the present tense verb *keeps*, which is consistent with *have*.

#13 Solid Mud Walls

(A) Parallelism (*X and Y*)
(B) Parallelism (*X and Y*)
(C) Parallelism (*X and Y*)
(D) CORRECT
(E) Modifier (*which were laid*)

First Glance

The medium-length underline contains multiple commas, signaling likely Parallelism, Structure, Modifier, or Meaning issues.

Issues

(1) Parallelism: *X and Y*

This sentence is complex! Try to understand the meaning before diving in. The sentence initially states that *there are several ways to build solid mud walls* and then describes *the most extensively used method* of doing so. The underlined section explains the two parts to this method: forming the bricks *and* then laying them in the wall. The parallelism marker *and* signals the *X and Y* structure.

Check for parallelism in the description of the wall building method:

(A) *has been* **the forming** *of bricks*	*and* **they are laid**
(B) *has been* **forming** *the mud or clay*	*and* **to lay**
(C) *has been* **having bricks formed**	*and* **they were laid**
(D) *has been* **to form** *the mud or clay*	*and* **to lay**
(E) *has been* **that bricks were formed,**	*which were laid*

Answers (A), (B), (C), and (D) contain the parallel marker *and*, but answers (A), (B), and (C) are not structurally parallel. Answer (D) is parallel because the infinitive *to form* matches the infinitive *to lay*. Eliminate answers (A), (B), and (C).

Note that, in answer (E), the *and* becomes a *which*. *Which* signals the start of a modifier, not a parallel structure, so that modifier needs to be investigated.

(2) Modifier: *which were laid*

Answer (E), unlike the others, uses *which* instead of *and* to link the two steps together. Although you would expect a parallel structure here (see the discussion of parallelism for more), can the *which* also be correct?

What is the modifier describing? Examine this section of the sentence:

bricks were formed from mud or clay, which were laid

Logically, the bricks were laid. This structure, though, illogically implies that the mud or clay was laid somewhere. Eliminate answer (E).

Note that the GMAT test writer was really clever. An adverbial modifier (*after some preliminary air drying or sun drying*) is sitting right in the middle of the noun modifier. This is completely acceptable from a grammar standpoint and makes it much harder to spot the problem with the noun modifier.

The Correct Answer

Correct answer (D) states the two steps of the most common method for creating a solid mud wall in an appropriately parallel way.

#14 Rising Inventories

> (A) Meaning (*correspondingly*)
> (B) Subject–Verb (*leads*)
> (C) Verb (*were*)
> (D) Meaning (*correspondingly*); Subject–Verb (*leads*)
> **(E) CORRECT**

First Glance

The underline contains one comma, and another is placed just before the underline, signaling likely Structure, Modifier, or Meaning issues.

Issues

(1) Subject–Verb: *leads*

 The answers change between *can lead* (which can be singular or plural) and *leads* (which is singular). What subject goes with this verb?

 The subject of the sentence, *inventories*, is plural and so needs a plural verb, *can lead*. Answers (B) and (D) use the singular *leads*; eliminate both.

(2) Verb: *were*

 Most of the answers don't include a verb in the modifier portion set off by commas, but answer (C) includes the past tense plural verb *were*. The tense should generally match or make sense with the main action in the sentence.

 The simple past tense *were* indicates that the action was completed in the past: *The rising inventories were unaccompanied by sales increases*. However, the main clause says that rising inventories *can lead* to production cutbacks in the future. The action hasn't happened yet! These two verb tenses are not compatible with each other. Eliminate answer (C).

(3) Meaning: *correspondingly*

The long modifier, *when … sales*, is clearly describing inventories, but changes across the five answers:

     (A) *when unaccompanied correspondingly by increases in sales*
     (B) *when not accompanied by corresponding increases in sales*
     (C) *when they were unaccompanied by corresponding sales increases*
     (D) *if not accompanied by correspondingly increased sales*
     (E) *if not accompanied by corresponding increases in sales*

When or *if*? This split is actually a red herring because either *when* or *if* is acceptable. Likewise, *unaccompanied* versus *not accompanied* is a red herring; both versions are acceptable.

What about *corresponding* and *correspondingly*? *Corresponding* is an adjective and it does logically describe the noun *increases*. The *rising inventories* go with a *corresponding increase in sales*. *Correspondingly*, though, is an adverb, and so must modify something other than a noun—but no verb or adjective or other non-noun word in the sentence is *corresponding*, or going along with, *inventories*. Eliminate answers (A) and (D).

A̶
B
C
D̶
E

The Correct Answer

Answer (E) correctly uses the adjective *corresponding* to describe the noun *increases* and maintains the proper subject–verb match (*inventories can lead*).

#15 Credit Card Borrowing

(A)	Comparison (*not as X, rather Y*)
(B)	Comparison (*not as X, yet as Y*)
(C)	Comparison (*not as X, but Y*)
(D)	**CORRECT**
(E)	Comparison (*not as X, but also as Y*)

First Glance

The medium-length underline is preceded by a comma and starts with the word *rather*, suggesting a Comparison issue.

Issues

(1) Comparison: *not as X, rather Y; not as X, yet as Y; not as X, but Y; not as X, but also as Y*

The original sentence has this core structure: *many experts regarded the increase not as a sign that … , rather a sign*. Check the comparison to ensure that it is both idiomatically correct and parallel.

MANHATTAN
PREP

The basic structure is this: *regarded the increase not as X, rather Y.* This idiom is incorrect; the construction needs a conjunction that indicates contrast, such as *not X, but Y.*

Answers (A) and (B) use incorrect comparison idioms (*not X, rather Y* or *not X, yet Y*). Answer (E) uses *not X, but also Y.* This is a trap. *Not only X, but also Y* is a correct idiom; *not X, but also Y* (without the word *only*) is incorrect. Eliminate answers (A), (B), and (E).

Further, the comparison contains yet another idiom: *regarded as.* The *as* is located at the start of the X portion, so it also needs to be used at the start of the Y portion: *regarded not as a sign* of something, *but as a sign* of something else.

(A)	*not* *as a sign*	*rather* *a sign*
(B)	*not* *as a sign*	*yet* *as a sign*
(C)	*not* *as a sign*	*but* *a sign*
(D)	*not* *as a sign*	*but* *as a sign*
(E)	*not* *as a sign*	*but also* *as a sign*

Answers (A) and (C) are missing the word *as* for the Y portion.

(A)	*not* *as a sign*	*rather* *a sign*
(C)	*not* *as a sign*	*but* *a sign*

Essentially, the second half of the comparison says *regarded a sign* (rather than *regarded as a sign*). Eliminate answers (A) and (C).

The Correct Answer

Correct answer (D) uses the right comparison structure *not X, but Y* and places the word *as* at the start of each parallel portion to complete the idiom *regarded as.*

#16 New Home Sales

(A)	**CORRECT**
(B)	Subject–Verb (*suggests*); Comparison (*so weak as*)
(C)	Subject–Verb (*have*)
(D)	Structure; Comparison (*so weak as*)
(E)	Structure

First Glance

The underline doesn't contain any punctuation marks or other obvious clues. Be ready for anything!

Issues

(1) Subject–Verb: *suggests; have*
Structure

 The first three answers begin with the noun *claims* followed by a verb that changes from plural to singular: *suggest* or *suggests*.

 The subject is *a surge and a drop*. The subject is therefore plural and needs a plural verb: *suggest*. Eliminate answer (B).

Answer (C) correctly uses the plural *suggest* but uses a second plural verb later in the sentence: *the economy is not as weak as* [the economy] *have been thought* [to be]. *The economy* is singular; it can't match with the plural *have*. Eliminate answer (C).

Answers (D) and (E) change the structure more substantially: the verb *suggest* changes into a "comma -ing" modifier. A sentence has to have a verb. No verb goes with the subject *a surge and a drop*; eliminate answers (D) and (E) because both are sentence fragments.

A
B̶
C̶
D̶
E̶

(2) Comparison: *so weak as*

 The sentence makes a comparison. In some answers, the comparison takes the form *as weak as*; in others, it takes the form *so weak as*.

 As weak as is a correct comparison structure. It is also possible to say *so X as to result in Y* or *so X that Y results*. Answers (B) and (D) use *so weak as*, though, which is not a correct structure. Furthermore, note that in the two correct *so* examples given above, the *X* action leads to or results in the *Y* action; this meaning does not apply to the sentence given in the problem. Eliminate answers (B) and (D).

A
B̶
C
D̶
E

The Correct Answer

Correct answer (A) pairs the plural subject with a plural verb, *suggest*, and uses a proper comparison structure, *as weak as*.

#17 Sunspots

(A)	**CORRECT**
(B)	Meaning; Structure
(C)	Structure
(D)	Structure
(E)	Modifier / Meaning (*which*)

First Glance

The underline starts with a verb. Glance at the first word of each answer choice; the verbs *are* and *appear* are both plural (so subject–verb is not the problem) and in the present tense (so Verb Tense is not the problem either). Keep an eye on Structure and Parallelism issues.

Issues

(1) Meaning

 The original sentence describes a contrast: sunspots are visible (they've been seen on the surface of the Sun) but they can't be seen at the poles or the equator. Examine the meaning of this portion of answer (B): *visible as dark spots that never have been sighted.*

 This language says that the *spots* are both *visible* and *have never been sighted.* Both of those things can't be true at once. Rather, the spots have been sighted in some locations but not in others. Eliminate answer (B).

(2) Structure
Modifier / Meaning: *which*

 When examining the Meaning issue, above, you might also spot a Structure issue in answer (B): *spots that have never been sighted on the surface of the Sun the Sun's poles or equator.*

 Ignoring the illogical meaning for a moment, the sentence appears to discuss a list of three things: *the surface of the Sun, the Sun's poles,* or *the equator.* At the very least, the list is missing commas. Eliminate answer (B).

Check the other answers for Structure issues:

(A)	*sunspots are visible*	*but have never been sighted*
(C)	*sunspots appear*	*although never sighted*
(D)	*sunspots appear,*	*although never having been sighted*
(E)	*sunspots appear,*	*which have never been sighted*

The answers all use parallel structure (the words in grey text are verbs that apply to the subject *sunspots*), but the structure changes in the middle. It's acceptable to use a coordinating conjunction (*but*) to connect the two halves because both verbs, *are visible* and *have been sighted*, have the same subject, *sunspots.* Consider this structurally similar example: She likes milk *but* never drinks it.

It's not okay, however, to use a subordinating conjunction (*although*) in this situation because a subordinating conjunction requires a clause (its own subject and verb). Consider this example: She likes milk *although* she never drinks it. Answers (C) and (D) don't provide a subject after the word *although*. Eliminate answers (C) and (D).

Answer (E) uses the relative pronoun *which*, which is a noun modifier. This modifier should refer to the closest main noun that precedes it. The sentence reads: *Sunspots appear as dark spots, which have never been sighted*. How can something appear and yet never be sighted? This same mistake was also made in answer (B). Eliminate answer (E).

The Correct Answer

Correct answer (A) uses a parallel structure with an appropriate conjunction to connect the two halves of the sentence. It also clearly conveys the idea that the sunspots are visible sometimes, but not at the poles or equator.

#18 National Academy of Sciences

(A) Structure / Parallelism (*creating*)

(B) Structure / Parallelism (*creating*); Meaning (*takes*)

(C) Structure / Parallelism (*creating*);
    Idiom (*for taking*)

(D) Idiom (*for taking*)

(E) CORRECT

First Glance

The underline starts with a "comma -ing" structure. Look for Modifier, Meaning, Parallelism, or Structure issues.

Issues

(1) Structure / Parallelism: *creating*

The original sentence appears to contain a list of three things with a faulty structure:

> *The NAS has urged the nation to revamp, institute, creating.*

While it might be tempting to say that the sentence is only making the first two verbs (*revamp, institute*) parallel, this is impossible because the sentence would need to include the word *and*: *revamp and institute*. That portion of the sentence isn't underlined, so it can't be changed. The sentence, then, must be providing a list of three things (*X, Y, and Z*), but the word *and* is missing before the third item. Also, that third item (*creating*) is not parallel to the first two (*revamp, institute*). Eliminate answers (A), (B), and (C) for faulty parallel structure.

(2) Meaning: *takes*
   Idiom: *for taking*

 The idiom at the end of the sentence changes from choice to choice:

(A) *an organization* *to take* *charge*
(B) *an organization* *that takes* *charge*
(C) *an organization* *for taking* *charge*
(D) *an organization* *for taking* *charge*
(E) *an organization* *to take* *charge*

 The intended meaning is this: create an organization in order to *take charge* of something. The idiom *to take charge* is acceptable. The idiom *for taking charge* is incorrect. Eliminate answers (C) and (D).

Answer (B) is more subtle. The sentence says that the National Academy of Sciences has urged the nation to act. This answer choice specifically calls for a new organization that *takes* charge of something. But *takes* is a present tense verb, implying that the organization already does take charge. That doesn't make any sense! Eliminate answer (B) for illogical meaning.

A
~~B~~
~~C~~
~~D~~
E

The Correct Answer

Correct answer (E) fixes the initial parallel structure error by inserting the word *and*. It also ensures that the third item, *create*, is parallel to the first two.

#19 Nellie Bly

(A) Modifier (*A pioneer journalist,*)
(B) CORRECT
(C) Structure
(D) Subject–Verb (*are*)
(E) Meaning

First Glance

The sentence begins with a few words and then a comma. Look for a Modifier issue.

Issues

(1) Modifier: *A pioneer journalist*

 An opening modifier should refer to the main subject after the comma.

 In the original sentence, the *pioneer journalist* refers to *Nellie Bly's exploits*, not *Nellie Bly* herself. The other answers change the structure around, so you can't reuse this particular reason to eliminate; do examine the other answers for similar structural or modifier issues, though. Eliminate answer (A).

A
B
C
D
E

(2) Structure

 The remaining answers are so dissimilar that you'll simply have to read each one. Answer (C) reads:

> (C) *Nellie Bly was a journalist including in her exploits the circling the globe faster than Fogg.*

 Technically, there should be a comma just before the word *including*, but commas are sometimes judgment calls. Luckily, there's a bigger issue: sentence structure. At the very least, the sentence would need to say *the circling* of *the globe*. Eliminate answer (C) for faulty structure.

(3) Subject–Verb: *are*

 Answer (D) contains an inverted sentence structure: the subject appears after the verb. Here's the sentence flipped around the "right" way:

> (D) *Circling the globe faster than Fogg are included in Bly's exploits.*

 The subject is actually the word *circling*. Gerunds (-ing words functioning as nouns) are singular, so the verb should be *is*, not *are*.

Note: The official explanation states that *are* should be in past tense, but it is possible to say that, today, a list of Bly's exploits includes (present tense) this incident of circling the globe. The subject–verb mismatch is a stronger reason to eliminate answer (D).

(4) Meaning: *the journalist's exploits of Bly*

 Answers (A) through (D) make clear that *Bly* is the *journalist*. Answer (E) talks about the *journalist's exploits of Bly*.

 Is Bly also the journalist? Or is a journalist describing or discussing Bly? If it's the latter, then who circled the globe faster than Fogg: the journalist or Bly? Eliminate answer (E) for unacceptable ambiguity in meaning.

The Correct Answer

Correct answer (B) fixes the original modifier error with the structure *exploits of Bly, a journalist.*

MANHATTAN
PREP

#20 Retail Sales

(A)   Verb / Meaning (*doubled*); Comparison (*that of*)
(B)   CORRECT
(C)   Structure; Verb / Meaning (*doubled*)
(D)   Comparison (*that of*)
(E)   Structure; Comparison (*that of*)

First Glance

The underline begins with the word *that*, indicating likely Modifier, Meaning, or Structure issues.

Issues

(1) Verb / Meaning: *doubled*

 The original sentence talks about *intensifying expectations that* something *more than doubled*.

 You have expectations for the future, not for the past. It's illogical to say that the retail sales patterns are intensifying expectations that something already happened in the past. Eliminate answers (A) and (C).

(2) Comparison: *that of*

 The sentence makes a comparison: *personal spending in one quarter more than doubled that of the growth rate in personal spending in the previous quarter.* What does *that of* refer to?

 Both logic and parallelism dictate that the phrase *that of* refers to *personal spending*. The original sentence, then, reads *personal spending in one quarter more than doubled personal spending of the growth rate in personal spending in the previous quarter. Personal spending of the growth rate in personal spending*? You can't *spend* a *growth rate*; this is illogical. Eliminate answers (A), (D), and (E) for an illogical comparison.

(3) Structure

 Answers (C) and (E) both split out the last part of the sentence into its own clause:

> *Retail sales rose, intensifying expectations of personal spending, that it* (*more than doubled | would more than double*).

 Consider this example: The company's sales rose, intensifying expectations of success, that it would increase.

If the portion after the last comma (*it would increase*) is an independent clause, then it should be connected to the rest of the sentence by a coordinating conjunction (such as *and*). If, on the other hand, the *that* clause is either part of the original core structure or a modifier, it should not be set off by a comma (and other changes would need to be made). In either case, something is wrong. Eliminate answers (C) and (E).

The Correct Answer

Correct answer (B) fixes the initial Verb / Meaning error by replacing *more than doubled* with *would more than double*, appropriately conveying both a future time frame and uncertainty (the word *expectations* implies something that may or may not happen in the future).

#21 Natural Foods

(A)   Meaning (*nothing*)
(B)   Parallelism (*X, Y, or that Z*)
(C)   Meaning (*nothing; and*)
(D)   CORRECT
(E)   Meaning (*and*)

First Glance

With an underline this short, look at the answers before reading the original sentence. The *and* versus *or* and *nothing* versus *anything* splits signal a Meaning or Idiom issue. Verb tense might be an issue (*has been* versus *is*).

Issues

(1) Meaning: *nothing; and*

The original sentence describes *foods that do not contain additives, preservatives, or nothing that has been synthesized.* Shorten the sentence: *foods that do not contain nothing that has been synthesized.*

Both *do not* and *nothing* are negatives. It's not acceptable to use two negatives in a row; this is called a double negative and it's always wrong. Eliminate answers (A) and (C).

Check the *and* versus *or* issue that you spotted when comparing the answers:

> *do not contain additives, preservatives, or anything synthesized*
> *do not contain additives, preservatives, and anything synthesized*

The *and* option means that the food cannot contain all three bad things at once—but a food that has only one or two of the three would still be considered *natural*. This doesn't make logical sense. It's more logical to say that the food cannot contain any of the bad ingredients. Eliminate answers (C) and (E).

A
B
E
D
E

(2) Parallelism: *X, Y, or that Z*

The sentence contains a list of three items; check for parallelism.

The list consists of nouns that describe bad things that could be added to food. Answers (A), (C), (D), and (E) all offer a noun (*anything* or *nothing*), but answer (B) is problematic. It could be interpreted in two different ways:

MANHATTAN
PREP

Option 1: *additives, preservatives, or that has been*
Option 2: *that do not contain X, Y, or that has been Z*

Option 1 is a list of three items, but the third is not parallel to the first two. In option 2, the sentence contains two parallel *that* clauses: *that do not contain* and *that has been*. In this case, the first portion would have to be *that do not contain X* or *Y*. The word *or* is missing! Under either interpretation, the sentence isn't constructed properly. Eliminate answer (B).

~~A~~
~~B~~
C
D
E

The Correct Answer

Correct answer (D) eliminates the double negative by changing the word *nothing* to *anything*.

#22 Plants Acquiring Carbon

(A) Modifier (*in the form of*)
(B) Modifier (*in the form of*); Comparison (*X than Y*)
(C) CORRECT
(D) Structure
(E) Comparison (*X than Y*); Parallelism (*X and Y*)

First Glance

The underline doesn't contain any obvious clues, but the sentence isn't very long. Just dive right in!

Issues

(1) Modifier: *in the form of*

 The sentence contains the prepositional phrase *in the form of carbon dioxide*. What is this phrase modifying?

 Prepositional phrase modifiers are flexible. They can modify nouns (in which case, they should be placed as close to the noun as possible) or they can modify the main clause to which they're attached. Check the text before the modifier to find an acceptable noun or adverbial modifier structure:

(A) *Plants are more efficient at acquiring carbon than are fungi, in …*
(B) *Plants are more efficient at acquiring carbon than fungi, in …*
(C) *Plants are more efficient than fungi at acquiring carbon, in …*
(D) *Plants, more efficient than fungi at acquiring carbon, in …*
(E) *Plants acquire carbon more efficiently than fungi, in …*

Note: *plants* and *fungi* are two categories of organisms. An example of a fungus (fungi and funguses are both acceptable plural forms of fungus) is a mushroom.

Logically, the *carbon* is found *in the form of carbon dioxide*. In answers (A) and (B), if the phrase is a noun modifier, then it must be modifying the closest noun, *fungi*. If the phrase is an adverbial

~~A~~
~~B~~
C
D
E

modifier, then it must be modifying the sentence core: *plants are more efficient*. Either way, the phrase is not modifying *carbon*. Eliminate answers (A) and (B).

The other options offer a logical meaning based on either the sentence core or the noun before the comma. Notice something important, though: answer (D) doesn't have a sentence core. See the Structure issue below for more.

(2) Comparison: *X than Y*

The comparison structure in the first two answers changes slightly:

> (A) *Plants are more efficient at acquiring carbon than are fungi.*
> (B) *Plants are more efficient at acquiring carbon than fungi.*

Answer (B) drops the second instance of the verb *are*—and thereby completely changes the meaning! Consider this example:

Example	This means:
Cats hate dogs more than mice do.	cats hate dogs more than mice hate dogs
Cats hate dogs more than they do mice.	cats hate dogs more than cats hate mice
Cats hate dogs more than mice.	Ambiguous: could be interpreted in either of the ways above

Apply this understanding to the problem.

(A) Plants are more efficient at acquiring carbon than fungi are efficient at acquiring carbon.	Plants and fungi are both categories of organisms. The two are compared in terms of how well they each acquire carbon. This is a logical comparison.
(B) Plants are more efficient at acquiring carbon than plants are efficient at acquiring fungi.	Plants can acquire carbon efficiently (implying intent / purpose). While a plant could become infected by a fungus, plants don't efficiently acquire (on purpose) a fungus. This is illogical! Or it could mean the same as (A); at the very least, the meaning is ambiguous.

Answer (E) uses the same structure as answer (B), so eliminate both answers for having an illogical comparison. Note that this issue is very subtle; other reasons to eliminate answers (B) and (E) exist.

(3) Structure

 While examining the prepositional phrase issue above, you might have spotted a Structural issue with answer (D):

> (D) *Plants, more efficient than fungi at* something*, in the form of* something*, and converting it to* something.

 No verb exists for the subject *plants*! *More efficient* and *in the form* are both modifiers. Any verb would have to come before *and converting*. Eliminate answer (D) because it is a sentence fragment.

(4) Parallelism: *X and Y*

 The sentence contains the parallelism marker *and*. What is parallel to *and converting it*?

 Answers (A), (B), (C), and (D) all contain a parallel structure: *acquiring carbon and converting it*. Answer (E) does not contain anything parallel to *converting it*. Eliminate answer (E).

The Correct Answer

Correct answer (C) fixes the initial modifier error by placing the word *carbon* just before the modifier *in the form of carbon dioxide*.

#23 Iroquois

| (A) Structure |
| (B) Meaning (*and*); Structure; Verb (*had*) |
| (C) Meaning (*and*); Structure |
| **(D) CORRECT** |
| (E) Structure |

First Glance

With such a short underline, definitely start with the answers. First, there's a split between *but* or *although* (contrast) and *and* (no contrast), signaling a Meaning issue. Next, the *supplementing* versus *supplemented* split indicates a Structure or Meaning issue.

Read for Meaning

Here's how a 99th percentile test-taker might read the sentence:

First Read: Original Sentence	Thoughts
The Iroquois were primarily planters, but	I've got an independent clause, followed by a comma and the word *but*. I'm expecting two things: some kind of contrast should follow, and that contrast should be in the form of an independent clause.
supplementing their cultivation	This isn't an independent clause.
of maize, squash, and beans with fishing and hunting.	There is a contrast—although they primarily planted, they did do some fishing and hunting.
	The contrast word *but* works (and I don't want the word *and* here), but the portion after the *but* isn't a complete sentence. Answer (A) is wrong.

Issues

(1) Structure

As the test-taker's thoughts above show, the independent clause followed by *but* setup signals a second independent clause.

Answers (A) and (E) fail to provide an independent clause after the word *but*.

Answers (B) and (C), which use *and*, also require an independent clause after the conjunction; the word *although* in answer (D) is more flexible:

> (B) *The Iroquois were planters, and had supplemented X with Y.*
> (C) *The Iroquois were planters, and even though they supplemented X with Y.*
> (D) *The Iroquois were planters, although they supplemented X with Y.*

Answers (C) and (D) both contain a full independent clause after the conjunction. Answer (B) provides only a verb, not a subject. This error is extremely subtle; the structure would be fine if there weren't a comma before the word *and*. Don't feel badly if you missed it. The test writers won't make you choose based solely on this.

Answer (C) would have been fine without the word *and*. With *and even though*, however, the structure now requires a subordinate clause followed by an independent clause:

> She worked hard, but even though she was diligent, she didn't get the promotion.

Eliminate answers (A), (B), (C), and (E).

(2) Meaning: *and*
   Verb: *had*

As the test-taker explained above, the sentence requires some kind of contrast word: the *Iroquois primarily planted* food, *but they* sometimes fished and hunted.

Answers (B) and (C) use *and*, which doesn't convey a contrast. This is especially true in answer (B), where the past perfect verb *had supplemented* emphasizes some kind of change: *they had supplemented* their plant food *with fishing and hunting, but* later they *were primarily planters*. Eliminate answers (B) and (C).

The Correct Answer

Correct answer (D) fixes the original error by using the contrast word *although* and inserting the needed independent clause *they supplemented*.

#24 Honeybees and Yellow Jackets

(A) Comparison / Idiom (*as contrasted with X, Y*)
(B) Comparison / Parallelism (*in contrast to X, Y*)
(C) Comparison / Parallelism (*unlike X, Y*)
(D) Comparison / Parallelism (*unlike X, Y*)
(E) CORRECT

First Glance

The underline is short enough to start with the answers. A Comparison issue pops up: *as contrasted with X, Y* versus *in contrast to X, Y* versus *unlike X, Y.*

Issues

(1) Comparison / Idiom: *as contrasted with X, Y*

The original sentence contains the comparison idiom *as contrasted with X, Y.* This is not a valid construction.

Eliminate answer (A) and check the other answers. *In contrast to X, Y* is an acceptable comparison idiom, as is *unlike X, Y.*

(2) Comparison / Parallelism: *in contrast to X, Y; unlike X, Y*

Any comparison requires the *X* and *Y* portions to be parallel; the words must be structurally similar and logically comparable. The *Y* portion must be *yellow jacket* (it's not underlined). Examine the *X* portions of the answers:

(A) *the honeybee*
(B) *the honeybee's*
(C) *the sting of the honeybee*
(D) *that of the honeybee*
(E) *the honeybee*

The honeybee is logically comparable to the yellow jacket; answers (A) and (E) are acceptable.

In answer (C), the *sting* of an insect is not logically comparable to *yellow jacket*. In answer (D), the *X* portion is *that*. It's not necessary to determine the antecedent for this pronoun. The word *that* must be referring to something other than *the honeybee*—the sentence can't say *the honeybee of the honeybee*—so *that* cannot be logically comparable to *yellow jacket*.

Answer (B) is tricky. The apostrophe-s structure signals a possessive noun, so some unknown main noun is implied to follow *honeybee's*. As with answer (D), this choice can't say the *honeybee's honeybee*, so the main noun (whatever it is) can't be parallel to *yellow jacket*. Eliminate answers (B), (C), and (D).

The Correct Answer

Correct answer (E) fixes the original error by inserting a valid comparison idiom: *unlike X, Y.*

#25 Neuroscientists

(A) **CORRECT**
(B) Structure; Meaning (*over the past twenty years*)
(C) Structure; Meaning (*over the past twenty years*)
(D) Structure / Meaning (*now*)
(E) Structure / Meaning (*now*)

First Glance

The underline is quite long and contains two commas. Chances are good that Structure, Meaning, or Modifiers will be at issue.

Issues

(1) Structure

 The sentence begins with a subject (*Neuroscientists*), followed immediately by a modifier, and finally the verb (*are*). The underline extends to this point, so check the remaining answers for the subject–verb core of the sentence:

> (B) *Neuroscientists, (modifier), and are*
> (C) *Neuroscientists (modifier), and are*
> (D) *Neuroscientists have amassed (modifier), now drawing*
> (E) *Neuroscientists have amassed, (modifiers), now drawing*

 Answers (A), (D), and (E) all contain a subject–verb core: *Neuroscientists are drawing* or *neuroscientists have amassed*. Answers (B) and (C), though, use the structure *Neuroscientists, and are*. The structure *and are* indicates a second main verb—but where is the first one? Consider this example: The university, and announced. The structure is not a complete sentence. Eliminate answers (B) and (C).

(2) Structure / Meaning: *now*

While examining the Structure issue above, you might spot another issue with answers (D) and (E). The modifier *now drawing* changes the time frame. *Have amassed* is present perfect, but *now* is simple present.

Normally, a "comma -ing" modifier takes on the time frame of the main clause: The university has amassed a strong reputation, drawing on the expertise of its professors. The *drawing on* action takes place in the same time frame as the *has amassed* action. Try to change the time frame: The university has amassed a strong reputation, and is now drawing on the expertise of its professors to further cement its status.

It would be necessary to insert a new clause: and is now drawing. Answers (D) and (E) don't do this. Eliminate both for faulty structure.

A
B
C
~~D~~
~~E~~

(3) Meaning: *over the past twenty years*

The modifier *over the past twenty years* moves around in the answer choices.

A time frame modifier should be clearly attached to one particular action: what happened *over the past twenty years*?

The *neuroscientists amassed knowledge over* the twenty-year period. Answers (A), (D), and (E) all place *over the past twenty years* close to *amassed knowledge*. Answers (B) and (C), however, place *over the past twenty years* just after the description *its development from birth to adulthood*. The *adulthood* occurred *over the past twenty years*? The *development* occurred *over the past twenty years*? Neither interpretation is logical. Eliminate answers (B) and (C) for illogical meaning due to bad modifier placement.

A
~~B~~
~~C~~
D
E

The Correct Answer

Correct answer (A) is a complete sentence and correctly places the modifier *over the past twenty years*.

#26 Tropical Bats

(A) Parallelism (*X; Y; and Z*)
(B) CORRECT
(C) Parallelism (*X; Y; and Z*)
(D) Parallelism (*X; Y; and Z*)
(E) Parallelism (*X; Y; and Z*); Idiom (*helping the producing*)

First Glance

The sentence contains two semicolons and multiple commas. Check for Structure, Parallelism, and Meaning issues.

Note: Your first instinct might be to cross off answer (A) because of the two semicolons, but scan the answers. They all contain the semicolons, so you're stuck with them.

Issues

(1) Parallelism: *X; Y; and Z*

 The sentence contains a very unusual structure: two semicolons! When you read the original sentence, pay attention to the overall meaning; this will help you to determine how these semicolons are used.

> *Tropical bats play important roles in the ecosystem,*
> *aiding in the dispersal of seeds;*
> *pollinating trees;*
> *and help produce tequila by pollinating plants.*

 The sentence contains a list of three roles played by the *tropical bats*. The first one, *aiding*, is not underlined, so the other two have to match. In answer (A), the third item is not parallel to the first two. Eliminate answer (A).

Scan the other answers. Eliminate answers (D) and (E) for using *they pollinate* (which is not parallel to *aiding*). Eliminate answers (C) and (D) for using *they help* or *help* (neither of which is parallel to *aiding*).

A̶
B
C̶
D̶
E̶

(2) Idiom: *helping the producing*

 Answer (E) uses the structure *helping the producing of tequila*.

 This structure is an incorrect idiom. It's possible to say *helping to produce* but not *helping the producing*. Eliminate answer (E).

A
B
C
D
E̶

The Correct Answer

Correct answer (B) is the only one to offer a parallel structure: *aiding*; *pollinating*; *and helping*.

It is possible (though unusual) to use semicolons to separate items in a list. This sentence probably used that structure because two of the items on the list also contained lists themselves; using only commas would have been confusing.

Note: The test writers did not actually test you on this issue. All five of the answers used the semicolons.

#27 Causes of Crime

(A)   Meaning / Parallelism
(B)   Meaning / Parallelism; Subject–Verb (*has*)
(C)   Meaning / Parallelism
(D)   CORRECT
(E)   Meaning / Parallelism

First Glance

The underline is as short as it gets, so look at the answers first. Some kind of Verb or Meaning issue is at play.

Issues

(1) Meaning / Parallelism
   Subject–Verb: *has*

 The sentence uses a parallel structure to describe a puzzling phenomenon: *why most of the people* in one group *do not commit crimes and, conversely, why so many of those* in the opposite group *have.*

 Though the full verb structure is not repeated, the words *commit crimes* are understood to apply to the second half as well: *most* in one group *do not commit crimes and many of those* in the opposite group *have commit crimes.* That structure is incorrect; it would need to say *have committed crimes.* It's not permissible to repeat words with a change in the structure; rather, the exact structure, *commit crimes,* must be repeated.

Test the other answers. Answer (B) not only contains the same error as answer (A) but it also uses the singular *has* when the subject is the plural *many.* Eliminate answers (A) and (B).

Answers (C), (D), and (E) can all re-use the structure *commit crimes* in that exact form: *shall commit crimes, do commit crimes, could commit crimes.* The meaning of the sentence, though, is illogical in answers (C) and (E). The question is not why some people *don't commit crimes* today while others *shall commit crimes* in the future. Nor is it why some people *don't commit crimes* today while others *could commit crimes* (but do they?). The issue is why one group *does not commit crimes* while another group *does.* Eliminate answers (C) and (E) for an illogical meaning.

The Correct Answer

Correct answer (D) corrects the error by using the same verb in the same tense for the second group: *do.*

#28 Dioxin

(A)   Meaning (*organism's trying*)
(B)   Meaning (*organism's trying*); Idiom (*trying that*)
(C)   Meaning (*attempt to try*)
(D)   Meaning (*attempt to try*);
        Meaning / Structure (*try and metabolize*)
(E)   **CORRECT**

First Glance

The underline contains a couple of commas, so keep an eye out for Modifier or Meaning issues.

Issues

(1) Meaning: *organism's trying*
    Idiom: *trying that*

 The initial sentence contains the construction *the organism's trying to metabolize.*

 The official test writers typically reject this construction (*organism's trying*, a possessive noun followed by gerund) as awkward, but it is not necessarily always wrong. At least one official Sentence Correction question does contain this type of construction in the correct answer.

What to do? If another choice offers a regular noun (not a gerund) and is otherwise correct, choose the regular noun over the gerund. In this case, three answers do offer the construction *the organism's attempt*. Set answer (A) aside until you have examined those other answers; if a choice using *attempt* is also otherwise correct (as is the case in this problem), then eliminate answer (A).

Answer (B) also uses *organism's trying,* but this answer actually crosses the line into an outright error. *Trying that it* do something is idiomatically incorrect; the proper structure is *trying to* do something. Eliminate answer (B).

(2) Meaning: *attempt to try*
    Meaning / Structure: *try and metabolize*

 Answers (C) and (D) use the structure *attempt to try,* while answer (E) says *attempt to metabolize.*

 An *attempt* already means *to try* to do something, so it is redundant to say *attempt to try*. Eliminate answers (C) and (D).

Answer (D) also introduces a meaning error with the structure *try and metabolize* (rather than *try to metabolize*). Consider this example: She attempted to meet her friends for only an hour and study afterwards, but her plan failed. The use of the word "and" separates the two actions: she attempted to meet her friends and, separately, she attempted to study. In the given problem, the separation would mean that the *organism attempted to try* something *and* (separately) *attempted to*

metabolize something—but then the sentence fails to say what the *organism* is *trying* to do. Common sense indicates that the organism is *trying to metabolize* something, so don't separate the two actions with the word *and*. Eliminate answer (D).

The Correct Answer

Correct answer (E) fixes the initial awkwardness by replacing the gerund *trying* with the regular noun *attempt*. It also drops *to try* because *attempt* means the same thing.

#29 Emily Dickinson

(A) Meaning / Modifier (*outnumbering*)
(B) Verb / Parallelism / Structure
(C) Verb / Parallelism / Structure
(D) Verb / Parallelism / Structure
(E) CORRECT

First Glance

The underline is very long, so look for Structure, Meaning, Modifier, or Parallelism issues.

Issues

(1) Meaning / Modifier: *outnumbering*

 The original sentence structure is complex:

> *The letters were written over a period beginning X and ending Y, outnumbering her letters to anyone else.*

 A "comma -ing" modifier refers to the main subject and verb of the sentence. In this case, the sentence says that the fact that the letters were written *over a long period* resulted in those letters *outnumbering* her letters to others. This is nonsensical; it's possible to write 3 letters spaced over a long period or 3,000. Eliminate answer (A) for an illogical meaning.

(2) Verb / Parallelism / Structure

 Following from Issue (1) above, answers (C) and (D) also use *outnumbering* but both place an *and* beforehand, altering the sentence structure. Given the long and complex sentence structure in general, examine the overall structure of the remaining answers:

> (B) *The letters were written over a period that begins X and ended Y, outnumber her letters to anyone else.*
> (C) *The letters, written over a period beginning X and that ends Y and outnumbering her letters to anyone else.*
> (D) *The letters, which were written over a period beginning X, ending Y, and outnumbering Z.* (Note: Parallel structure dictates a list of three things in this choice!)
> (E) *The letters, which were written over a period beginning X and ending Y, outnumber her letters to anyone else.*

A
B
C
D
E

Stripping the answers down to the core reveals quite a bit. First, the sentence structure contains some parallelism (*X and Y*). Answer (B) pairs an earlier action in present tense (*begins*) with a later action in past tense (*ended*). The *period* can't begin in the present and end in the past. Answer (C) violates parallelism by using *beginning and that ends*. Eliminate answer (B) for an illogical meaning and answer (C) for faulty parallelism.

Further, in answer (B), the *outnumber* portion of the sentence is no longer constructed as a modifier. If *outnumber* is meant to be part of the core, though, then a coordinating conjunction is needed: the *letters were written and outnumber*. Answer (B) can also be eliminated for bad structure.

Answer (C) lacks a main verb entirely—everything following the word *written* is part of a modifier. Answer (D) has the same error—everything after *which* is part of a modifier. Eliminate answers (C) and (D) because they are sentence fragments.

The Correct Answer

Correct answer (E) fixes the initial modifier / meaning error by making *outnumber* the main verb: *The letters outnumber her letters to anyone else.* The information in between is introduced as a *which* modifier and the *X* and *Y* portions (*beginning and ending*) are parallel.

#30 Paleontologists

(A) Idiom (*at*)
(B) Idiom (*as being*); Subject–Verb (*provides*)
(C) Idiom (*that it is*); Subject–Verb (*provides*)
(D) CORRECT
(E) Idiom (*as*); Subject–Verb (*provides*)

First Glance

The underline doesn't contain any obvious punctuation or other clear clues; be prepared for anything!

Issues

(1) Idiom: *at; as being; that it is; as*

The original sentence uses an incorrect idiom: *estimated at 40 to 44 million years old.* Note that the underline begins with *at* and all five of the answers differ at this location.

The correct idiom to use when estimating a number is *estimated to be.* Only answer (D) offers this option; if you know this idiom, then you're done in one step! Eliminate answers (A), (B), (C), and (E).

(2) Subject–Verb: *provides*

 A verb changes from the plural *provide* to the singular *provides* in various answers. What's the subject?

 The sentence contains two subjects: *paleontologists* (which pairs with the verb *believe*) and *fragments*, which should pair with the plural verb *provide*. Eliminate answers (B), (C), and (E).

Note that *jawbone* cannot be the subject because this noun is part of the prepositional phrase *of a primate jawbone*. A noun in a prepositional phrase is not eligible to be the main subject of a sentence.

The Correct Answer

Correct answer (D) uses the correct idiom *estimated to be* and also properly matches *fragments* with *provide*.

#31 Barbara McClintock

<table>
<tr><td>(A) Comparison (unlike X, Y)</td></tr>
<tr><td>(B) Idiom (of the conviction of)</td></tr>
<tr><td>(C) Idiom (being convinced)</td></tr>
<tr><td>(D) CORRECT</td></tr>
<tr><td>(E) Idiom (convinced of genes being)</td></tr>
</table>

First Glance

When a long sentence contains an underline right at the beginning, as in this problem, an obvious error might pop up early on. If so, you might choose to alter the normal process and jump to the answers before finishing the entire sentence.

Issues

(1) Comparison: *unlike X, Y*

 Unlike = comparison! When *unlike* is at the beginning of the sentence, the structure will usually be Unlike *X, Y* … so the next step is to find the *X* and the *Y*. In this case, *X* is *the conviction* and *Y* is *Barbara McClintock*.

 Comparisons are supposed to be logically comparable—that is, the two things should be similar types of things —but a person and a non-person are definitely not similar. How could this be fixed? Notice that *the conviction* is underlined, while *Barbara McClintock* is not; you're stuck with Barbara, then, and need to change the other half of the comparison to a person or people. Eliminate answer (A).

(2) Idiom: *of the conviction of; convinced of genes being; being convinced*

 The original sentence doesn't contain any errors beyond the comparison error. What to do? Try a vertical comparison of the answers to spot differences that might help point to specific errors. The ends of the five answer choices show a split between *that genes were* and *of genes being*.

 Take a look at answer (B) first; it attempts to use the idiom *to be of the conviction that*, but incorrectly finishes off the idiom with the word *of* rather than *that*. Further, the word *being* here is incorrect; the sentence requires a regular verb construction (such as *that genes were*). Either reason is good enough to eliminate answer (B).

Answers (C), (D), and (E) change the noun *conviction* to the verb *convinced*. How does this change the idiom? Someone can be convinced *that genes were* something (convinced + that + subject + verb), or someone can be convinced *of the simplicity of* a noun (convinced + of + noun or noun phrase, but not a verb). In all three remaining answers, the sentence tries to use a subject + verb after the word *that*, so the correct construction must be *convinced that*. Eliminate answer (E) (which uses *convinced of* + subject + verb).

Answer (C) correctly uses *convinced that* but contains a different idiom error: *contrary to many being convinced*. The people were not perpetually in the process of being convinced; rather, they were already convinced prior to this point in time. A correct construction might be: *contrary to many of her colleagues, who were convinced that genes were …* Eliminate answer (C).

The Correct Answer

Correct answer (D) fixes the original error (the person-to-nonperson comparison) and does not introduce any new errors, as answers (B), (C), and (E) do. The structure convinced + that + subject + verb is idiomatically correct.

#32 Galileo

(A) Comparison (*to X as Y*)
(B) CORRECT
(C) Structure; Pronoun (*it*)
(D) Pronoun (*it*); Meaning
(E) Structure; Meaning

First Glance

The underline is extremely short, so examine the answers first. Punctuation is at issue, so also keep a broader eye on Structure issues.

Issues

(1) Comparison: *to X as Y*

 The sentence employs a comparison structure: *Phenomena would appear the same to someone* (in one position) *as a person* (in another position).

Although it might seem like the structure *the same to X as Y* is parallel, it isn't. The correct structure is *the same to X as to Y*. The other answers correctly insert the word *to* before the *Y* portion. Eliminate answer (A).

(2) Structure

 Answers (C) and (E) both use a semicolon. Are the portions before and after the semicolon both independent clauses (could each portion stand alone as a complete sentence)?

 In answers both (C) and (E), the portion before the semicolon is an independent clause. Here are the portions after the semicolon:

> (C) *Just as it would to a person standing on land.*
> (E) *Just as to the person standing on land.*

Neither of these is a complete sentence. Eliminate answers (C) and (E).

(3) Pronoun: *it*

 Answers (C) and (D) use the pronoun *it*. Which noun goes with this pronoun?

 Parallelism dictates that *it would* reflects the earlier sentence structure *phenomena would*. This next part is tricky: *Phenomena* is plural. Phenomenon is the singular form. A singular pronoun can't refer to a plural noun; eliminate answers (C) and (D).

(4) Meaning

 The first three answers compare *someone* to *a person*. The final two answers compare *someone* to *the person*. What's the difference?

 As a general rule, *a person* means any unspecified person. *The person* refers to one specific person, possibly a person who has been mentioned previously.

> A person is walking down the street.
> The person walking down the street is her friend.
> A color-blind person can't distinguish certain colors. The person will think two different colors are the same.

In the sentence, two generic people are discussed: *someone* on a ship and *a person* on land. Answers (D) and (E), though, say that something *would appear the same to someone on a ship as to the* (same) *person* on land—a much more restrictive message than the original. Eliminate answers (D) and (E).

The Correct Answer

Correct answer (B) fixes the initial comparison error by adding a *to*: *Phenomena would appear the same to X as to Y.*

#33 Computer Chips

(A) **CORRECT**
(B) Subject–Verb (*is*)
(C) Meaning / Modifier (*which*)
(D) Meaning / Modifier (*due to*)
(E) Meaning / Modifier (*due to*)

First Glance

The underline covers just the beginning of the sentence, up to the first comma. The word *because* signals a subordinate clause, so expect Modifier or Meaning issues.

Note: If the original sentence seems fine, how can you find a starting point? Compare it to the next answer down, answer (B). The differences will tell you where to start.

Issues

(1) Subject–Verb: *is*

Compared to answer (A), the structure of answer (B) changes substantially:

    (A) *Because an oversupply has sent prices plunging,*
    (B) *Because of plunging prices, which is due to an oversupply,*

Answer (B) splits the wording into two modifiers. The *which* modifier refers to the main noun in the preceding text, *plunging prices*. This noun, though, is plural, while the modifier uses the singular verb *is*. The modifier can't refer to *chips* either, because *chips* is also plural. Mismatch! Eliminate answer (B).

A
~~B~~
C
D
E

(2) Meaning / Modifier: *which*

Answer (C)'s structure is similar to that of (B), so examine (C) next. Once again, check for the referent of the *which* modifier.

In this sentence, *plunging* is a verb, so the *which* portion must refer to the noun *prices*—but note that, this time, *prices* refers to the original prices, not the lowered prices! The original prices didn't result from an oversupply. The *plunging prices* were the problem. Eliminate answer (C) for bad meaning.

A
B
~~C~~
D
E

(3) Meaning / Modifier: *due to*

Answers (D) and (E) change the structure more substantially; time to start fresh but keep an eye out for the same issues you already found earlier.

    (D) *Due to plunging prices from an oversupply,*
    (E) *Due to an oversupply, with the result that prices have been sent plunging,*

A
B
C
~~D~~
~~E~~

Due to X modifies a noun. For example: Her high score was due to diligent study. "Due to diligent study" modifies "high score." In the problem, an oversupply leads to plunging prices, so a correct construction might be something such as *the plunging prices were due to an oversupply*. In answer (D), though, the *due to* construction modifies the noun *manufacturer*. The *manufacturer* was not *due to plunging prices*; this is nonsensical. Likewise, in answer (E), neither the original *prices* nor the *manufacturer* was *due to an oversupply*. (Note: It's not okay to say that the fact that *the manufacturer will cut production* was *due to plunging prices*—then, *due to* would modify a clause, not a noun.) Eliminate answers (D) and (E) for faulty use of a noun modifier.

The Correct Answer

Correct answer (A) uses the conjunction *because* to signal a cause-effect relationship between two clauses.

#34 Cash Flow Crisis

(A) Idiom (*depends on if*)
(B) CORRECT
(C) Idiom (*whether or not*); Structure
(D) Idiom (*ability for*)
(E) Meaning (*the ability for it*)

First Glance

The underline is relatively short; glance down the beginning of each answer choice. Some choices start with *whether* versus *if*. Look for Idiom or Meaning issues.

Issues

(1) Idiom: *depends on if; whether or not; ability for*

 The original sentence uses the incorrect construction *depends on if*.

 It's possible to use *depends on* whether it can or *depends on* its ability to. The phrase *whether or not* is common in speech but is considered redundant because the word *whether* already means whether or not. Eliminate answers (A) and (C) for incorrect idiom usage.

Note the last two answers, which use the form *depends on its / the ability*. The correct idiom to continue this structure is *ability to* do something. Answer (D) uses the incorrect idiom *ability for*. Note that answer (E) might appear to make the same error, but *to broaden* does appear later in the sentence. Eliminate answer (D) for incorrect idiom usage.

(2) Structure

     Meaning: *the ability for it*

 The answers use different constructions for the final parallelism structure:

(A) *it can* **broaden**	*and* **leave**
(B) *it can* **broaden**	*and* **leave**
(C) *it has the capability to* **broaden**	*and* **can leave**
(D) *its ability for* **broadening**	*and* **leaving**
(E) *the ability to* **broaden**	*and* **leave**

All are parallel on the surface but one has a problematic structure and one a problematic meaning. Answer (C) is similar to answers (A) and (B) but broadens the parallelism: *has the capability to broaden* and *can leave*. From a technical standpoint, nothing is wrong with answer (C). The parallel structure *broaden* and *leave*, though, is much simpler than the structure *has the capability to broaden* and *can leave*. The parallel structure in answers (A) and (B) is cleaner, and at least one, answer (B), does not have any other errors or problems. Eliminate answer (C).

Answer (E) introduces a Meaning issue. The *ability* in question is the museum's ability, logically, so it should be expressed as such with a possessive. The phrase *the ability for it* should therefore be replaced by *its ability*. Eliminate answer (E).

The Correct Answer

Correct answer (B) fixes the initial idiom error by replacing *if* with *whether*.

#35 Jacqueline Cochran

(A)	Meaning
(B)	Meaning
(C)	Modifier (*where*)
(D)	Modifier (*in which*);
	Idiom (*so X such that Y were Z*)
(E)	**CORRECT**

First Glance

The underline begins with a comma followed by the word *and*; check the beginning of each answer. The split between *and* + clause, *earning*, and *earned* points to some kind of Modifier or Structure issue.

Issues

(1) Meaning

 The original sentence discusses *a time when aviation was still so new for many of the planes.* Compare that to this example: The concept was so new for many of the students that they struggled to understand.

MANHATTAN
PREP

The structure *X is new for Y* implies that *Y* is having the new experience. The students are learning a new concept. Are the planes just learning about or experiencing aviation for the first time? That meaning is nonsensical. Eliminate answers (A) and (B) for implying that *the planes* found *aviation new*.

(2) Modifier: *where; in which*

 The answers differ in the way that they introduce the time frame: *at a time when, at a time that, at a time where,* or *at a time in which.*

 The word *when* is perfectly appropriate when discussing a time frame. It's also acceptable to say *at a time that* (though *when* would probably be preferred in this sentence). The word *where*, though, refers to a location not a time frame. It's also inappropriate to say *at a time in which* (though perhaps *at a time during which* could work). Eliminate answers (C) and (D).

(3) Idiom: *so X such that Y were Z*

 Answer (D) uses the construction *so new such that many planes were of experimental design.*

 This choice mixes two idioms. It's possible to say that *aviation was so new that many planes were of experimental design* (*so X that many Y were Z*). It's also possible to say that the history of aviation was such that planes were still dangerously new (*X such that Y*). It's not correct, though, to jumble the two together. Eliminate answer (D).

The Correct Answer

Correct answer (E) fixes the initial meaning error by changing the word *for* to *that*: *Aviation was so new that many of the planes were of dangerously experimental design.*

#36 Producer Prices

(A)	Idiom (*like it is*); Pronoun (*it*)
(B)	Idiom (*as if*); Structure
(C)	**CORRECT**
(D)	Structure
(E)	Structure

First Glance

The underline is very short; glance through the answers before reading the sentence. Three answers begin with *like* or *as*, so there may be a Comparison issue. The other two answers are different, though, so be flexible.

Issues

(1) Idiom: *like it is; as if*

 The original sentence contains the idiomatic structure *sales figures seem like it is indicative.* What is this portion of the sentence trying to convey?

Consider this example: His test result seems like it is indicative of intelligence. At the most basic level, it would be necessary to use the idiom *seems as though,* not *seems like* (although people do speak that way in casual speech). Eliminate answer (A) for using an incorrect idiom.

Likewise, in answer (B), it would be necessary to say that *the sales figures seem as though* they are something or have some characteristic, not *as if.* Eliminate answer (B).

(2) Pronoun: *it*

 While examining the idiom issue, you might also spot the pronoun problem: *sales figures seem like it is indicative.* What is *it*?

 The pronoun *it* refers back to *sales figures*—but *it* is singular and *figures* is plural. (It's also a bit clunky to say that *the sales figures seem like the sales figures are indicative that X.* Why repeat the term *sales figures* as a pronoun?) Eliminate answer (A) for a bad pronoun match.

(3) Structure

 The final clause is introduced in one of three ways:

> (A) *it is indicative that the economy is not nearing a recession*
> (B) *as if to indicate the economy is not nearing a recession*
> (C) *to indicate that the economy is not nearing a recession*
> (D) *indicative of the economy is not nearing a recession*
> (E) *an indication of the economy is not nearing a recession*

 Let's slightly change the example used during the discussion of the Idiom issue: His test result seems like it is indicative of he is intelligent. In the original example, it was appropriate to use the preposition *of* because only a noun followed: *indicative of intelligence.* In this new example, though, a clause follows: *he is intelligent.* The preposition *of* cannot be followed by a clause. Eliminate answers (D) and (E) for a faulty sentence structure.

Answer (B) also makes an error in structure. *To indicate* can be followed by just a noun (his test results seem to indicate intelligence) or by a clause. When followed by a clause, it's preferable to insert the word *that*: his test results seem to indicate that he is intelligent. While there is some debate in the real world as to when the word *that* is required, the GMAT test writers have not yet published a question in which the correct answer does not insert the word *that* before the clause in a similar setup. Eliminate answer (B).

The Correct Answer

Correct answer (C) fixes the original idiom and pronoun errors and appropriately introduces the final clause with the word *that.*

MANHATTAN
PREP

#37 Deborah Sampson

(A) CORRECT	
(B) Parallelism / Meaning (*while being*)	
(C) Parallelism / Meaning (*discharged*)	
(D) Parallelism / Meaning (*injured*)	
(E) Meaning (*having been*)	

First Glance

The underline contains two commas; check for Parallelism, Modifier, Structure, or Meaning issues.

Issues

(1) Parallelism / Meaning: *while being; discharged; injured*

 The original sentence provides a list of three things relating to Deborah Sampson; other answers change this structure:

> (A) *Sampson joined, was injured, and was discharged*
> (B) *Sampson joined, was injured, while being discharged*
> (C) *Sampson joined and was injured, and discharged*
> (D) *Sampson joined, injured, and was discharged*
> (E) *Sampson joined, having been injured and discharged*

 The original *X, Y, and Z* list is correctly constructed. Answer (B) changes the list to what appears to be two items followed by a modifier (*while being discharged*); this introduces two problems. First, a two-item list still needs an *and* between the two items: *Sampson joined and was injured*. Answer (B) is missing the *and*. Second, the sentence now indicates that Sampson was in the midst of being discharged on all three (separate) occasions when she was injured. The meaning is nonsensical. Eliminate answer (B).

Answer (C) also changes the structure: *Sampson joined and was injured, and discharged*. Aside from the fact that it's wordy to use *and* twice, *Sampson* didn't discharge herself from the army; she *was discharged*. Answer (D) contains a similar error: *Sampson joined, Sampson injured, and Sampson was discharged*. Sampson *was injured*. Eliminate answers (C) and (D) for illogical meanings in the parallel portion of the sentence.

A̶
B̶
C̶
D̶
E

(2) Meaning: *having been*

 Answer (E) changes the parallel structure so substantially that it deserves a separate discussion. *Sampson joined in 1782, having been injured and discharged in 1783.*

 Consider this example: Riga joined the company in March, having been offered a substantial raise. When was she offered the raise and when did she join the company? "Comma -ing" modifiers pick up the time frame of the main verb in the sentence (in this case, the past tense *joined*). In this case, Riga either had already been offered the raise or was offered the raise pretty much at the moment she joined.

A
B
C
D
E̶

Likewise, in answer (E), the *having been* actions should take place before or in the same time frame as the *joined* action. This is impossible, though, because Sampson joined in 1782 but wasn't injured or discharged until 1783. Consider this: Riga joined the company in March, having been offered a promotion three months later in June. That's nonsensical! Eliminate answer (E) for an illogical meaning.

The Correct Answer

Correct answer (A) employs a list with appropriate meaning for the three parallel verbs.

#38 Tagore and Gandhi

(A) Parallelism (*X and also as Y*)	
(B) CORRECT	
(C) Meaning / Idiom (*not only X and Y*)	
(D) Idiom (*admiration of*)	
(E) Idiom (*admiration of*); Meaning / Idiom (*not only X and Y*)	

First Glance

The underline contains a "comma" but structure. Look for possible Structure, Parallelism, Meaning, or Idiom issues.

Issues

(1) Parallelism: *X and also as Y*
   Meaning / Idiom: *not only X and Y*

 The sentence contains a parallel structure, which in some answers appears with an idiomatic structure as well:

(A) *the person*	*and also as a politician*	
(B) *as a person*	*and as a politician*	
(C) *not only as a person*	*and as a politician*	*but Tagore*
(D) *as a person*	*and as also a politician*	
(E) *not only as a person*	*and as a politician*	*but Tagore*

 Answer (A) is incorrect due to a lack of parallelism between the *X* and *Y* elements: either both portions should begin with a preposition (*as*) or neither should. Further, the word *also* is redundant in the construction *X and also Y*. Eliminate answers (A) and (D).

Answers (C) and (E) are setting a very tricky trap. Both begin with *not only* and each answer does contain the words *but also*; superficially, the sentence appears to use the construction *not only X but also Y*. In this case, though, *X* is *as a person* while *Y* is *Tagore*; the two portions aren't parallel.

Alternately, you could interpret the construction as *not only X (as a person) and Y (as a politician)*. *Not only X and Y* is an incorrect idiom. Either way, answers (C) and (E) are wrong.

(2) Idiom: *admiration of*

Some choices note that *Tagore had admiration for Gandhi*; others say that he *had admiration of Gandhi*. Are both acceptable?

When describing a person, the correct idiom is *admiration for*, as in: She had the greatest *admiration for* her teacher. Eliminate answers (D) and (E) for using the wrong preposition.

A
B
C
~~D~~
~~E~~

The Correct Answer

Correct answer (B) fixes the original parallelism and verb tense errors while avoiding the idiomatic and meaning errors present in the other choices.

#39 Schistosomiasis

(A) CORRECT
(B) Idiom (*such X, Y*); Meaning (*economical*)
(C) Idiom (*so X as to Y*)
(D) Idiom (*such is X, Y*); Meaning (*economical*); Verb / Meaning (*becomes*)
(E) Meaning (*economical*)

First Glance

The underline begins right after a comma; keep an eye out for Modifier, Structure, Meaning, and Parallelism issues.

Issues

(1) Idiom: *such X, Y; such is X, Y; so X as to Y*

The original sentence uses the construction *so X that Y: it is so debilitating that it has become a drain*. The *Y* portion describes or further elucidates *X*. Other answers change this construction:

(B) *it is of such* debilitation,	*it has become*
(C) *so* debilitating is it	*as to become*
(D) *such is* its debilitation,	*it becomes*
(E) *there is so much debilitation*	*that it has become*

The structure in answer (A) is correct. Answers (B) and (D) are missing the word *that*; the idiom is *of such debilitation that*. Furthermore, the constructions *such X, Y* and *such is X, Y* are both incorrect. Eliminate answers (B) and (D).

Answer (C) uses the idiom *so X as to Y*; the correct idiom is *so X that Y*. Eliminate answer (C).

A
~~B~~
~~C~~
~~D~~
E

(2) Meaning: *economical*

The original sentence describes an *economic drain*, as does answer (C). Answers (B), (D), and (E), however, talk about an *economical drain*.

Economic and *economical* don't have the same meaning! *Economic* refers to the economy; an *economic drain* is a monetary drain, or a loss of money. *Economical*, on the other hand, typically means "in a frugal or cost-effective manner." *Economical drain*, then, means the *drain* is actually *cost-effective*—which is illogical. The sentence is discussing the fact that this disease costs countries money. Eliminate answers (B), (D), and (E).

(3) Verb / Meaning: *becomes*

The original sentence describes the disease in the present tense (*it is not often fatal*) but notes that it became an *economic drain* sometime in the past and that this condition continues today (*has become*, the present perfect tense). Most of the other answers maintain this tense, but answer (D) changes to the simple present *becomes*.

The disease isn't just becoming an economic drain right at this very moment. The phenomenon must have already been observed. Eliminate answer (D).

The Correct Answer

Correct answer (A) employs the valid idiom *so X that Y* and also uses the appropriate adjective, *economic*, to describe the drain.

#40 OPEC

| (A) Meaning (*but*); Verb (*were*) |
| (B) Meaning (*but*); Meaning (*is trimmed*) |
| (C) Meaning (*would be trimmed*); Verb (*would be*) |
| (D) Verb (*were*) |
| **(E) CORRECT** |

First Glance

The underline contains many commas; keep an eye out for Parallelism (particularly lists) as well as Modifier and Structure issues.

Issues

(1) Meaning: *but*

Strip the original sentence down to its core structure:

> *OPEC had been expected to announce X, but officials announced that the group will do X, but only if Y.*

The double use of the "comma but" structure should raise an alarm bell. The first instance is used correctly to introduce a new independent clause. In the second instance, the words *but only* are redundant; it is sufficient to say that *the group will do X only if Y*. Eliminate answers (A) and (B).

(2) Verb: *were; would be*

 The verb tense changes from choice to choice: *were to trim, is trimmed, would be trimmed, were trimming,* or *trim.*

 The group will only pare production if some other countries first reduce output, so this reduction in output could not have occurred yet. It's inappropriate, then, to use past tense for this portion of the sentence. Eliminate answers (A) and (D).

It's also inappropriate to use the hypothetical *would be trimmed*. The *officials announced* an intention to do a certain thing *if non-OPEC nations trim output*. This intention is not hypothetical. Eliminate answer (C).

(3) Meaning: *is trimmed; would be trimmed*

 For a portion of the sentence, the answers switch from active to passive voice:

(A) *if non-OPEC nations were to trim output*
(B) *if the output is trimmed*
(C) *if the output would be trimmed*
(D) *if non-OPEC nations were trimming output*
(E) *if non-OPEC nations trim output*

 This issue is very subtle. Although many people prefer active voice to passive voice, passive voice is grammatically correct; don't eliminate just for this reason. Do, though, examine the meaning.

The meaning of the original sentence is that OPEC will do *X* if nations agree to reduce output. In other words, the organization first wants these nations to agree to take a certain action themselves. The active construction *if nations trim output* conveys this meaning. By contrast, the passive construction *if the output is trimmed* does not indicate who is responsible for trimming the output. The nations themselves are no longer the ones who must agree to do so; perhaps the international community or OPEC will force the countries to do so. Eliminate answers (B) and (C) for introducing this ambiguity in who performs the action.

The Correct Answer

Correct answer (E) fixes the initial verb tense issue by using the simple present *trim*; in addition, answer (E) removes the redundant word *but*.

#41 Lucretia Mott

(A)   Meaning; Structure / Meaning
(B)   Meaning
(C)   Parallelism (*advocate X and for Y*)
(D)   Parallelism (*advocate X and for Y*)
(E)   CORRECT

First Glance

The underline begins with a "comma -ing" modifier. The word *and* appears just after the underline ends. Keep an eye out for Modifier and Parallelism issues.

Issues

(1) Meaning

Answers (A) and (B) read: *Lucretia Mott published her Discourse on Women, arguing in a treatise …* What does this mean? Is *Discourse on Women* the *treatise*? Or is the treatise something else?

If *Discourse on Women* is the treatise, then there is no need to include the phrase *in a treatise*; the *arguing* action described refers to the entire previous clause, which includes *Discourse on Women*. If, on the other hand, the *treatise* is a different piece of work, then the sentence is confusing; why is the modifier talking about something other than what was discussed in the main clause? Eliminate answers (A) and (B) for creating this problem!

Note that answers (C), (D), and (E) fix this problem by placing *a treatise* immediately after the comma. In these choices, *a treatise* is a straight noun modifier, referring to the noun just before the comma in a manner similar to this construction: She likes Rover, the basset hound that Luciano bought.

~~A~~
~~B~~
C
D
E

(2) Parallelism: *advocate X and for Y*
Structure / Meaning

The sentence contains a parallel structure:

(A)	*arguing* **for women to have rights**	*and* **for changes**
(B)	*arguing* **for equal rights**	*and* **for changes**
(C)	*that advocates* **equal rights**	*and* **for changes**
(D)	*advocating* **equal rights**	*and* **for changes**
(E)	*argued* **for equal rights**	*and* **for changes**

Tackle the most obvious mismatch first: answers (C) and (D) use the structure *advocates X and for Y*. The second parallel item should be *changes*, not *for changes*. Eliminate answers (C) and (D).

Superficially, the other three are fine, but the structure in answer (A) is not quite right. The treatise argues for two things: *equal rights* and *changes*. Pretend someone's reading answer (A)

A
B
~~C~~
~~D~~
E

aloud: *arguing in a treatise for women …* (pause) *… to have rights.* The treatise was written for women? The treatise was intended to be read by women? The treatise wants women to have rights? Who knows! In order to eliminate this potential ambiguity in meaning, say either (1) *a treatise* argues *for equal rights* (*for* + noun), or (2) *a treatise* argues *that* women should have *equal rights* (*that* + clause). Eliminate answer (A).

The Correct Answer

Correct answer (E) fixes the initial meaning error by turning the modifier into a standard noun modifier: *Discourse on Women, a treatise that argued.* It also uses a parallel structure: *argued for equal rights and for changes.*

#42 Population Forecasts

(A) Verb / Meaning (*have*); Comparison (*X more than Y*)
(B) Verb / Meaning (*have*); Meaning (*economical*)
(C) Meaning (*economical*)
(D) CORRECT
(E) Comparison (*X more than Y*)

First Glance

The underline starts with the verb *have*; the choice is between *have* and *would have*. Some kind of verb tense is at issue.

Issues

(1) Verb / Meaning: *have*

The first split in the answers is between the simple present tense *have to know* and the conditional *would have to know.*

The sentence discusses a hypothetical situation: the demographers currently don't know the information that they *would* need to know in order to make certain forecasts. In this case, use the conditional *would have to know.* Eliminate answers (A) and (B) for using a tense that does not convey this conditional meaning.

~~A~~
~~B~~
C
D
E

(2) Comparison: *X more than Y*

The underline contains a comparison marker, *X more than Y.* When you spot a comparison, check the *X* and *Y* portions to make sure that they are logically comparable—that is, the two things should be similar things.

In the original sentence, the *X* portion is what the demographers *would have to know* and the *Y* portion is *now.* These two things aren't comparable; the proper comparison is between what they *would have to know* and what they actually *do know.* Note: This trap was set specifically for native speakers, who will typically understand what the sentence is trying to convey and overlook the fact that the comparison itself is not exact. Eliminate answers (A) and (E) for an illogical comparison.

~~A~~
B
C
D
~~E~~

(3) Meaning: *economical*

 Answers (A), (D), and (E) end with the word *economic.* Answers (B) and (C) use *economical.* These two words do not mean the same thing!

 Economic refers to the economy; *economic determinants* is a synonym for business factors. *Economical,* on the other hand, can relate to the economy but more commonly means "in a frugal or cost-effective manner." *Economical determinants,* then, means *cost-effective determinants.* The word *cost-effective* is illogical in this context. The sentence is trying to discuss the social and business factors that affect fertility. Eliminate answers (B) and (C).

The Correct Answer

Correct answer (D) fixes the original comparison error with this structure: *would have to know a great deal more than they do now.* It also correctly uses the conditional verb *would* and the adjective *economic.*

#43 Laos

(A) Comparison; Modifier (*where*); Modifier / Meaning *(many)*	
(B) Comparison; Meaning / Meaning *(many)*	
(C) Structure	
(D) Meaning / Meaning *(many)*	
(E) **CORRECT**	

First Glance

The underline begins with the words *about the same as;* check for Comparison issues.

Issues

(1) Comparison

 The original sentence indicates that Laos's *land area* is *about the same as Great Britain.* It's illogical to compare the land area of a country to an actual country—compare either land area to land area or country to country.

 Scan the other answers for the same issue. Answer (B) also compares Laos's *land area* to *Great Britain.* Eliminate answers (A) and (B).

Answer (D) compares Laos's *land area* to Great Britain's *size.* While this comparison can technically be made, *size* is a more vague term—it could refer to area, yes, but also to other things, such as population. Be suspicious of this answer.

(2) Modifier: *where*

The original sentence contains a modifier beginning with the word *where*; this modifier provides information about the characteristics of members of the *population*.

Population is not a location; it's inappropriate to refer to *population* using a modifier that starts with the word *where*. Eliminate answer (A). None of the other answers repeat this error.

(3) Modifier / Meaning: *many*

The original sentence talks about *many* who *are members of hill tribes*. *Many* what? People, presumably—but the modifier specifically refers to the population. The sentence essentially says that *many populations are members of hill tribes*.

Populations aren't *members* of anything; individuals are. Eliminate answers (A), (B), and (D) for implying that the *populations* are *members of the hill tribes*.

(4) Structure

This last issue is pretty subtle; many people won't spot it. All of the answers change the structure of the second half of the underline; answer (C) changes the most significantly:

> (C) ... , *but in Laos with a population of only four million people, many of them are members.*

The conjunction *but* can introduce a new clause, and *many of them are members* is a clause, so that works. It is also acceptable to say *in Laos, many of them are members* (as long as the sentence contains an antecedent somewhere for *them*). The problem in (C) lies with the pronoun, *them*, and the placement of the antecedent, *people*. Consider the meaning of this example: In a country with too many people, overcrowding is common. It's evident that the overcrowding results from there being too many people in the country.

In answer (C), the implication is that because *Laos has four million people, many of them are members of hill tribes*. This cause-effect relationship doesn't make sense. Eliminate answer (C).

The Correct Answer

Correct answer (E) fixes the original comparison error by inserting the pronoun *that*: Laos's *land area is comparable to that* (the land area) *of Great Britain*. This choice also inserts the word *people* so that the sentence can then logically refer to *many of* the people.

#44 The Bostonians

(A) Idiom (*between X with Y*)
(B) Idiom (*X against Y*)
(C) CORRECT
(D) Idiom (*between X with Y*)
(E) Meaning

First Glance

The underline contains four commas! Keep an eye out for Modifier or Parallelism issues.

Issues

(1) Idiom: *between X with Y; X against Y*

 The original sentence uses the idiom *between Olive with her cousin*. *Olive* and *her cousin* are parallel, but the idiom *between X with Y* is incorrect.

 The entire idiom is underlined, so you can't know exactly how the correct answer will fix the issue. Possibly it will use the correct idiom *between X and Y*. Possibly it will discuss *Olive's rivalry with her cousin*. Possibly it will use some other construction entirely.

Answers (A) and (D) use the incorrect idiom *between X with Y*. Answer (B) uses another incorrect idiom: *the rivals Olive against Basil*. The correct idiom would be *the rivals Olive and Basil*. Eliminate answers (A), (B), and (D).

(2) Meaning

 You might spot this issue while examining the choices for the Idiom issue discussed above. Answer (E) says that *the plot centers on the feminist and the rivalry with her cousin*.

 While we know from the original sentence that the rivalry is between Olive and Basil, answer (E) does not actually convey that information. This answer merely indicates that Basil is part of a rivalry, but the reader is left to guess with whom. Eliminate answer (E) for an ambiguous meaning.

The Correct Answer

Correct answer (C) fixes the original idiom error by using the proper idiom *between X and Y*.

Note that answer (C) introduces a new verb, *develops*. The *when* clause at the end of the sentence is an adverbial modifier, providing additional information about some action earlier in the sentence. In answer (C), that action is *develops*: *the rivalry develops when they find themselves* … The other answers contain only the verb *centers*; those sentences say that *the plot centers on* (something) *when they find themselves* … Pairing the *when* modifier with the verb *develops*, as in answer (C), is more clear.

#45 Quasars

(A)	Structure
(B)	**CORRECT**
(C)	Structure
(D)	Structure
(E)	Structure

First Glance

The underline is very short; examine the answers before reading the full sentence. The verb keeps changing, so some sort of verb structure is at issue.

Issues

(1) Structure

Chop out the modifier separated out by commas and examine the sentence core:

(A) *Quasars believed to be the cores of galaxies in an early stage of development.*

The sentence is missing a verb. The word *believed* is a past participle; it can't function as the verb by itself. Consider this simpler example: Shelley believed to be the smartest woman in the world.

In both the original sentence and the simpler example, some form of the verb *to be* is needed: Shelley is believed to be. *Quasars are believed to be.* Answer (A) is not a complete sentence.

Answer (B) correctly inserts the verb *are*. What about the other answers?

(C) *Quasars some believe them to be the cores*
(D) *Quasars some believe they are the cores*
(E) *Quasars it is believed that they are the cores*

These answers do insert a verb, but they also insert additional subjects. A sentence can't have two subjects simply running together in this way: Shelley some believe she is the smartest. Eliminate answers (A), (C), (D), and (E) for a faulty core sentence structure.

The Correct Answer

Answer (B) offers one subject paired with one verb: *Quasars are believed.* It is the only choice that offers a proper sentence core.

#46 Ancient Thailand

(A) Parallelism (*X and Y*); Idiom (*for*); Pronoun (*they*)
(B) CORRECT
(C) Parallelism (*X and Y*)
(D) Meaning
(E) Meaning

First Glance

Nearly the entire sentence is underlined. Be prepared for Big 4 issues: Structure, Meaning, Modifiers, or Parallelism.

Issues

(1) Parallelism: *X and Y*
Meaning

 The original sentence contains the word *and*. What is it trying to make parallel? The parallel structure appears to be this: *Much energy was expended for* **the creation** *and* **when they constructed**.

 The writer is setting a trap. Superficially, the sentence might sound fine, but the construction is not actually parallel because the *X* portion is a simple phrase (*creation of images*) and the *Y* portion is a full clause (*they constructed*). Answer (C) contains a similar error: *Energy was expended on* **the creation** *as well as* **constructing**. Eliminate answers (A) and (C).

Answers (D) and (E) switch up the subject of the sentence, also changing the parallel structure:

(D) *creating images accounted for* energy *and also* constructing and decorating
(E) *the creation of images accounted for* energy *as well as* construction and decoration

In both cases, the sentence says that the *creation of images accounted for* two things: *energy*, and *construction and decoration*. This is illogical; the *creation of images* did not account for the *construction and decoration of the temples*. Rather, the *artisans' energy was expended on* these things. Eliminate answers (D) and (E) for illogical meaning.

(2) Idiom: *for*

 The original sentence contains the words *energy was expended for*.

 When explaining how the energy was used, the correct idiom is the *energy was expended on* something. Answers (B) and (C) both fix this error. Answers (D) and (E) use a different construction entirely. Eliminate answer (A).

It can also be correct to say something such as this: The battery's energy was *expended for* the good of science. However, the meaning of this example is very different from the intended meaning of the original sentence. This alternate example explains why the energy was expended; the original sentence explains how the energy was expended.

(3) Pronoun: *they*

The original sentence includes the pronoun *they*. What is its antecedent?

Logically, the pronoun *they* should refer to the noun *artisans*—the *artisans* are the ones who *constructed the temples*. The word *artisans*, though, is not a noun in this sentence; instead, the word *artisans'* is an adjective, in the same way that the word *cat's* is an adjective in the phrase the cat's toy. Whose *energy*? The *artisans' energy*. Whose toy? The *cat's* toy.

This leaves the plural noun *images* to match with the word *they*, but that match is illogical. Eliminate answer (A).

The Correct Answer

Correct answer (B) fixes the initial parallelism error and uses the correct idiom: *Energy was expended* **on the creation** *and* **on construction and decoration**. It also eliminates the illogical pronoun *they*.

#47 Alexander Pope

(A) Structure / Parallelism (*X and Y*)
(B) CORRECT
(C) Verb (*had taken*); Structure / Parallelism (*X and Y*)
(D) Meaning; Structure / Parallelism (*X and Y*)
(E) Meaning; Verb (*had taken*); Structure / Parallelism (*X and Y*)

First Glance

The long underline contains many commas (four!), so keep an eye out for Modifier, Meaning, Parallelism, and Structure issues.

Issues

(1) Structure / Parallelism: *X and Y*

The original sentence starts with an independent clause (*Pope began … Iliad*) and follows it up with a modifier (*a work that*). The modifier has a confusing structure:

Original Sentence:

                  (modifier)

             taking him 7 years until completion,

a work that, ↗

      and   (parallelism!)

(a work) that Johnson pronounced

Essentially, the sentence says *Pope began his translation of the Iliad, a work that and that Johnson pronounced*. In the structure *a work that X and that Y*, there is no *X* portion at all.

 Answer (A) is definitely wrong. Eliminate (A).

Check the other answers to see how they handle this construction:

(B) *a work* **that took**	*and* **that Johnson pronounced**
(C) *a work* **that had taken**	*and* **that Johnson pronounced** *it* *as*
(D) *a work* **that took**	*and* **that Johnson pronounced** *it* *as*
(E) *a work* **that had taken**	*and* **Johnson pronounced** *it*

On the surface, all of the remaining choices appear to be parallel. There is one problem though. The words *a work*, which appear before the parallelism starts, must apply to both the *X* and *Y* portions of the sentence. Try this with answer (B): *a work that took and (a work) that Johnson pronounced*. No problem. Now try answer (C): *a work that had taken and (a work) that Johnson pronounced it*. What is *it*?

It is the work! Answer (C) really reads *a work that Johnson pronounced the work*. This is redundant, if not downright illogical. Answers (C), (D), and (E) all contain this error, so eliminate them.

(2) Verb: *had taken*

 Some answers say that *the work took seven years to complete*; others say *the work had taken seven years to complete*. Are both versions acceptable?

 Pope began his translation in 1713. The completion happened after that, so the past perfect can't be used in that sense. The sentence also talks about another past event: *Johnson pronounced*. It's possible that Johnson made his pronouncement well after the work was done, in which case *the completion* might properly be written in the past perfect. Johnson, though, was Pope's contemporary; he might have made the pronouncement before the work was even fully completed. Because the sequence of events isn't clear, and either possibility is reasonable, it's better to keep the two actions in simple past. Eliminate answers (C) and (E).

(3) Meaning

 The first three answer choices talk about a *translation of the Iliad*. The final two change the noun *translation* to a verb: *Pope began translating the Iliad*. Recall that a noun modifier (*a work that*) follows.

 In answers (D) and (E), *a work* must refer to *the Iliad*, because *translating* is not a noun. Pope did not create *the Iliad* itself, however; he created a *translation of the Iliad*. The modifier is also clearly talking about the *translation*, not the original work, because Johnson pronounced Pope's work *the greatest translation*. Eliminate answers (D) and (E).

The Correct Answer

Correct answer (B) fixes the original parallelism error; in fact, it turns out to be the only answer that offers a correctly constructed parallel modifier.

#48 Landlocked Caspian

(A)	Modifier (*which*)
(B)	Modifier (*which; actually*)
(C)	**CORRECT**
(D)	Structure
(E)	Meaning

First Glance

The underline contains two commas. Keep an eye out for Modifier, Meaning, and Structure issues.

Issues

(1) Modifier: *which; actually*

 The original sentence says that *the Caspian is the largest lake on Earth, which covers.* Does the *which* modifier refer to *the Earth* or to *the largest lake*?

 If the *which* modifier does refer to *the Earth*, then the meaning is illogical; the Earth isn't four times the size of a lake on the Earth. If, on the other hand, the *which* modifier refers to *the largest lake*, the meaning is logical, but the structure is odd. *The largest lake* refers to *the Caspian*, so why not use the simpler and completely unambiguous structure *the Caspian is the largest lake and covers*? Eliminate answer (A) for creating this dilemma in the first place.

When one meaning issue due to modifier placement exists, look for similar issues in the other answers. The word *actually*, an adverb, moves around the sentence. What does it modify? In this case, the *Caspian* is *called a sea* but it is *actually the largest lake.* Answer (B) places *actually* with the *landlocked Caspian*, not *the largest lake.* Eliminate it.

(2) Structure

 Answer (D) begins with the word *though*, signaling a subordinate clause. Such opening modifiers can either be complete sentences (*Though he studied all night, he still failed his test the next day*) or non-clause modifiers (*Though tired, she studied for another hour*).

 In answer (D), the opening subordinate clause offers both a non-clause modifier (*called a sea*) and a complete sentence (*it actually is the largest lake*). This isn't allowed—the sentence should either say something along the lines of *though called a sea but actually the largest lake on Earth* (two non-clause modifiers) or *though it is called a sea, it is actually the largest lake on Earth* (two clauses). Eliminate answer (D) for faulty structure.

(3) Meaning

The meaning issue in answer (E) is very subtle; this one is tough to spot.

> *Despite being called a sea, the largest lake … is actually the Caspian.*

Consider this example:

> Despite being called a pie, the best cake in the store is actually the chocolate dessert.

Think about how you would convey that same meaning in a sentence yourself. Perhaps you'd say something similar to this: Despite being called a pie, that chocolate dessert right there is actually a cake. The contrast is between pie and cake, the two possible types of dessert. The example sentence above, though, appears to contrast the category pie and one specific chocolate dessert. Simplify the faulty example even more:

> Despite being called a pie, it is actually the chocolate dessert.
> *Despite being called a sea, it is actually the Caspian.*

This structure doesn't offer a logical contrast. The sentence should say something such as *despite being called a sea, it is actually a lake.* Eliminate answer (E) for an illogical meaning.

A
B
C
D
~~E~~

The Correct Answer

Correct answer (C) fixes the initial modifier error by using a "comma -ing" modifier, *covering*, which refers to the main noun, *the Caspian.*

#49 Conveyor-Belt System

(A) Idiom (*of assembling*)	
(B) Meaning (*being*); Meaning (*down to*)	
(C) Meaning (*being*); Meaning (*X to Y*)	
(D) CORRECT	
(E) Structure	

First Glance

The underline starts with the word *from*, indicating a possible Meaning issue.

Issues

(1) Idiom: *of assembling*

The original sentence uses the idiom *the required time of assembling.*

The correct idiom is *the time required to* do something, or *time required + infinitive.* In this case, the sentence should read *the time to assemble* or *the time required to assemble.* Eliminate answer (A).

~~A~~
B
C
D
E

MANHATTAN
PREP

(2) Meaning: *being*

 Being gets its own category because it's so very odd. In this case, answers (B) and (C) both use *the time being required*.

 As a general guideline, if you can remove the word *being* and the sentence is still structurally correct and makes sense, then do so. Because both answers (B) and (C) could correctly say *the time required* (the exact same structure without the word *being*), the insertion of the word *being* is unnecessary.

Note that when used correctly, *being* most often indicates either an ongoing action in the passive voice or a characteristic of something; neither is the case here. Eliminate answers (B) and (C).

(3) Meaning: *down to; X to Y*

 The answers differ slightly in the way that they present the portion *from a day and a half to 93 minutes*. Answer (B) inserts extra meaning with *down to 93 minutes*. Answer (C) omits the word *from*.

 The non-underlined portion of the sentence already indicates that the time has been *reduced*. Further, *from* a longer time frame *to* a shorter one reinforces the idea that the time has gone down. It's redundant, then, to add the word *down*. Eliminate answer (B).

The sentence is trying to convey a change: *from X* (one time frame) *to Y* (another time frame). The structure *X to Y* does not convey the same meaning, so eliminate answer (C).

(4) Structure

 Strip out the *which* modifier (along with both of its commas) and examine answer (E):

> *The system reduced from a day and a half to 93 minutes, the time required for the assembling of a Model T.*

 Why is that comma there? The test writers are hoping you fall into the trap of thinking that there is also a comma between reduced and from, like this: *the system reduced, from X to Y, the time required*. That would be okay—but it's not what answer (E) says.

With only the one comma, though, the portion before the comma should now be able to stand alone as its own sentence, while the portion after the comma would be a modifier. *The system reduced from a day and a half to 93 minutes.* What did it reduce? Itself? The core of the sentence no longer makes sense. Eliminate answer (E).

The Correct Answer

Correct answer (D) fixes the initial idiom error by using the correct form *required to assemble*.

#50 Soft Landing

(A) CORRECT
(B) Idiom (*confidence in*); Modifier (*what*);
      Structure / Meaning (*X rather Y*)
(C) Idiom (*confidence in*); Meaning
(D) Idiom (*confidence in*)
(E) Structure / Meaning (*X with Y*)

First Glance

The underline doesn't contain any obvious punctuation but does start with the word *that*, signaling possible Structure or Modifier issues.

Issues

(1) Idiom: *confidence in*

The sentences contain a split at the beginning:

> (A), (E): *confidence that the economy will avoid*
> (B), (C), (D): *confidence in the economy ('s ability) to avoid*

It is possible to use either *confidence that* or *confidence in* correctly in a sentence, as long as you follow some rules. Someone has *confidence in* a noun: She has confidence in your ability. Alternately, someone has *confidence that* something more complex will occur: She has confidence that you will get a good score on the GMAT. In the given answers, the more complex structure exists, so use *confidence that*, not *confidence in*. Eliminate answers (B), (C), and (D).

A
B̶
C̶
D̶
E

(2) Modifier: *what*

Answer (B) changes the restrictive modifier *that many had feared* into a non-restrictive modifier (set off by commas) beginning with the word *what*.

What and *that* are not interchangeable; *what* is not a regular relative pronoun and can't be used to start this kind of noun modifier. None of the other answers repeats this error, so eliminate answer (B).

A
B̶
C
D
E

(3) Structure / Meaning: *X rather Y; X with Y*

Answers (B) and (E) change the structure so that the sentence no longer contains the *X and Y* parallelism marker:

> (B) *in the economy* to avoid X   *rather* to come in for Y
> (E) *the economy will* avoid X   *with it instead* coming in for Y

The word *rather* is an adverb, not a conjunction (such as *and*), so *to come in for Y* is never properly connected to the rest of the sentence. This is the equivalent of saying *confidence in the economy to avoid X, to come in for Y*. Note that *rather* is not the same thing as *rather than*.

In answer (E), the prepositional phrase *with it coming* does not clearly convey the idea that *the economy will avoid X and instead do Y*. Further, the wording seems to indicate that the economy is definitely *coming in for a "soft landing"* already, where the original sentence says merely that there is growing confidence that this will occur. Eliminate answers (B) and (E).

(4) Meaning

Answer (C) changes the placement of *earlier in the year*:

> the recession, something earlier in the year many had feared

Placing *earlier in the year* right after *something* makes it sound like *something* (in this case, *the recession*) actually happened then. Rather, the action that occurred *earlier in the year* was the fear: *Many had feared* that something would happen *earlier in the year*. The recession itself did not actually occur, though. Eliminate answer (C) for a confusing meaning.

The Correct Answer

Correct answer (A) uses the correct idiom, *confidence that + clause*, and employs a clear parallel structure to convey the idea that the *economy will* probably *avoid X and instead come in for Y*.

#51 Conversational Pace of Life

(A) Idiom (*ability for*); Structure / Meaning
(B) CORRECT
(C) Structure / Meaning
(D) Structure / Meaning
(E) Idiom (*ability for*); Structure / Meaning

First Glance

The underline contains two commas, with the word *and* appearing before the first. Keep an eye out for Parallelism, Modifier, Meaning, or Structure issues.

Issues

(1) Idiom: *ability for*

The original sentence contains the clause *it hampers the ability for distinguishing*. The correct idiom is *ability to* do something, not *ability for* doing something. If you don't spot the error on your initial read-through, you have a second chance when comparing the answers; some use *ability for* while others use *ability to*.

Eliminate answers (A) and (E) for using the incorrect idiom *ability for*.

(2) Structure / Meaning

The ends of the answer choices differ. All begin with the same lead-in words:

hampers the ability of some children …

(A) *for distinguishing X*	*and, the result is, to make Y*
(B) *to distinguish X*	*and, as a result, to make Y*
(C) *to distinguish X*	*and, the result of this, they are unable to make Y*
(D) *to distinguish X*	*and results in not making Y*
(E) *for distinguishing X*	*resulting in being unable to make Y*

The meaning of the original sentence is illogical. The sentence is structured as two different clauses, each with its own subject and verb. The first clause asserts that the brisk pace of life hampers kids' ability to distinguish sounds. The second clause indicates that as a result, the kids can make sense of speech. Think about what that means. Shouldn't the opposite be true? If they have trouble distinguishing sounds, that should make it harder for them to make sense of speech, not easier. Eliminate answer (A) for an illogical meaning.

This reasoning would seem to mean that you should eliminate answer (B) as well because the two answers look fairly similar. Be careful! Don't fall into the trap. In answer (B), the parallel structure allows you to apply the verb *hampers* to the last part of the sentence:

It hampers the ability of some children **to distinguish sounds** *and, as a result,* **to make sense of speech.**

Both *X* and *Y* are hampered. Answer (B) is okay. What about the remaining answers?

Answer (C) is similar to (A) in construction, but the subject is missing a verb: *The result of this* [is that] *they are unable to make sense of speech.* Eliminate answer (C) for containing a subject without a matching verb.

Answers (D) and (E) change the ending structure more substantially. In both cases, the *results* portion is no longer talking about the children. In answer (D), the wording *and* [it] *results in not making sense of speech* conveys only that someone is not making sense of speech, but who? Perhaps it's the case that adults can't make sense of the children's speech.

In answer (E), the "comma -ing" modifier *resulting* refers to the main subject and verb: *the pace of life may be so brisk.* Again, this fails to convey who is now *unable to make sense of speech.* Eliminate both (D) and (E) for ambiguous meaning.

The Correct Answer

Correct answer (B) fixes the original error by changing the clause *the result is* to the modifier *as a result*, and by ensuring that parallelism allows the verb *hampers* to apply to both described actions: *hampers the ability to distinguish sounds and* [hampers the ability] *to make sense of speech.*

#52 Josephine Baker

(A)	Modifier (*to Josephine Baker*)
(B)	Modifier (*for Josephine Baker*)
(C)	Idiom (*to be*)
(D)	**CORRECT**
(E)	Idiom (*being*)

First Glance

The underline contains two commas and begins with a short modifier. Keep an eye out for Modifier, Meaning, or Structure issues.

Issues

(1) Modifier: *to Josephine Baker; for Josephine Baker*

The original sentence begins with a short opening modifier, *to Josephine Baker*. Answer (B) has a similar structure, but answer (C) changes the structure to make *Baker* the subject of the sentence. In answers (D) and (E), the sentence is back to starting with an opening modifier. Check both modifier placement and meaning.

In order for a sentence to start with a modifier such as *to Josephine Baker* or *for Josephine Baker*, the main clause has to be something that is true *to* or *for Baker*. Consider this example: To Josephine, olives tasted too salty. You can flip that sentence around: Olives tasted too salty to Josephine.

Can you do this with the original sentence? *To Josephine, Paris was her home.* Paris was her home to Josephine. The sentence seems to say that someone else's Paris home felt like home to Josephine. The sentence should say *To Josephine, Paris was home* (Paris was home to Josephine). The same problem exists with the construction *for Josephine Baker*; eliminate answers (A) and (B) for ambiguous meaning.

(2) Idiom: *to be; being*

The answers differ in the way that they present this portion of the sentence:

(A) *before* **it was fashionable to be** *an expatriate*
(B) *before* **it was fashionable to be** *an expatriate*
(C) *before* **to be** *an expatriate* **was fashionable**
(D) *before* **it was fashionable to be** *an expatriate*
(E) *before* **it was fashionable being** *an expatriate*

Fashionable to be is an acceptable idiom, but *fashionable being* is not. In order to move the verb *to be* earlier in the sentence, as in answer (C), you would have to say *before being an expatriate was fashionable* (and that construction would probably still be considered awkward). Eliminate answers (C) and (E).

The Correct Answer

Correct answer (D) fixes the original modifier error by making *Josephine Baker* the subject of the sentence. It also uses the correct idiom *fashionable to be*.

#53 Humphry Davy

(A)	CORRECT
(B)	Pronoun (*his*); Parallelism (*X and also Y*)
(C)	Parallelism (*X and Y*)
(D)	Parallelism (*X and also Y*)
(E)	Pronoun (*his*); Meaning

First Glance

The underline doesn't contain any obvious punctuation or other markers right at the beginning of the underline. Be ready for anything!

Strategy Tip

You might not find anything to attack in the original sentence. If so, where do you start? The underline is on the shorter side, so start by comparing the answer choices vertically. The issues below are presented in the order in which they would be found using a vertical comparison from the beginning of each answer choice.

Issues

(1) Parallelism: *X and also Y; X and Y*

 The first difference is a split between *a critique* and *critiquing*. What's the difference between the two forms?

 The original sentence offered two commentaries about the "Essay on Heat and Light": It was *a critique* of something *as well as a vision* of something else. The two pieces, then, should be parallel: *X as well as Y* or (in other choices) *X and Y*. Check all of the answers for parallelism:

(A) *a critique*	*as well as* **a vision**
(B) *a critique*	*and also* **his envisioning**
(C) *a critique*	*and* **envisioning**
(D) *critiquing*	*and also* **a vision**
(E) *critiquing*	*as well as* **his own envisioning**

Answers (B), (C), and (D) are definitely not parallel; eliminate them. Answer (E) does have two -ing words, so it's parallel on the surface, but this one needs to be examined more closely; see the Meaning issue on the next page.

A
~~B~~
~~C~~
~~D~~
E

(2) Meaning

When examining the choices for Parallelism, you might pick up on an ambiguous Meaning issue in answer (E). The sentence could be read to mean *critiquing X as well as Y*; that is, Davy *critiqued* two things, rather than *critiquing* one thing and *envisioning* another.

Technically, you don't have to know which meaning Davy really intended; this isn't a history test. It's enough to eliminate answer (E) because it's not clear whether the sentence is trying to say that he critiqued one thing and envisioned something else or that he critiqued two things. Eliminate answer (E) for an ambiguous meaning.

(3) Pronoun: *his*

This issue is probably the hardest to spot, but you might have noticed the use of the pronoun *his* when examining answer (E) for the Meaning issue. Does *his* refer to *Boyle* or to *Davy*?

Answers (B) and (E) use the pronoun *his* after the mention of both *Davy* and *Boyle*. In either answer choice, it's entirely possible for the pronoun to refer to either man. Eliminate both answers (B) and (E) for ambiguity.

The Correct Answer

Correct answer (A) conveys the needed meaning in a parallel and unambiguous manner. Note that some people might eliminate answer (A) because *all chemistry since Robert Boyle* can sound awkward. It is not actually incorrect, though.

#54 Hospital Report

(A) Verb (*should*); Parallelism (*X, Y, and Z*)	
(B) Verb (*should*); Parallelism (*X, Y, and Z*)	
(C) Verb (*should*); Parallelism (*X, Y, and Z*)	
(D) Parallelism (*X, Y, and Z*)	
(E) **CORRECT**	

First Glance

The underline contains two commas, the second of which comes right before the word *and*. Is Parallelism an issue?

Issues

(1) Verb: *should*

When verbs, such as *recommended*, are followed by the word *that*, the subsequent verb should be in the subjunctive: The teacher recommended that she study every night. The original sentence, however, uses the construction *should eliminate*, rather than the subjunctive form of the desired verb, *eliminate*.

Answers (A), (B), and (C) all incorrectly use the structure *recommended that the hospital should*. Eliminate them. Answers (D) and (E) both correctly use *recommended that the hospital eliminate*.

(2) Parallelism: *X, Y, and Z*

 The original sentence appears to contain a list of three recommendations made by the report (*X, Y, and Z*), though the three items are so far from parallel that it's hard to anticipate what the correct answer will contain.

 Eliminate answer (A) for lack of parallelism. Examine the other answers to see whether they maintain the *X, Y, and Z* structure. If so, cross off any that aren't parallel.

> (B) *should* **eliminate** *beds,* **services** *should be consolidated,* **and space** *be used*
> (C) *should* **eliminate** *beds,* **services** *should be consolidated,* **and to use** *space*
> (D) **eliminate** *beds,* **consolidate** *services,* **and space** *used*
> (E) **eliminate** *beds,* **consolidate** *services,* **and use** *space*

All of the answers do attempt to use an *X, Y, and Z* structure, but only option (E) offers a parallel set of three. The other answers mix verbs and nouns. Eliminate answers (A), (B), (C), and (D).

~~A~~
~~B~~
~~C~~
~~D~~
E

The Correct Answer

Correct answer (E) fixes both of the original errors. It uses the subjunctive *eliminate* following *recommended that* and it is also the only choice with a properly parallel *X, Y, and Z* list.

#55 Rent-to-Buy Programs

(A) Meaning (*to be able*)
(B) CORRECT
(C) Structure
(D) Subject–Verb (*enables*); Meaning (*applying*)
(E) Meaning (*to be able*); Meaning (*applying*)

First Glance

A significant portion of the sentence is underlined. Keep an eye out for Structure, Meaning, Modifier, or Parallelism issues.

Issues

(1) Meaning: *to be able*

 The issue in the original sentence is tough to spot because the sentence is so wordy, but look closely at the extract below:

> *rent-to-buy programs that enable a family … to be able to move*

The verb *enable* means the same thing as the phrase *to be able to*; using both words is redundant.

Answers (B), (C), and (D) strip out the *to be able* language and correctly say that the *programs enable a family to move.* Eliminate answers (A) and (E) for redundant language.

(2) Structure

Answer (C) introduces a semicolon after the word *programs.* The first portion is a complete sentence. What about the second portion?

The second portion of the sentence is problematic, but, interestingly, it can be considered a complete sentence. The word *that* refers back to the entire first clause (the portion before the semicolon), and it is actually logical to say that because builders offer these rent-to-buy programs, families are enabled to move into new housing.

The end of the sentence, though, tacks on a comma followed by *to apply.* How does this structure relate to the rest of the sentence? It's unclear. The parallelism marker *and* has been removed, and the only thing in its place is a comma, which doesn't indicate how *to apply* matches up with the rest of the sentence. Eliminate answer (C) for unclear structure.

(3) Subject–Verb: *enables*

Answer (D) says *programs, which enables*; answer (E) says *programs, which enable.* Does the sentence need a singular or plural verb?

A *which* modifier typically refers to the main noun immediately preceding the comma—in this case, *programs.* The plural *programs* should match with the plural verb *enable.* Eliminate answer (D) for a subject–verb mismatch.

(4) Meaning: *applying*

Answers (A), (B), and (C) contain *to apply* at the end of the underline. Answers (D) and (E) change the form to a comma, followed by *applying.*

Don't automatically cross off answers (D) and (E) simply because *to move* and *applying* are no longer parallel. These answers also remove the parallel marker *and,* so perhaps parallelism isn't required any longer.

A "comma -ing" modifier refers to the main clause (main subject and verb) in the sentence. You should be able to remove any other extra modifiers (even ones in between) and the sentence should still make sense:

> *Many house builders offer rent-to-buy programs, applying part of the rent to a purchase later.*

This illogically implies that the *builders* are *applying part of the rent,* not the families buying the homes. Eliminate answers (D) and (E).

MANHATTAN
PREP   121

The Correct Answer

Correct answer (B) fixes the initial error by dropping the redundant words *to be able*.

#56 Elizabeth Barber

(A) Parallelism (*both X and Y*): Meaning
(B) Parallelism (*both X and Y*); Meaning;
     Idiom (*authority about*)
(C) Parallelism (*both X and Y*); Idiom (*account about*)
(D) Parallelism (*both X and Y*); Meaning;
     Idiom (*authority about, account about*)
(E) CORRECT

First Glance

The underline contains two commas, so you should check for Modifier, Meaning, or Parallelism issues.

Issues

(1) Parallelism: *both X and Y*

The original sentence contains the parallel structure *both X and Y*. The *Y* portion is underlined, so check to see whether it is parallel with *X*.

(A) *of both Prehistoric Textiles*	*and also of Women's Work*
(B) *of both Prehistoric Textiles*	*and also Women's Work*
(C) *of both Prehistoric Textiles*	*and of Women's Work*
(D) *of both Prehistoric Textiles*	*and of Women's Work*
(E) *of both Prehistoric Textiles*	*and Women's Work*

The *X* portion consists solely of the title of one work, *Prehistoric Textiles*, so the *Y* portion should match. Only answer choice (E) offers the simple title *Women's Work*. Answers (A), (C), and (D) incorrectly repeat the word *of*, which was already used before the *both X and Y* parallelism began. Answers (A) and (B) insert the word *also*, which means the same thing as *and*. Using *and also* is redundant; the correct idiom structure is *both X and Y*. Eliminate answers (A), (B), (C), and (D).

(2) Meaning

The original sentence calls *Elizabeth Barber* an *expert authority* on something. The two words mean the same thing.

Answers (C) and (E) both use just one word, *authority*. Eliminate answers (A), (B), and (D) for using the redundant description *expert authority*.

A
B
C
D
E

A
B
C
D
E

(3) Idiom: *authority about; account about*

 Some answers say that *Barber* is an *authority on textiles*; others say she is an *authority about textiles*. Some answers say that the second book is a *general account of cloth manufacture*; others say that the book is a *general account about cloth manufacture*. Which versions are correct?

 For the first idiom in question, use *authority on*. A person is an *authority on* a certain subject. Eliminate answers (B) and (D). For the second idiom, a book can be about a topic, but a book is *an account of* a topic. It's incorrect to use the phrase *account about*. Eliminate answers (C) and (D).

The Correct Answer

Correct answer (E) is the only one that offers a viable parallel construction for the *both X and Y* portion of the sentence. It also uses the correct idioms *account of* and *authority on*.

#57 Kushan Empire

(A) Modifier (*Empire, fashioned*); Parallelism (*either X or Y*)
(B) Modifier (*Empire, fashioned*); Parallelism (*either X or Y*)
(C) Modifier (*f Empire, ashioned*); Parallelism (*either X or Y*)
(D) Parallelism (*either X or Y*); Verb (*fashioned*)
(E) CORRECT

First Glance

The sentence and underline are both of medium length, and a glance at the answers shows that they start off in similar fashion—no obvious clues here.

Issues

(1) Modifier: *Empire, fashioned*

 The structure *Empire, fashioned* (a comma followed by an -ed word) is a big noun-modifier clue; the information after the comma, the modifier, should refer to the closest main noun before the comma. In this case, that noun is *empire*. An entire empire was fashioned from sandstone? Maybe the buildings, but not the empire itself; that's illogical.

 If the empire was not fashioned from sandstone or schist, what was? The images. Eliminate answer (A) and scan the remaining choices. Answers (B) and (C) repeat this error so they can be eliminated.

(2) Parallelism: *either X or Y*

 The word *either* is always paired with the word *or* in the structure *either X or Y*. In addition, the *X* and the *Y* have to be parallel.

(A) *either* from sandstone   *or* schist
(B) *either* sandstone   *or* from schist
(C) *either* fashioned from sandstone   *or* schist
(D) *either* fashioned from sandstone   *or* from schist
(E) *either* from sandstone   *or* from schist

 Answers (A), (B), (C), and (D) all break parallelism. Only answer (E) provides *from + noun* for both *X* and *Y*.

Answer (E) is not the only way to make *X* and *Y* parallel. The authors could have written:

fashioned from either **sandstone** *or* **schist**

(3) Verbs: *fashioned*

 Answers (D) and (E) both correct the original modifier error by inserting the word *and* after the word *Empire*. This creates a second main verb and a parallel structure:

(D) *Many of the images date from X and fashioned from Y.*
(E) *Many of the images date from X and were fashioned from Y.*

 The subject is *many of the images.* Did these images themselves perform the action of fashioning something? Or were they fashioned by someone or from something? The images didn't fashion anything; rather, they *were fashioned from* one of two substances. The sentence requires the passive *were fashioned*. Eliminate answer (D).

Note that the correct answer is in passive voice. Based upon the meaning of the sentence, active voice would be illogical. Don't cross off passive voice simply because it's passive!

The Correct Answer

Correct answer (E) fixes both original errors. The insertion of the word *and* after *Empire* corrects the original modifier error: *Many of the images date* (from a certain time) *and were fashioned* (from one of two materials). The structure *either X (from sandstone) or Y (from schist)* is parallel.

#58 Alvin Toffler

(A)   Idiom (*can hardly be said*)
(B)   Meaning
(C)   Meaning
(D) CORRECT
(E)   Meaning; Idiom (*can hardly be said*)

First Glance

The underline ends at a colon. The information following the colon should provide context for the meaning of the underlined portion. Look out for Idiom or Meaning issues.

This sentence has such an unusual structure that it can be hard to understand the intended meaning. The sentence essentially says that people shouldn't blame the educators for failing to anticipate the impact of microcomputers because even Alvin Toffler (someone who would have known) failed to do so.

Issues

(1) Idiom: *can hardly be saidt*

 The original sentence uses an unusual construction: *That [X is true] can hardly be said that it is Y.* The correct idiomatic structure is *that [X is true] can hardly be said to be Y.*
(Note: *Can hardly be said* means that the thing is not true—these people are not at fault.)

 Eliminate answer (A) for using the incorrect idiom. Answer (B) does use the correct idiom. Answer (E) is missing the ending portion of the idiom: *to be Y.* Answers (C) and (D) use a different structure, *it can hardly be said that*; the idiom is used correctly in both of those answers. Eliminate answers (A) and (E).

(2) Meaning

 When examining the Idiom issue, you may have noticed some related Meaning issues. In answer (B), while the idiom itself is correct, the meaning of the *Y* portion is illogical:

> *That educators have not* (done something) *can hardly be said to be at fault.*

Who is not at fault? Technically, this sentence says that *the fact that* the educators didn't anticipate something is *not at fault.*

 The meaning of answer (B) is illogical. The *educators* are the ones who are *not at fault.* Answer (E) also contains an illogical meaning: *the fact that educators are at fault* indicates that these people really are in the wrong. However, this doesn't match the information after the colon; the sentence should say that the educators are not really at fault. Eliminate answers (B) and (E).

In answer (C), the clause *it is the fault of educators who* introduces an ambiguous meaning. The *who* modifier simply defines which educators are under discussion. The sentence essentially says: *it*

is [not] the fault of those particular *educators*. What is not their fault? The pronoun *it* can't refer to the descriptive modifier, so now the reader doesn't know what *it* is. Eliminate answer (C).

The Correct Answer

Correct answer (D) fixes the original idiom error by using a different construction: *it can hardly be said that educators are at fault for* something. This meaning, *the educators* are not *at fault*, agrees with the meaning of the example given after the colon.

#59 Adam Smith

(A) Modifier (*a leading figure*)
(B) Modifier (*a leading figure*); Comparison (*X is to Y like A is to B*)
(C) Modifier (*a leading figure*); Comparison (*X is to Y just as A is to B*)
(D) Comparison (*X is to Y similar to A is to B*)
(E) CORRECT

First Glance

The underline starts just after a comma. Look for Modifier, Meaning, or Parallelism issues.

Issues

(1) Modifier: *a leading figure*

 The original sentence begins with an opening noun modifier: *a leading figure*. This text should modify the subject after the comma. In the construction *Adam Smith's books*, *Smith's* is not a noun; it's an adjective describing the *books*, which are the subject of the sentence.

 It's illogical to say that *the books* were *a leading figure*; rather, *Adam Smith* was *a leading figure*. Eliminate answers (A), (B), and (C) for an illogical match between the modifier and the noun.

(2) Comparison: *X is to Y like A is to B; X is to Y just as A is to B; X is to Y similar to A is to B*

 The problem uses an unusual comparison idiom that changes a bit in the five answers:

> (A) *Smith's books are to democratic capitalism what Marx's book is to socialism*
> (B) *Smith's books are to democratic capitalism like Marx's book is to socialism*
> (C) *Smith's books are to democratic capitalism just as Marx's book is to socialism*
> (D) *books are to democratic capitalism similar to Marx's book is to socialism*
> (E) *books are to democratic capitalism what Marx's book is to socialism*

 What does this comparison idiom mean? Here's a simpler example: McDonald's is to the fast food industry what Coke is to the soft drink industry. The sentence is saying that McDonald's and Coke play similar roles in their respective industries.

MANHATTAN
PREP

Similarly, the given problem is saying that Smith's books and Marx's book play similar roles in their respective forms of government. The correct structure to use is *X is to Y what A is to B*. Eliminate answers (B), (C), and (D) for using an incorrect word in place of the word *what*.

The Correct Answer

Correct answer (E) fixes the initial modifier error by making the subject *Adam Smith*. It also uses the correct comparison idiom *X is to Y what A is to B*.

#60 Olympic Games

(A)	Idiom (*festival's month*)
(B)	Modifier (*proclaiming*); Idiom (*festival's month*)
(C)	Pronoun (*they*); Meaning
(D)	**CORRECT**
(E)	Meaning

First Glance

The underline is relatively short and doesn't contain any immediately obvious punctuation or clues right at the start of the underline. Be ready for anything!

Issues

(1) Idiom: *festival's month*

 The original sentence indicates that the *truce* took place *during the festival's month*. Other answer choices use the wording *the festival month* or *the month of the festival*.

 The possessive apostrophe-s is used when the possessive word owns or possesses the following noun, as in the example *Jun's car*. Jun possesses the car.

In the given sentence, does the festival possess the month? Consider this example: April is spring's month. This is incorrect because spring does not actually possess the month. In this problem, the *festival* does not actually possess the *month*. Eliminate answers (A) and (B).

(2) Modifier: *proclaiming*

 Answer (B) introduces a "comma -ing" modifier: *proclaiming a truce*. This kind of construction modifies the main subject and verb, in this case, *the Olympic Games helped to keep peace*.

 The "-ing" form *proclaiming* refers to someone or something performing an action. But who performed that action? Did the Greek world proclaim a truce? Did the people proclaim a truce? Did the Olympic Games organizers proclaim a truce? Eliminate answer (B) for an ambiguous meaning

(3) Pronoun: *they*

 Answer (C) introduces a pronoun: *they proclaimed a truce*. Who *proclaimed the truce*?

 The sentence contains two plural nouns: *the Olympic Games* and *the pugnacious states*. The subject pronoun *they* appears to refer to the subject *Olympic Games*. Consider this example: The cars were stolen when they were left unlocked. Structurally, the words "when they" point right back to the original subject.

A
B
C
D
E

In the given problem, though, this meaning would be illogical—the *Games* themselves can't proclaim something. Only the *states* would work logically, but structurally, the pronoun *they* seems to point to the *Games*. Eliminate answer (C) for ambiguity.

(4) Meaning

 Some answers indicate that the truce took place *during* the relevant month; others say that the truce was *for* the relevant month. Are both variations acceptable?

 Answers (C) and (E) both say that *the truce [was] for* the given time frame. Technically, this means that the truce was in favor of the time frame. Consider this example: Alan was for the new law. This would mean that Alan approved of the new law (i.e., he wanted to see it pass or succeed). This *for* construction doesn't convey the same meaning as *for the duration of* or *during*, the intended meaning of the sentence. Eliminate answers (C) and (E) for conveying an illogical meaning.

A
B
C
D
E

The Correct Answer

Correct answer (D) fixes the original error by removing the possessive and using *the month of the festival*. This answer also makes clear that the truce lasted *during* the relevant month. Notice that the correct answer contains two independent clauses, *The Olympic games helped to keep peace* and *a sacred truce was proclaimed,* joined by a comma and the coordinating conjunction *for*. The correct answer would be a run-on sentence if that *for* weren't there.

#61 Industrial Waste Problems

(A)   Subject–Verb (*determines*)
(B)   Pronoun (*their*)
(C)   Structure; Subject–Verb (*determines*)
(D)   Subject–Verb (*determines*); Meaning
(E)   CORRECT

First Glance

The long underline increases the chances that there are Structure, Meaning, Modifier, or Parallelism issues. The only word before the underline is *while*, indicating some kind of contrast or comparison.

Issues

(1) Subject–Verb: *determines*

 The subject of the main clause is *the predominating industries and the regulatory environment*. This plural subject needs a plural verb, but the corresponding verb in the original sentence is the singular *determines*.

 Note that both the subject and verb are underlined, so you'll need to check both in the other answers. It turns out that every answer uses the same plural subject, but the verb switches back and forth between *determines* and *determine*. Eliminate answers (A), (C), and (D) for using the singular *determines* with a plural subject.

(2) Pronoun: *their*

 While checking the subjects, you may have noticed that some answers say *their industries* instead of *the industries*. Check the pronoun.

 Answer (B) uses *their* incorrectly. The plural pronoun needs to point to a plural noun, but *each state* is singular. Answer (C) also uses *their*, but this time the pronoun correctly points to the plural *all states*. Eliminate answer (B).

(3) Structure

 Answer (C) contains a semicolon; always check for proper usage whenever you see a semicolon. This punctuation mark can be used only if the part before is a complete sentence and the part after is a complete sentence.

 In this case, the portion of the sentence that appears before the semicolon (*while all states face a similar industrial waste problem*) is not a complete sentence. Eliminate answer (C).

(4) Meaning

 This issue is pretty subtle; you might not spot it. The sentence is attempting to contrast two things: *while all states* are alike in a certain way, *each state* differs in another way.

 This contrast is made more clear if the *states* are lumped together, plural, when discussing the way in which they're alike, and separated out (*each state*) when discussing the way in which they're different. It's not necessarily incorrect to write this in a different way, but notice that the correct answer is written this way.

Answers (A), (C), and (E) appropriately talk about *all states* when discussing the similarity. Answers (B) and (D), though, use *each state*. Answer (D) further confuses things by using *each state* a second time, during the portion of the sentence discussing the differences. The two halves of the sentence describe a contrast; using *each state* twice, though, makes the two halves seem more similar. Eliminate answer (D) for introducing ambiguity and put a question mark next to answer (B) for using *each state* where *all states* would be more clear.

The Correct Answer

Correct answer (E) matches the plural subject with the plural verb *determine* and makes the similarity (*all states*) and contrast (*each state*) clear.

#62 Terra-Cotta Warriors

(A)	**CORRECT**
(B)	Modifier (*rivaling the pyramids*); Meaning
(C)	Modifier (*rivaling the pyramids*); Meaning
(D)	Modifier (*rivaling the pyramids*)
(E)	Modifier (*rivaling the pyramids*)

First Glance

The very long underline signals likely Structure, Meaning, Modifier, or Parallelism issues.

Issues

(1) Modifier: *rivaling the pyramids*

 The original sentence begins with a modifier: *Rivaling the pyramids or the cities as an achievement*. The information is talking about something that has not yet been mentioned. What is rivaling the pyramids?

 The *pyramids of Egypt* are works of art. What else in the sentence is a work of art or can be described as *an achievement*? *An army of terra-cotta warriors* makes sense and should be placed right after the comma, so the original sentence is fine. The other answers offer various other illogical options as the noun following the comma:

(B) *Qin Shi Huang* (a person is not a work of art)
(C) *it* (referring to how long the warriors took to make)
(D) *artisans* (people are not works of art)
(E) *36 years* (a length of time is not a work of art)

Eliminate answers (B), (C), (D), and (E) because each uses an illogical noun following the comma.

(2) Meaning

 The sentence contains a lot of modifiers; the placement of some modifiers in answers (B) and (C) confuse the meaning.

 In answer (B), the pronoun *it* refers to the *army*, so that the sentence reads: *an army that was created by artisans who took 36 years to complete the army*. This is an equivalent example: the cake that was created by the chef who spent 3 hours to make the cake. As though the second cake is a different cake!

The sequence of modifiers in answer (C) is confusing:

(C) *to create an army of warriors more than 2,000 years ago that would protect Huang*

What happened *more than 2,000 years ago*? The army was *created*. The *warriors* didn't just appear, nor were they *protected* 2,000 years ago. The modifier should more clearly point to the action that occurred *more than 2,000 years ago*. Further, the placement interrupts another noun and modifier pair: *the warriors (more than 2,000 years ago) that would protect Qin Shi Huang*. The two halves not in parentheses should be right next to each other; *the warriors*, not some *years ago*, are the ones who *would protect Huang*.

Eliminate answers (B) and (C) for confusing modifier placement.

A̶
B̶
C̶
D̶
E̶

The Correct Answer

Correct answer (A) is the only one that completes the opening modifier structure correctly: *rivaling the pyramids as an achievement, the army of warriors*. Further, the placement of the many modifiers is logical.

#63 Grain Restrictions

(A) Meaning (*try and establish*); Parallelism (*X and Y*); Idiom (*establish restrictions for*)
(B) Meaning (*try and establish*); Parallelism (*X and Y*); Meaning (*able to be*)
(C) Idiom (*establish restrictions for*); Parallelism (*X and Y*)
(D) Meaning (*capable of being*); Parallelism (*X and Y*)
(E) CORRECT

First Glance

The underline begins with the word *and*. Keep an eye out for Parallelism or Structure issues.

Issues

(1) Meaning: *try and establish*

The original sentence has a meaning problem: members *will try and establish restrictions*. Whenever you see an *X and Y* structure with two verbs (like this one), check whether the logical meaning is actually *will try to establish restrictions*.

How to know which it is? When the parallel marker *and* is used, the sentence is discussing two parallel but separate verbs: the *members will try* and, separately, the *members will establish*. In this case, the meaning is illogical. The members are trying *to establish*; they have the intention *to establish* these restrictions. Eliminate answers (A) and (B).

Although people will use *try and establish* in casual conversation all the time, the meaning is still illogical. The test writers are trying to get you to fall for false parallelism, but the sentence shouldn't have a parallel structure here.

Answer (C) is suspect; *establishing* might be okay, but the construction in answers (D) and (E) (*try to establish*) is better. Put a question mark next to answer (C).

(2) Idiom: *establish restrictions for*

The original sentence uses the idiom *establish restrictions for* the amount of something. The correct idiom is to *establish restrictions on* the amount or usage of something.

Eliminate answers (A) and (C) because they use the incorrect idiom *establish restrictions for*.

(3) Parallelism: *X and Y*

The original sentence also contains a real instance of the parallelism marker *X and Y*:

(A) *will try and establish*   *and to encourage*
(B) *will try and establish*   *and encouraging*
(C) *will try establishing*   *and to encourage*
(D) *will try to establish*   *and encouraging*
(E) *will try to establish*   *and to encourage*

Answers (A) and (B) use the form *will establish* for the *X* portion. Neither *to encourage* nor *encouraging* is an acceptable match for the *Y* portion. Answers (C) and (D) pair a participle with an infinitive; both are not parallel. Only answer (E) offers a parallel structure: *to establish and to encourage*. Eliminate answers (A), (B), (C), and (D).

(4) Meaning: *able to be*; *capable of being*

Answers (A), (C), and (E) indicate that the government is trying to restrict what some people will be *allowed to grow*. Answer (B) talks about what is *able to be grown* and answer (D) talks about what is *capable of being grown*. Are all versions acceptable?

Allowed means permitted: the government permits the farmers to grow a certain amount of grain. What farmers are *able to grow* or *capable of growing* is a different issue. One farmer might be *able to grow* more than the restrictions would allow while another farmer might be *capable of growing* less than the restrictions allow. The government can't determine this; it just depends how much land a farmer has, how good she is at growing grain, and so on. Eliminate answers (B) and (D) for an illogical meaning.

The Correct Answer

Correct answer (E) fixes the original meaning issue by using the construction *will try to establish*. It also offers the parallel construction *to establish and to encourage*.

#64 Genetic Predispositions

<table>
<tr><td>

(A) CORRECT

(B) Idiom (*X but also Y*); Meaning (*aggravating*)

(C) Idiom (*X but also Y*); Meaning (*aggravating*)

(D) Idiom (*not only X, Y*); Meaning (*aggravating*)

(E) Verb (*doing*); Meaning (*aggravating*)

</td></tr>
</table>

First Glance

In the original sentence, the underline begins with the words *not only*. Check for Idiom issues.

Issues

(1) Idiom: *X but also Y; not only X, Y*

 The original sentence uses the idiom *not only X but also Y*. This is a correct idiom, but check the other answers to see what form they use. Also check the *X* and *Y* portions for parallelism.

(A)	*not only do damage*	*but also aggravate*
(B)	*do damage*	*but also are aggravating*
(C)	*are damaging*	*but also are aggravating*
(D)	*not only do damage*	*they are also aggravating*
(E)	*are doing damage*	*and they are also aggravating*

 The idiom *not only X but also Y* means that the *X* and *Y* portions go in the same direction. In other words, these *factors do damage* and *aggravate genetic predispositions*. Answers (B) and (C) unacceptably change the meaning of the sentence by using the idiom *X but also Y*. *But* is a contrast: She likes ice cream but hates chocolate. The *X* and *Y* portions no longer go in the same direction. Answer (D) is wrong for a similar reason. The *X* portion starts with *not only* but the *Y* portion doesn't start with any idiom marker at all. Eliminate answers (B), (C), and (D).

(2) Meaning: *aggravating*

 The original sentence uses the verb *aggravate*. The other answer choices use the form *aggravating*.

 To aggravate means to cause something to get worse. The adjective *aggravating*, on the other hand, is most commonly used to mean irritating or annoying. In a sentence structure such as *the factors are aggravating*, it can be difficult to tell whether *aggravating* is used as a verb (causing something

to get worse) or as an adjective (irritating, in the colloquial usage). Such ambiguity is bad and the GMAT writers prefer to avoid this construction. Eliminate answers (B), (C), (D), and (E).

(3) Verb: *doing*

 Answer (E) uses the present progressive verb *doing* rather than the simple present *do*.

 The sentence is trying to convey a general "truth": these three factors *do damage. Are doing damage* implies that the three factors are only having this effect at this very moment (rather than in general). Eliminate answer (E).

The Correct Answer

Correct answer (A) uses an appropriate idiom, *not only X but also Y*, and the simple present verb form of the words *do* and *aggravate* to convey the desired meaning.

#65 China Sediments

(A) Modifier (*digging in sediments*); Meaning (*suggesting*)	**First Glance**
(B) Modifier (*digging in sediments*)	
(C) CORRECT	The majority of the sentence is underlined, signal-
(D) Meaning (*that which*)	ing potential Structure, Meaning, Modifier, or
(E) Meaning (*that*)	Parallelism issues.

Issues

(1) Modifier: *digging in sediments*

 The original sentence begins with an opening "comma -ing" modifier: *digging in sediments in northern China*. The main noun following this structure should indicate who or what was *digging*—but it's illogical to say that the *evidence* was *digging*.

 Because the underline starts with the word *evidence*, scan the beginning of each answer. There are only two options: *evidence* (definitely wrong) and *scientists*. The word *scientists* is acceptable: the *scientists* were *digging*. Eliminate answers (A) and (B).

(2) Meaning: *suggesting*

 The original sentence contains *suggesting* as an ambiguous modifier: *evidence has been gathered by scientists suggesting that*. Is the evidence suggesting something or are the scientists suggesting something?

When an "-ing" word functioning as a modifier isn't separated out by a comma, then that modifier typically modifies the noun right before it; this modifier may or may not have anything to do with other nouns in the sentence. Consider this example:

> Evidence has been gathered by people living in France.

The evidence isn't living in France; the people are. The evidence isn't even necessarily being collected in France; these people live in France, but they might be collecting evidence in Indonesia. Similarly, the original sentence implies that the *evidence* was collected by *scientists* who also happen to be *suggesting* a separate theory about something else. This is theoretically possible but not very logical.

It would be more logical, then, to say that the *evidence suggests* (or indicates) something. Eliminate answer (A).

(3) Meaning: *that which; that*

  The sentence makes a comparison between what the new evidence suggests and what was previously thought to be true. Some of the comparisons include a pronoun structure (*that* or *that which*).

(A) *life-forms emerged*	*earlier than **they had previously thought***
(B) *earlier emergence*	*than **had been previously thought***
(C) *life-forms emerged*	*earlier than **previously thought***
(D) *earlier emergence*	*than **that which was previously thought***
(E) *earlier emergence*	*than **that previously thought***

The structure is pretty complex. The comparison signal is *earlier than*, but what is the actual comparison? Here's where the difficulty comes in: these answers all imply something for the second half that was already stated in the first half. It's possible to say that something *emerged* (verb) earlier than it was previously thought to *have emerged* (an implied verb). It's also possible to say that the *emergence* of something *occurred* earlier than it was previously thought to *have occurred* (another implied verb). In both cases, the implied verb is explicitly used in the first half of the comparison. Parallelism allows you to assume that the verb repeats in the second half.

Answers (D) and (E) mess up the comparison by introducing an unneeded pronoun: *that*. This pronoun seems to refer to *emergence*, but if you substitute *emergence* in place of *that*, the illogic of the comparison becomes apparent, as in the case of (D): *earlier emergence … than the emergence which was previously thought*. This substitution implies that there were two separate emergences. However, there was only one emergence, one that simply happened earlier *than previously thought*. Choice (E) also inserts the word *that*; eliminate answers (D) and (E).

The Correct Answer

Correct answer (C) fixes the opening modifier error by making *scientists* the subject of the sentence. This choice also correctly indicates that the *evidence* is *suggesting* something and the comparison structure is parallel: *life-forms emerged earlier than* [*they were*] *previously thought* [*to have emerged*].

#66 Beach Erosion

(A) Parallelism (*X and Y*)
(B) Parallelism (*X and Y*); Meaning (*act like*)
(C) CORRECT
(D) Parallelism (*X and Y*)
(E) Parallelism (*X and Y*); Meaning (*acting like*)

First Glance

The underline is very short; compare the answers before reading the original sentence. The first word splits between *act* and *acting*, and the word right before the blank is *and*, indicating possible Parallelism issues. Other answers split between a clause (*it absorbs*) and a modifier (*absorbing*), indicating possible Structure issues.

Issues

(1) Parallelism: *X and Y*

The sentence contains this parallel structure:

> (A), (B), (C): *a breakwater that would* **rise**   *and* **act**
> (D), (E): *a breakwater that would* **rise**   *and* **acting**

The form *act* is parallel to *rise*; *acting* is not. Eliminate answers (D) and (E) for breaking parallelism.

Because you've spotted one parallelism issue already, check to see whether there are any others. A second parallel structure, *X and Y*, begins later in the underline: *it absorbs and protecting*. The *Y* portion, *protecting*, is not underlined, so the *X* portion must be made to match. Answers (A), (B), and (E) do not use the word *absorbing*; eliminate all three for breaking parallelism.

(2) Meaning: *act like; acting like*

Answers (A), (C), and (D) use the idiom *act(ing) as a buffer*. Answers (B) and (E) use *act(ing) like*. Are both acceptable?

It is possible to use both *act as* and *act like* correctly in a sentence, but the two mean different things. *Act as* is used when something performs a certain function: Her GMAT book acts as the perfect sleep aid (because she falls asleep whenever she starts to study!). *Act like*, on the other hand, describes how someone behaves: He acts like a jerk sometimes, but he's actually a nice guy. In this sentence, the *breakwater* is functioning *as a buffer*, so use the form *act as*. Eliminate answers (B) and (E).

The Correct Answer

Correct answer (C) maintains the proper meaning by using *act as*. It also corrects the original parallelism error by changing *it absorbs* to *absorbing*.

#67 Dolphin Species

> **(A) CORRECT**
> (B) Meaning (*growing*); Meaning (*as big as*)
> (C) Meaning (*growing*)
> (D) Subject–Verb (*includes*); Meaning (*as big as*)
> (E) Subject–Verb (*includes*)

First Glance

The underline includes a comma followed by *which*, indicating possible Modifier or Meaning issues.

Issues

(1) Meaning: *growing*

 Three answer choices contain the comma followed by *which*, the other two change to "comma -ing." Does the sentence require a noun modifier or an adverbial modifier?

 What *can grow* or is *growing*? The *killer whale*. Because the noun *killer whale* already appears right before the comma, the sentence should use a noun modifier (*which*) after the comma. The adverbial modifier, *growing*, would modify the verb *include*, implying that the killer whale is *growing* as a result of the fact that the *32 species include* them. This is illogical. Eliminate answers (B) and (C).

(2) Meaning: *as big as*

 The five answers differ in their description of the whale's possible length:

> (A) *can grow **to be** 30 feet long*
> (B) *growing **as big as** 30 feet long*
> (C) *growing **up to** 30 feet long*
> (D) *can grow **as big as** 30 feet long*
> (E) *can grow **to be** 30 feet long*

 It is acceptable to say that something grows *to be 30 feet long* or *up to 30 feet long*. The third variation, however, is the wrong word choice (and redundant besides). It's incorrect to use *as big as* for a length; rather, use *as long as*. However, even if the correct idiom had been used, this would make the full phrase *as long as 30 feet long,* which is redundant. Eliminate answers (B) and (D).

(3) Subject–Verb: *includes*

 Answers (A), (B), and (C) start with the plural verb *include*; answers (D) and (E) begin with the singular *includes*. Which is correct?

 Find the subject. The subject is not *whales*, nor is it the *dolphin family*. The subject is all the way at the beginning: *species*. This word is a little tricky, because the singular and plural versions are identical. Two clues indicate that *species* is plural in this sentence: the number *32* and the double-verb structure. The sentence reads: *The 32 species are X and include Y.* Eliminate answers (D) and (E) for using a singular verb.

The Correct Answer

Correct answer (A) uses a plural verb to match the plural subject. It also correctly employs a noun modifier structure (comma followed by *which*) to provide additional information about the *killer whales*.

#68 Troubled Conglomerate

(A) Modifier (*outlining his strategy*);
     Idiom (*plans for cutting*)
(B) Modifier (*outlining his strategy*)
(C) Modifier (*outlining his strategy*);
     Idiom (*plans for cutting*)
(D) CORRECT
(E) Modifier / Meaning

First Glance

The opening split is between *executive's plans* and *executive.* Look for Subject–Verb, Modifier, Structure, or Pronoun issues.

Issues

(1) Modifier: *outlining his strategy*

 The original sentence contains a classic opening modifier structure: *Outlining his strategy, the executive's plans were announced.* When the underline includes any portion of an opening modifier or the main clause that follows an opening modifier, check the structure.

 Such opening modifiers must refer to the subject right after the comma, but *the plans* didn't develop a *strategy.* The *executive* did. (Note that the pronoun *his* also can't refer to the *plans*!) Eliminate answers (A), (B), and (C).

(2) Idiom: *plans for cutting*

 The original sentence talks about the *plans for cutting the debt.*

 First, note that the word *plans* is a noun in this sentence, not a verb. It is possible to talk about *the plans for* a noun: the plans for the house. If you want to talk about the *plans* for an action, though, then that action should be in verb form: the plans to launch a new product.

In this sentence, the *plans* are designed *to cut the debt,* so the idiom should be *plans to cut.* Eliminate answers (A) and (C) because they use *plans for cutting.*

Answer (D) uses the correct idiom. Answers (B) and (E) don't use the idiom at all.

(3) Modifier / Meaning

 The final issue is subtle, but you might have spotted it when examining the idiom issue discussed above. Answer (E) says:

The executive announced plans that are to cut the debt by selling assets.

 The *that* modifier refers to the preceding noun, *plans*. In other words, *the plans are to cut the debt by selling assets*. This may sound perfectly fine, because people speak this way in the real world, however, the meaning is illogical.

In the structure *the plans are to* do something, the *plans* themselves are about to undertake the described action. The meaning is similar to this: The executive announced the team that is to launch the new product. The team members themselves are the ones who will carry out the action. In the same way, according to the given sentence, the plans themselves are literally the ones who are going to carry out the action. This doesn't make sense; the plans can't execute themselves. Eliminate answer (E).

A
B
C
D
E̶

The Correct Answer

Correct answer (D) fixes the opening modifier error by changing the subject to *executive*. It also presents a logical meaning.

#69 Gibraltar

(A) Verb (*was*)	
(B) CORRECT	
(C) Verb (*was*); Pronoun (*it*)	
(D) Pronoun (*that*); Meaning	
(E) Pronoun (*it*)	

First Glance

The underline begins with the word *if*. Some kind of conditional verb structure might be an issue.

Issues

(1) Verb: *was*

 The original sentence uses the conditional structure *if X, (then) Y*. Conditional structures require certain verb tenses, depending on the intended meaning of the sentence. (Note: Some answers don't specifically use the word *if*, but the conditional nature of the meaning is still clear.)

 In this case, the *if* portion is in past tense (*if they did not hold it*) and the full meaning is hypothetical: They did not know what was going to happen after that. The second half of the structure, then, should be in the present conditional form: *Their grip would be insecure.* Answers (A) and (C) both incorrectly use simple past *was* for the conditional portion of the sentence; eliminate them.

A̶
B
C̶
D
E

(2) Pronoun: *it; that*

Four of the five answers use the pronoun *it*; answer (D) uses the pronoun *that*. The word *it* is a personal pronoun; the word *that* is a demonstrative pronoun.

When demonstrative pronouns are used alone, not in conjunction with a noun, such as "that car," they should not refer to a noun that is located within the same main clause. In answer (D), the pronoun *that* refers to *Morocco*, which is in the same main clause. Eliminate answer (D).

The other four all use *it*, so they must all be correct, right? Not so fast. Answers (A) and (B) do correctly use *it*; first, the noun *Morocco* appears, then the pronoun *it*, which refers to *Morocco*, and finally *Algeria* (so it's clear that *it* does not refer to *Algeria*). In answers (C) and (E), however, the pronoun *it* does not appear until the end of the sentence. Do the French need to hold *Morocco* or *Algeria*? The sentence is no longer clear. Eliminate answers (C) and (E).

A
B
C̶
D̶
E̶

(3) Meaning

The original sentence says that *their grip was insecure.* Answer (B) conveys a similar meaning, this time with the correct conditional tense: *Their grip would never be secure.* In both cases, the *grip* is the thing that is (or is not) *secure.* Answer (D) changes this structure: The French *could never be secure about their grip.* What's the difference?

The meaning in answer (D) no longer indicates whether the grip actually is secure. Rather, this choice talks about how the French feel about the situation. For example: The dog could not be secure about his grip on the bone (he wasn't sure he had a good grip on the bone). The dog's grip on the bone was not secure (he definitely did not have a good grip on the bone). The two sentences convey different meanings. Eliminate answer (D).

A
B
C
D̶
E

The Correct Answer

Correct answer (B) fixes the initial tense error by changing *was* to the conditional *would be.*

#70 Tell Hamoukar

(A) Idiom (*evidence for*)
(B) Subject–Verb (*yields*)
(C) Idiom (*simultaneously of*)
(D) Idiom (*evidence of*); Subject–Verb (*yields*); Idiom (*simultaneously of*)
(E) **CORRECT**

First Glance

It's important to read the extra-long original sentence in full, even though it will take longer than usual. Be very diligent about comparing portions of the (long!) answer choices vertically; you do not want to read each one in full!

MANHATTAN
PREP

Issues

(1) Idiom: *evidence for; evidence of*

 The core of the sentence is contained within the first two lines: *The trenches … have yielded evidence*. After that, the sentence becomes almost impossibly complex:

Original Sentence:

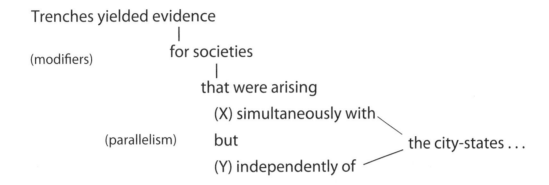

The structure isn't technically incorrect, but there is a potential idiom issue: *yielded evidence for*.

 Something can *yield evidence for* a noun, for example: Her poor performance yielded damning evidence for her boss. It's also possible to *yield evidence of* a noun: Her poor performance yielded evidence of incompetence. If, though, the intention is to talk about a more complex result presented in the form of a clause, then the proper structure is *yield evidence that*: Her poor performance yielded damning evidence that she was not qualified to do the job. Eliminate answers (A) and (D).

(2) Subject–Verb: *yields*

 The original sentence does not underline the subject but does underline the verb. Further, this verb changes in format from answer to answer: *have yielded* in answers (A), (C), and (E) versus *yields* in answers (B) and (D).

 The subject, *trenches*, is plural. The verb *have yielded* is plural but the verb *yields* is singular (he yields versus they yield). Eliminate answers (B) and (D) for lack of subject–verb agreement.

(3) Idiom: *simultaneously of*

 Answers (C) and (D) both state that the *societies* arose *simultaneously but independently of the city-states*. The parallel structure *X but Y* requires that either *the city-states* or *of the city-states* apply to both items.

 It is possible to say *independently of the city-states*, but it is not correct to say *simultaneously of the city-states* or *simultaneously the city-states*. The correct idiom is *simultaneously with the city-states*. Eliminate answers (C) and (D).

The Correct Answer

Answer (E) correctly uses *yielded evidence that* followed by a clause; the choice does not introduce any new errors, as answers (B), (C), and (D) do. Answer (E) does chop out some extraneous words (*cut* in place of *that were cut, arose* in place of *that were arising*) but note that these substitutions are only preferred, not strictly necessary.

#71 Major Rivers

> (A) Verb (*endure*); Idiom (*endure in*);
>   Meaning (*combination of X and Y both*)
> **(B) CORRECT**
> (C) Meaning (*combination of X and Y*);
>   Verb (*have encouraged*)
> (D) Meaning (*combination of X and Y*);
>   Idiom (*endured*)
> (E) Meaning (*combination of X and Y both*)

First Glance

The underline starts just after the word *and*. Look for Parallelism issues.

Issues

(1) Verb: *endure; have encouraged*

 In the original sentence, the time sequence is illogical: *Traditions endure [for] 6,000 years.* The traditions don't just *endure* today. They *have endured* for a long period of time.

 Because the traditions began in the past, either the simple past should be used (if those traditions are no longer in place today) or the present perfect should be used (if those traditions are still in place today). Eliminate answer (A).

Scan the other answers for verb issues. Answer (C) also mixes up the timeline: *Conditions have encouraged traditions that endured.* If the conditions are continuing to encourage certain traditions now, then those traditions still endure today and present perfect must be used. Eliminate answer (C).

(2) Idiom: *endured in; endured*

 The original sentence talks about *traditions that endure in 6,000 years.*

 Endure in a time period is an incorrect idiom. Rather, the traditions *endure for* a period of time. Eliminate answer (A).

Answers (B), (C), and (E) all correctly use *for.* Answer (D), though, does not use a preposition at all: *traditions that endured 6,000 years.* A person can endure some kind of trial; for example, a

MANHATTAN
PREP

person endured a serious illness. Traditions (or people) cannot endure a time period, though. Rather, something *endures for* a period of time. Eliminate answer (D).

(3) Meaning: *combination of X and Y; combination of X and Y both*

The original sentence contains the parallel structure *X and Y.* The form of *Y* differs in the five answers:

(A), (B): *combination of a supply*   *and good growing conditions*
(C), (D), (E): *combination of a supply*   *and of good growing conditions*

Further, answers (A) and (D) use the word *both* in this construction, but this word is dropped in the other choices.

What represents the *X* portion? Is it *of a reliable supply* or just *a reliable supply*? Be very careful; the test writers are setting a trap here.

The trap is to think that both the *X* and *Y* portions should start with *of.* The *of,* though, is part of the idiom *combination of* and shouldn't be repeated. How do you know? Meaning. Consider this simpler example:

The combination of peanut butter and jelly tastes very good. (Correct)
The combination of peanut butter and of jelly tastes very good. (Incorrect)

The second (incorrect) sentence appears to be talking about two different combinations: that of peanut butter and that of jelly. This is illogical; rather, the combination is "of peanut butter and jelly" together.

Likewise, in the problem, it is illogical to say that the *combination of a water supply and* (separately) *of good conditions* led to something else. Eliminate answers (C), (D), and (E).

Further, note that answers (A) and (D) add the word *both* to the sentence. That word could begin its own idiom (*both X and Y*), but this structure doesn't exist in the sentence. Alternately, *both* could refer to the two things mentioned previously: *the combination of a supply and good conditions both encouraged* something. The addition of the word *both,* though, is redundant; the word *combination* means the same thing. Eliminate answers (A) and (D).

The Correct Answer

Answer (B) correctly uses *have endured* to indicate something that started enduring in the past and still endures today. It also uses the proper idiom *endured for 6,000 years.*

#72 Louis Agassiz

(A)	Verb (*had existed*); Meaning
(B)	**CORRECT**
(C)	Meaning
(D)	Verb (*had existed*); Meaning
(E)	Meaning

First Glance

The underline starts with *in which*. Glance at the answers to notice that other choices offer *when* instead. The sentence might contain a Modifier issue.

Issues

(1) Verb: *had existed*

 The original sentence uses the past perfect: *Ice sheets had existed*. Other answers use the simple past *existed*. Which is correct?

 Past perfect is used to denote the longer-ago of two past actions. In this case, the *had existed* action is paired with a comment about the climate in those same areas *now*. It's acceptable, then, to use the simple past *existed*; don't use a more complex tense when a simple tense is acceptable. Eliminate answers (A) and (D).

(2) Meaning

 In answer (A), *now currently* is redundant—both words mean the same thing. Eliminate answer (A), and examine the meaning in the other answers:

> (B) *existed in what are now temperate areas*
> (C) *existed where there were areas now temperate*
> (D) *existed in current temperate areas*
> (E) *existed in areas now that are temperate*

 Answer (D) drops *now* and switches from *currently* to *current*. That word is modifying the adjective *temperate*, so it needs to be in the adverb form (*currently*). The adjective form *current* can only be used to modify nouns. Eliminate answer (D).

The other answers drop *currently* and use only *now*. Answers (B) and (C) are okay, but answer (E) has a meaning problem. The word *now* must be tied to a particular action or event: Something happened *now*. In answer (E), the word now is actually tied to *existed*: *Sheets existed now that are temperate*. Something can't be simultaneously in the past (*existed*) and happening *now*. Eliminate answer (E).

Answer (C) also mixes two time frames: *were* and *now*. They *were [not] temperate* before; they *are temperate now*. Eliminate answer (C).

The Correct Answer

Correct answer (B) fixes the initial verb error by switching to the simple past *existed*. The construction *in what are now temperate areas* properly indicates that the climate has changed in these areas. They used to be cold; they are now temperate.

Miscellaneous

Note: The *in which* versus *when* split turned out to be a red herring! Both versions are acceptable.

#73 Virtual Leonardo

(A) Modifier (*which*)	
(B) Meaning	
(C) Pronoun (*it*)	
(D) CORRECT	
(E) Modifier (*which*)	

First Glance

The underline is very short; compare the answers before reading the original sentence. There is a split between *exhibit, which* (a modifier structure) and *exhibit and* (a parallel structure). Later, the sentence switches between *activates* and *activate*; one answer even changes to the noun form *activation*.

Issues

(1) Modifier: *which*

The original sentence switches between the modifier structure *exhibit, which* and the parallel structure *exhibit and*.

A "comma *which*" modifier must modify the preceding main noun. The exhibit doesn't activate itself, though. Logically, *thereby activates* is referring to the verb *touch*: The touch activates the exhibit. Eliminate answers (A) and (E).

(2) Meaning

Answer (B) doesn't use either the *exhibit, which* or the *exhibit and* structure. What is going on in answer (B)?

There are a couple of different ways to interpret answer (B). The general meaning is this: *The Project encourages visitors to "touch" each exhibit, in turn* causing something else to happen. It would be possible, then, to say *in turn activating the functions*. This answer uses the noun form *activation*, though. Possibly, the sentence is introducing a new clause, but then the sentence would need another verb, and it doesn't have one. Alternately, perhaps the phrase after the comma is modifying the preceding noun, *exhibit*. This is illogical, though. The *exhibit* isn't an *activation* of anything. Essentially, it's impossible to tell what *activation* means or is referring to in the sentence. Eliminate answer (B).

(3) Pronoun: *it*

Answer (C) introduces a new subject and verb in the second half of the parallel portion: *and it will activate*. What *will activate*?

Logically, the *touch* of a visitor should activate the *exhibit's functions*. The word *touch* can be a noun or a verb. In the given sentence, the word *touch* is used as a verb (to "*touch*"). A pronoun must refer to a noun, not a verb, so *it* can't refer to *touch* in answer (C). Nor can the noun be the word *exhibit* (the *exhibit* isn't activating itself), and no other noun in the sentence makes sense. Eliminate answer (C).

The Correct Answer

Correct answer (D) fixes the original error by replacing *which* with *and*. Now, two verbs are appropriately parallel: *The Project encourages visitors to (X) "touch" each exhibit and thereby (Y) activate the functions.*

#74 Earth's Crust

(A) Modifier (*covering the entire planet*); Structure
(B) Parallelism (*neither X nor Y, but Z*)
(C) Parallelism (*neither X nor Y, but rather Z*)
(D) CORRECT
(E) Modifier (*covering the entire planet*)

First Glance

Most of the sentence is underlined, likely signaling Structure, Modifier, Parallelism, or Meaning issues.

Issues

(1) Modifier: *covering the entire planet*

The original sentence begins with a modifier: *despite its covering the entire planet*. Opening modifiers should be followed by the words that they modify. In this case, does the opening modifier refer to the *Earth*?

It doesn't make sense to say that the *Earth covers the entire planet*—the Earth actually is the planet. It would make more sense to say that the *Earth's crust covers the planet*. Sure enough, a comparison of the answers shows that, in answers (B), (C), and (D), the opening modifier refers to the *Earth's crust*. Eliminate answers (A) and (E).

(2) Structure:

The original sentence contains two independent clauses: *Earth has a crust* and *it is fragmented*. Independent clauses have to be connected with a coordinating conjunction or an appropriate punctuation mark, such as a semicolon.

In this case, the two clauses are connected by the word *rather*, which is not a coordinating conjunction. This structure would be the equivalent of this sentence: The student was not tired, rather he was ready to study all night. Either the comma needs to be replaced by a semicolon or the word *rather* needs to be replaced by a coordinating conjunction, such as *and*. Eliminate answer (A).

(3) Parallelism: *neither X nor Y, but (rather) Z*

 Answers (B), (C), and (D) contain the idiom *neither X nor Y, but (rather) Z*. The *X*, *Y*, and *Z* portions should be parallel. Compare the parallel structure in the answers:

(B) *crust is neither* **seamless**	*nor* **is it stationary**	*but is*
(C) *crust is neither* **seamless**	*nor* **is it stationary**	*but rather*
(D) *crust is neither* **seamless**	*nor* **stationary**	*but rather*

In all three cases, the words immediately preceding the start of the idiom are *crust is*. These words, then, apply to all three items in the idiom. Answers (B) and (C) repeat the verb *is* for at least one of the later items; it's not possible to say *the crust is is it stationary* or *the crust is is fragmented*. Eliminate answers (B) and (C).

The Correct Answer

Correct answer (D) fixes the original modifier error by placing *Earth's crust,* not the *Earth* itself, after the comma. Further, it corrects the original run-on sentence error by turning the second independent clause into a subset of the main clause.

#75 The Arts

(A) CORRECT
(B) Meaning (*economically*)
(C) Meaning (*as a means of*); Parallelism (*X and Y*)
(D) Meaning (*economically*); Meaning (*as a means of*); Parallelism (*X and Y*)
(E) Idiom (*as a means for*); Parallelism (*X and Y*)

First Glance

The relatively short underline signals that you might want to compare the answers before beginning the sentence—possibly just the beginning and end of each choice.

Issues

(1) Meaning: *economically*

 A vertical comparison of the answers reveals a split between *economic* in answers (A), (C), and (E) and *economically* in answers (B) and (D). What is the difference between these two words?

Economic is an adjective, while *economically* is an adverb. The difference goes beyond form, however; these two words have different meanings. *Economic* refers to the economy; *economic development* is a synonym for business development. *Economically*, on the other hand, can relate to the economy but more commonly means "in a frugal or cost-effective manner." *Greater development economically*, then, means development done in a cost-effective way—not a logical meaning for the sentence. Eliminate answers (B) and (D).

A
~~B~~
C
~~D~~
E

(2) Idiom: *as a means for*
   Meaning: *as a means of*

 The first word of each answer changes; the options are *to*, *of*, and *for*. These prepositions are a part of the idiom *as a means* _____. Which is correct?

 Both *as a means to* and *as a means of* are valid idioms; *as a means for* is not. Eliminate answer (E).

A
B
~~C~~
~~D~~
~~E~~

The two valid idioms have different meanings. *X as a means to Y* indicates that *X* is used in order to make *Y* happen or to achieve *Y* result. *X as a means of Y* indicates that *X* is a type of *Y*. In this sentence, the cities are using the arts in order to help promote economic development; this meaning matches the idiom *as a means to*. Eliminate answers (C) and (D).

(3) Parallelism: *X and Y*

 A vertical comparison of the end of each answer indicates a split between *investing*, *invest*, and *the investment of*. The word *and* appears right before these options, indicating parallelism. In the idiom *X and Y*, what is the *X* portion?

 In answers (A) and (B), the *Y* form is *investing*; is there a parallel match? Yes—*cities are stressing* one thing and *investing* in another. The match is both structurally and logically parallel.

In answers (C) and (D), the *Y* form is *invest*; is there a parallel match? There isn't another similar verb form in the sentence; eliminate answers (C) and (D).

Answer (E) is interesting. Technically, *the investment of* is a structural match for *greater economic development*. It's illogical, however, to say that *cities are stressing the arts for X (economic development) and Y (investing millions)*. Rather, the cities are choosing to invest millions because they think this action will help economic development. Eliminate answer (E).

A
B
~~C~~
~~D~~
~~E~~

The Correct Answer

Correct answer (A) uses the appropriate idiom, *as a means to*, as well as the appropriate adjective to mean business development (*economic*). Further, the *X and Y* portion of the sentence is parallel.

#76 Paleolithic Neanderthals

(A) Meaning / Verb (*appear*);
     Idioms (*appear as; equipped for*)
(B) CORRECT
(C) Meaning / Verb (*appear*); Idiom (*appear as*)
(D) Idiom (*appear as*)
(E) Idiom (*equipped for*)

First Glance

A decent amount of text appears after the underline ends; make sure to read all the way to the end of the sentence.

Issues

(1) Meaning / Verb: *appear*

 The original sentence says that *Neanderthals appear* a certain way but also indicates that they became *extinct* a long time ago. If Neanderthals are extinct, they can't actually *appear* a certain way today.

At first glance, the verb split seems to be simple: *appear* versus *appeared*. Answers (B) and (E), though, have more complex verb structures: *appear(ed) to have been equipped*. If Stella *appears* happy, she is that way right now. If Stella *appears to have been* happy when she lived 100 years ago, then the sentence is referring to a past event or occurrence that appears to be true to people who are today examining that history.

Answers (A) and (C) use *Neanderthals appear* without the additional verbiage to indicate the past; eliminate both. Answer (B) uses *appear to have been equipped*; this choice properly indicates the time frame. It *appears* today that *the Neanderthals* were *equipped* in the past.

(2) Idioms: *appear as; equipped for*

 The original sentence uses the idioms *appear as (equipped)* and *equipped for (facing)*.

 The idiom *appear as* can be followed by a noun: She appeared as a witch in the school play. When followed by a verb, however, the idiom should say *appear to* (verb). In this case, the sentence would need something such as *appear to be equipped*. Eliminate answers (A), (C), and (D).

The idiom *equipped for* could also be followed by a noun: We are equipped for the pending apocalypse. When followed by a verb, however, the idiom should say *equipped to* (verb). In this case, the sentence should say *equipped to face*. Eliminate answers (A) and (E).

The Correct Answer

Answer (B) correctly conveys the time frame with *appear to have been equipped* and also uses the proper idioms (*appear to, equipped to*).

Miscellaneous

The split between *path* and *paths* is a red herring. Many will think that the sentence should use the plural *paths*, since *Neanderthals* is plural (and might use this reasoning to eliminate the correct answer!). It is also possible, however, to talk about the figurative *path* taken by the species as a whole. Instead of trying to decipher which meaning the sentence intends, concentrate on other issues.

#77 Phosphates in the Great Lakes

(A) Verb / Meaning (*had been*)
(B) Verb / Meaning (*had been*)
(C) Verb / Meaning (*have been*); Verb (*reduces*)
(D) CORRECT
(E) Verb (*reduces*); Idiom (*allowed for*)

First Glance

The sentence and underline are both of medium length and no punctuation jumps out; there are no solid clues at first glance.

Issues

(1) Verb / Meaning: *had been; have been*

 The initial sentence uses the past perfect tense *had been allowed* to refer to a change made in a 1972 agreement. How is past perfect used correctly?

 Past perfect refers to the longer-ago of two past actions. In this case, the 1972 agreement *reduced* a certain thing and that reduction would have to take place after the agreement, not before. It's incorrect to use past perfect for the later of the two actions; eliminate answers (A) and (B).

Note also that answer (B) drops the *allowed* wording. As a result, this answer is talking about the actual amount that was dumped (legally or illegally); further, the past perfect *had been dumping* means that they somehow reduced the amount that had been dumped in the past, prior to the 1972 agreement. What took place in the past can't be changed! Eliminate answer (B).

Answer (C) uses the present perfect *have been*. Present perfect refers to something that started in the past and still continues or is still true in the present. Did the *have been* event begin prior to 1972 or after 1972? It's not clear. Eliminate answer (C) for ambiguous meaning.

(2) Verb: *reduces*

 Answers (C) and (E) change the past tense *reduced* to the present tense *reduces*.

 The agreement took place in 1972. The verb tense in the original sentence, *reduced*, is properly in the past. The present tense *reduces* is illogical, as the action clearly occurred in the past. It would be acceptable to use the present perfect *has reduced*, but no answer choices offer this option. Eliminate answers (C) and (E).

(3) Idiom: *allowed for*

The four answers that use the *allowed* wording have different prepositions following that word. Answers (A), (C), and (D) all say *allowed to*. Answer (E) says *allowed for*. Are both idioms correct?

When the word *allowed* is followed by a verb, the correct idiom is *allowed to*. *Allowed for* is incorrect; eliminate answer (E).

A
B
C
D
E̶

The Correct Answer

Correct answer (D) fixes the initial verb error by changing the past perfect *had been allowed* to the present *are allowed*. Note that some people might eliminate this choice because they think the verb should be in past tense, but it is acceptable to use present tense here if the agreement itself is still in place in the present.

#78 Rhino Horns

> (A) Meaning (*and*); Pronoun (*their*); Verb (*are*)
> (B) Pronoun (*their; one*); Verb (*are*)
> **(C) CORRECT**
> (D) Meaning (*and*); Verb (*are*)
> (E) Pronoun (*one*)

First Glance

The sentence contains a semicolon but the underline is limited only to the second half. Do read the first half, as it will provide context for the intended meaning.

Issues

(1) Meaning: *and*

You might spot this in the original sentence or via a direct comparison of answers (A) and (B):

(A) *tourists will continue to* visit parks   ***and*** *see rhinoceroses*
(B) *tourists will continue to* visit parks   ***to*** *see rhinoceroses*

The *X and Y* structure in answer (A) does not require the two parallel portions to have anything to do with one another. Consider this example: *tourists will continue to visit* the pyramids in Egypt *and see* the Taj Mahal in India. Tourists will continue to do these two things, but the *X* and *Y* portions don't have anything to do with each other.

A̶
B
C
D̶
E

Similarly, in the original sentence, if the actions *visit game parks* and *see rhinoceroses* are connected by the word *and*, then they are completely separate. This doesn't make logical sense. *The tourists visit the parks* in order *to see the rhinoceroses*. Eliminate answers (A) and (D).

(2) Pronoun: *their; one*

 Some answers use the pronoun *their* while others use *the animals'* instead. Other answers change *rhinoceroses* to *one*.

 The pronoun *their* is ambiguous; it could refer to *rhinoceroses* or *tourists*. Consider this example: These tourists will travel to foreign countries and meet new people after their visas are approved. Whose visas need to get approved? The tourists, not the new people—the tourists are the ones who are traveling.

Because *their* could refer to tourists (it should refer to *rhinoceroses*), answer (A) is ambiguous. Answer (B) repeats this error; eliminate both.

Answers (B) and (E) replace *rhinoceroses* with the pronoun *one*. First, it's okay to use the number *one* to refer to a plural noun; this construction just means *one of those*. One of what, though? Logically, one *rhinoceros* makes sense, but maybe the question is whether tourists will continue to see *poachers* after the poachers have been discouraged from killing the rhinos—that's also a reasonable interpretation. The word *one*, then, is ambiguous. Eliminate answers (B) and (E).

(3) Verb: *are*

 A vertical scan of the end of each answer choice reveals a split between present tense *are* and past perfect *have been*. Are both acceptable?

 Verb tenses convey a time frame for an action and indicate when different actions happen relative to one another. In this sentence, the *trimming of the horns* must happen before a possible *visit* by tourists, so the simple present tense is inappropriate. The present perfect *have been* properly indicates that, at the time of a potential tourist visit, the horns must already have been trimmed. Eliminate answers (A), (B), and (D).

The Correct Answer

Correct answer (C) fixes the initial pronoun error by replacing *their* with *the animals'*. Furthermore, the sentence changes the *X and Y* construction to one with a more logical meaning: *the tourists visit parks to see rhinoceroses*.

Miscellaneous

Nowadays, *whether* and *if* are mostly used interchangeably. Formally, though, *whether* is used to indicate the meaning *whether or not*: Tell me whether you plan to go to the movies—I want to know whether you do or whether you don't. On the other hand, *if* is used for if–then (conditional) clauses: If you buy me an ice cream, I'll be happy.

To date, no published official GMAT questions have used *if* in a correct answer choice when the meaning technically matches the word *whether*. The official answer explanations, however, don't actually mention this issue. If you need to guess, don't pick an answer that uses *if* when the meaning is really *whether or not*.

MANHATTAN
PREP

#79 Akutagawa

(A) Parallelism (*X, Y, and Z*); Subject–Verb (*were*)
(B) Parallelism (*X, Y, and Z*); Idiom (*both X and Y*)
(C) CORRECT
(D) Meaning
(E) Subject–Verb (*were*); Idiom (*both X in addition to Y*)

First Glance

The underline is long, so there's a good chance that the question will test Modifier, Parallelism, or Meaning issues.

Issues

(1) Parallelism: *X, Y, and Z*

 There appears to be an *X, Y, and Z* list overlapping the underline: *The literatures of X (Europe), Y (China), and Z (____)*. Bingo—parallelism! *X* and *Y* are already parallel. Is *Z*?

 The first two items in the list are geographic locations (*Europe* and *China*). The third item should also be a location. *That of* refers to the word *literature*, but the list *Europe, China, and the literature of Japan* is not parallel. Eliminate answers (A) and (B).

(2) Subject–Verb: *were*

 The main subject of the original sentence is the word *knowledge*, which is singular. The main verb is *were*, which is plural.

 The subject, *knowledge*, is not underlined, so the correct answer must contain a singular verb. Scan the answers; answers (A) and (E) both use the plural verb *were*. Eliminate answers (A) and (E).

Note: Why isn't the subject *literatures*? That's the trap! The word *literatures* is part of a prepositional phrase —*of the literatures*—and a noun within a prepositional phrase can't be the subject of the sentence.

(3) Idiom: *both X as well as Y; both X in addition to Y*

 A vertical comparison of the answers reveals an idiom that's changing from answer to answer:

(A) *informing* his literary style   **as much as** the content
(B) *informed* **both** his literary style **as well as** the content
(C) *informing* **both** his literary style   **and** the content
(D) *informed* his literary style   **as much as** the content
(E) *informing* **both** his literary style   **in addition to** the content

Notice that the *X* (*his literary style*) and *Y* (*the content*) don't change, but the construction of the idiom itself does.

Answer (B) uses the structure *both X as well as Y*; answer (E) uses *both X in addition to Y*. When beginning with the word *both*, the correct idiomatic structure is *both X and Y*, as in answer (C). Eliminate answers (B) and (E).

(4) Meaning

 Answer (D) tosses in a lot of instances of the word *as*: *as a writer, as it informed his literary style as much as the content of his fiction*. Some might think that this sounds wordy or awkward. Why?

 The sentence is attempting to say that *Akutagawa's knowledge* informed two things: (1) *his style* and (2) *the content* of his work. The structure of answer (D) creates an ambiguous meaning. It might mean that his *knowledge* informed his *style* and that his *knowledge* also informed his *content*, both to the same extent or level. Alternately, it might mean that his *knowledge* informed his *style* and that his *content* also informed his *style*.

Consider this shorter example:

> The barking dog scared the mouse as much as the cat.

Did the barking dog equally scare both the cat and the mouse? Or did both the barking dog and the cat equally scare the mouse? It's not clear. Eliminate answer (D).

The Correct Answer

Answer (C) corrects the original parallelism error by dropping the *that of*, resulting in a correctly constructed *X, Y, and Z* list. In addition, this answer corrects the subject–verb error, changing the plural verb *were* to the singular verb *was* to match the singular subject *knowledge*.

#80 Frozen Citrus

(A) Pronoun (*them; they*)
(B) Pronoun (*they; them*);
      Parallelism (*the only way to X is to Y*)
(C) Pronoun (*them*);
      Parallelism (*the only way to X is to Y*)
(D) Pronoun (*they*);
      Parallelism (*the only way to X is to Y*)
(E) CORRECT

First Glance

The answers start with different prepositions; some kind of Idiom, Modifier, or Parallelism issue might be in play.

Issues

(1) Pronoun: *them; they*

 The word *citrus* is singular; the pronouns *them* and *they* are plural.

 Plural pronouns can't refer to a singular noun. The question writer wants some students to mistake *citrus* for a plural noun because it ends in the letter *s*. Answers (A), (B), and (C) all mistakenly use plural pronouns to refer to the singular *citrus*; eliminate all three. Similarly, answer (D) uses the plural pronoun *they* to refer to the singular noun *fruit*; eliminate (D).

(2) Parallelism: *the only way to X is to Y*

 The sentence uses the construction *the only way to X is to Y.* This idiom requires verbs in the infinitive form (i.e., *to salvage* and *to process*).

 Answers (A) and (E) correctly use the infinitive *to process*, which is parallel to the infinitive *to salvage*. Answers (B), (C), and (D) change the form; the *Y* portion is no longer parallel to the *X* portion. Eliminate answers (B), (C), and (D).

The Correct Answer

Correct answer (E) correctly changes the first plural pronoun to the singular pronoun *it*, to match with *citrus*, and changes the second plural pronoun to the noun *fruit*.

#81 Sloth Fossils

(A) Meaning
(B) Pronoun (*they*); Subject–Verb (*has*)
(C) Subject–Verb (*was*)
(D) CORRECT
(E) Structure / Meaning

First Glance

Most of the sentence is underlined, so look for Structure, Meaning, Modifier, or Parallelism issues.

Issues

(1) Meaning

 The core of the original sentence reads *fossils made it the earliest known mammal.* The meaning is illogical. The discovery of the fossils made the sloth the earliest known mammal, not the fossils themselves.

Eliminate answer (A) for an illogical meaning. The remaining answers don't repeat this error. Answer (B) does use the pronoun *it*, but *it* is part of the "comma -ing" modifier *making it*. The modifier refers to the entire clause *fossils [have] been dated at 34 million years old*, and it is accurate to say that the dating of the fossils makes the *sloth the earliest known mammal*.

(2) Pronoun: *they*

 Answer (B) introduces the pronoun *they*. Who are *they*?

 The sentence doesn't say. The only two plural nouns in the sentence are *fossils* and *islands*, neither of which could have found the fossils. Eliminate answer (B).

(3) Subject–Verb: *has; was*

 Some answers have singular verb forms; others have plural. Which should it be?

> (A) *Fossils … made it*
> (B) *Fossils … has been dated*
> (C) *Fossils … was dated*
> (D) *Fossils … have been dated*
> (E) *Fossils … was? Fossils … made the sloth?*

 Eliminate answers (B) and (C) for pairing a plural subject with a singular verb. Examine answer (E) more carefully (see the Structure issue, below).

(4) Structure / Meaning

 Answer (E) has a confusing structure. *Fossils of a sloth which was dated at 34 million years old, made the sloth the earliest known mammal.* The *sloth was dated at* a certain age? This doesn't make sense; the *fossils* are dated, not the *sloth* itself—but the sentence also can't say the *fossils was dated*. If *was dated* does go with *sloth*, then why is there a comma before the verb *made*, but not one before *which*, where a comma is required?

The modifier *found in Puerto Rico in 1991* is set off by a pair of commas. The third comma, between *old* and *made*, is extra—it's not part of a pair. Sentences shouldn't have a random comma separating the subject and verb: The sloth, took a nap (incorrect). A pair of commas should be in the middle only to separate out modifiers: The sloth, which was tired, took a nap (correct).

No acceptable subject–verb core exists in the sentence. Eliminate answer (E).

The Correct Answer

Correct answer (D) fixes the original meaning error by separating out the two actions: *fossils have been dated, making the sloth* (as a species) *the earliest known mammal.*

#82 Criminal Allergies

(A) Meaning / Modifier (*in attributing*)
(B) CORRECT
(C) Meaning / Modifier (*in attributing*)
(D) Idiom (*attribute X as Y*)
(E) Meaning / Modifier (*in attributing*);
       Idiom (*attribute X as Y*)

First Glance

The underline begins just after the word *but*, indicating some type of contrast and possibly a Structure issue.

(Note: It turns out that structure is not an issue in this problem.)

Issues

(1) Meaning / Modifier: *in attributing*

 The original sentence consists of two independent clauses connected by a coordinating conjunction (the word *but*): *Defense attorneys have argued X, but in attributing Y, the perpetrators are told Z.* Because the "comma -ing" modifier is after the word *but*, the modifier refers to the second half of the sentence. As a result, the *perpetrators* must be performing the action of *attributing* something, but this is illogical. If the perpetrators *are told* something, then someone else must be doing the *attributing*.

 The first half of the sentence indicates that the defense attorneys are the ones attributing the bad behavior to an allergy. Logically, then, an *in attributing* modifier should be placed with the first half of the sentence. The word *but* is not underlined, though, so this modifier has to stick with the second half of the sentence. The form *in attributing*, therefore, can't be used; eliminate answers (A), (C), and (E).

(2) Idiom: *attributed X as Y*

 The first three answers use the form *attributing (attributed) X to Y*. The final two answers use the form *attributing (attributed) X as Y*. Are both acceptable?

 In a word, no. *Attribute X to Y* is correct; *attribute X as Y* is not. Eliminate answers (D) and (E).

A
B
C
D̶
E̶

The Correct Answer

Correct answer (B) fixes the original modifier error by changing *in attributing X* to *if X is attributed*. The form *in attributing* requires the attached main subject (*perpetrators*) to perform that action; in this case, that meaning is illogical. The form *if X is attributed* doesn't require this (note that, in this second case, the sentence doesn't say exactly who is doing the attributing; that's okay).

#83 Dioxins

(A) Modifier (*much*)
(B) Modifier (*much*)
(C) Modifier (*much*); Meaning / Modifier
(D) Meaning / Modifier
(E) CORRECT

First Glance

The underline is of medium length and no obvious punctuation marks or other clues jump out. Be prepared for anything!

Issues

(1) Modifier: *much*

 The original sentence talks about *much of the dioxins*. Note: Mentally strip out the extra words (*currently uncontrolled*) in order to make sure that *much* and *dioxins* are well paired.

 Dioxins are countable: one dioxin, two dioxins, three dioxins. The modifier *much*, though, is used for uncountable nouns: there is much water, but there are many bottles of water. Answers (A), (B), and (C) all attempt to use the uncountable modifier *much* to talk about the countable word *dioxins*; eliminate them.

Note that answer (B) is also incorrect because the subject *much* is singular and the verb *come* is plural. This issue is moot, though, if you notice that *much* is the wrong modifier in the first place.

(2) Meaning / Modifier

 Answers (A), (B), and (E) present the information about dioxins and exposure as one long modifier, while answers (C) and (D) separate this portion into two parallel pieces of information:

> (A), (B), (E): *the currently uncontrolled dioxins (that / to which) North Americans are exposed*
> (C), (D): *the dioxins that are currently uncontrolled and (that) North Americans are exposed to*

What's the difference?

 When two pieces of information are placed in parallel, they are not required to have a logical connection with each other. For example: After studying all day, Sam concluded that geometry is his favorite topic and that he would learn more with a study partner. The two modifiers, "that geometry" and "that he would," don't have anything to do with one another directly (beyond the fact that Sam concluded both after studying all day).

Should the given problem separate these two pieces of information or keep them together? Logically, they go together: North Americans are exposed to the uncontrolled dioxins. Answers (C) and (D) make *that North Americans are exposed to* just a second, separate description of *dioxins*, so this connected meaning is lost; eliminate them.

The Correct Answer

Correct answer (E) fixes the original error by replacing *much* with *many* to match the countable noun *dioxins*. Note that this answer also changes the singular *comes* to the plural *come*, because *many* is plural.

#84 Stomach Ulcers

(A)   Parallelism (*not X but Y*)
(B)   Parallelism (*not X but Y*)
(C)   CORRECT
(D)   Parallelism (*not X but Y*)
(E)   Parallelism (*not X but Y*)

First Glance

The underline is fairly short; some answers start with *not caused* while others begin with *caused not*. Look out for a Parallelism issue.

Issues

(1) Parallelism: *not X but Y*

The original sentence contains the structure *not X but Y*, which requires parallelism. Compare the answers.

(A) *are not* **caused by stress**   *but* **a bacterium**
(B) *are not* **caused by stress**   *but* **are by a bacterium**
(C) *are caused not* **by stress**   *but* **by a bacterium**
(D) *are caused not* **by stress**   *but* **a bacterium**
(E) *are caused not* **by stress**   *but* **are by a bacterium**

Answers (A) and (B) include the verb *caused* within the *X* portion of the parallel structure, so this verb should be repeated for the *Y* portion. Neither does so; eliminate answers (A) and (B).

In answers (C), (D), and (E), the verb precedes the parallel structure and therefore already applies to both *X* and *Y*. The parallel portions themselves, then, should consist only of *by* plus the noun or nouns in question. Answer (D) breaks parallelism by not repeating the *by*; for the *Y* portion, the sentence reads *are caused a bacterium*. Likewise, in answer (E), the *Y* portion reads *are caused are by a bacterium*. Both are incorrect; eliminate answers (D) and (E).

The Correct Answer

Correct answer (C) is the only one to use proper parallelism: *ulcers are caused not by stress but (ulcers are caused) by a bacterium*.

#85 Freestanding House

(A) Comparison (*like that*)
(B) Comparison (*as that*)
(C) Comparison (*did*)
(D) Comparison (*have*)
(E) CORRECT

First Glance

The underline is very short; compare the answer choices before reading the original sentence. The first answer uses *like* while the others use *as*; a comparison is being tested.

Issues

(1) Comparison: *like that; as that; did; have*

The *like* versus *as* split in the answers indicates that the sentence contains a comparison. What is the comparison? Also check the comparison for parallelism.

The sentence compares two groups: *young adults* today and those of *earlier generations*. The heart of the comparison is the fact that *owning and living in a freestanding house on its own land is a goal* of both groups. In other words, the full comparison itself is a clause, so *as* should be used to make the comparison (*like* is used to compare nouns). Further, *as* is used to compare two clauses but the second half of the comparison in answer (B) does not include a verb. Eliminate answers (A) and (B).

Answers (C), (D), and (E) all correctly use *as* and include a verb in the second half of the comparison. Which is correct? Parallelism still rules the day. *Owning and living is a goal* today as *owning and living was a goal* in the past. Answer (C) uses the verb *did*; the *earlier generations did* a goal? Answer (D) uses the verb *have*; *owning and living have* earlier generations? Neither makes sense. Eliminate answers (C) and (D).

Note that *was* and *is* are different tenses, but the clauses are still parallel. The simple past tense *was* is appropriate for something that *was* a goal of young adults in past generations, just as the simple present *is* reflects something that *is* a goal of young adults now.

A̶
B̶
C̶
D̶
E

The Correct Answer

Correct answer (E) offers a parallel structure for the comparison. The pronoun *it* refers to the noun phrase *owning and living in a freestanding house on its own land,* and the verb *was* is parallel to the verb *is*.

#86 Prescription Drugs

(A) Parallelism (*not just X but Y*)
(B) CORRECT
(C) Parallelism (*not just X but Y*); Meaning
(D) Parallelism (*not just X but Y*)
(E) Parallelism (*not just X but Y*); Meaning

First Glance

The underline and answer choices don't contain any obvious characteristics that jump out at a glance; be prepared for anything.

Issues

(1) Parallelism: *not just X but Y*

 The original sentence contains the parallel structure *not just X but (also) Y*. (Note: The word *also* is optional; the structure is correct both with it and without it.) Check the answers for parallelism:

(A) *explained not just* **because of drugs**   *but* **by the fact that**
(B) *explained not just* **by the fact that X**   *but also* **by the fact that Y**
(C) *occurring not just* **because of drugs**   *but* **doctors are also writing**
(D) *which occurred not just* **because drugs**   *but* **doctors are also writing**
(E) *which occurred not just* **because of drugs**   *but* **because doctors**

 Answer (A) is not parallel. In addition, *a phenomenon that is explained because of* something is redundant: *Explained* and *because of* mean the same thing.

Answers (C), (D), and (E) are also not parallel. Eliminate all answers except for answer (B).

(2) Meaning

 Answers (C) and (E) introduce the word *also* in the second half of the parallel structure.

 In answers (C) and (E), the word *also* applies to the verb *written*: In addition to some other unnamed thing, the doctors have *also written prescriptions*. This meaning is illogical because the sentence doesn't describe some other action also taken by the doctors. The test writers are trying to set a trap for test-takers looking for a *not just X but also Y* construction; such a construction would be acceptable as long as the word *also* followed the word *but*. Eliminate answers (C) and (E) for an illogical meaning based on the placement of the word *also*.

The Correct Answer

Correct answer (B) is the only answer to offer a parallel construction for *not just X but also Y*.

#87 Northern Lights

(A)　Modifier (*which brightened*)
(B)　Parallelism (*X and Y*); Meaning (*and*)
(C)　CORRECT
(D)　Meaning (*from the Sun*)
(E)　Parallelism (*X and Y*); Meaning (*from the Sun*)

First Glance

Both the sentence and underline are long; there's a good chance that the question will test Modifier, Parallelism, or Meaning issues.

Issues

(1) Modifier: *which brightened*

A "comma *which*" construction always indicates a noun modifier. As a general rule, noun modifiers should refer to the closest main noun (almost always the noun immediately before the comma).

The closest main noun to *which brightened* is *Earth*. The Earth did not brighten the Northern Lights. Rather, the entire action of the previous clause (*the cloud triggered a storm*) resulted in the brightening of the Northern Lights. Because an entire action caused the result, a noun modifier cannot be used. Eliminate answer (A). No other answers repeat this error.

A
B
C
D
E

(2) Parallelism: *X and Y*

The word *and* always indicates parallelism: *X and Y*. The sentence structure shows a core followed by a comma and two modifiers that should be parallel: *A cloud triggered a storm, which brightened and also knocking.*

Check all of the answer choices in this location:

(A) *which* brightened	*and also* knocking
(B) *it brightened*	*and also* knocked
(C) *brightening*	*and* knocking
(D) *a storm* brightened	*and* it knocked
(E) *brightening*	*and* it knocked

Answers (A) and (E) definitely break parallelism; eliminate them. Answers (B) and (C) are both appropriately parallel.

Answer (D) is trickier. The structure of the sentence has changed more significantly. Now, the subject is *storm* (not *cloud*). The core sentence reads: *A storm brightened and it knocked.* This structure is potentially acceptable from a parallelism standpoint, although it is unnecessary to use the pronoun *it* before the second verb, as the subject (*storm*) applies to both verbs. As a general rule, do not use unnecessary words. You might choose to eliminate answer (D) at this point or to examine it further; see issue (4) on Meaning for further discussion.

A
B
C
D?
E

MANHATTAN
PREP

(3) Meaning: *and*

 When examining the parallelism issue, you might have noticed a couple of issues related to meaning. In answer (B), the structure *A cloud was what triggered a storm, and it brightened and also knocked* changes the initial meaning of the sentence.

 Changing a modifier (*which brightened*) into a separate sentence (independent clause) by replacing *which* with *and* usually alters the meaning of the sentence. What is the difference in meaning between these two sentences?

> (1) Her success triggered a bonus, which allowed her to buy a new car.
> (2) Her success triggered a bonus, and it allowed her to buy a new car.

In the first sentence, the bonus allowed her to buy the new car; otherwise, perhaps she couldn't have afforded it. In the second sentence, the pronoun "it" refers to "her success." Her success allowed her to buy the new car; she also, separately, earned a bonus.

The introduction of the conjunction *and* in answer (B) changes the meaning in a similar way: It no longer indicates that the large storm *caused* the brightening of the Northern Lights. Rather, the *cloud triggered a storm* and, separately, the *cloud ... brightened the Northern Lights*. Eliminate answer (B). The remaining answer choices do not contain this same error.

A
~~B~~
C
D
E

(4) Meaning: *from the Sun*

 When you discover one meaning error, such as the one in answer (B), examine the remaining answers for other possible meaning errors. Answers (D) and (E) both lack any reference to the Sun; the original sentence indicated that the particles were ejected *from the Sun*.

 As a general rule, the test writers prefer not to drop any information that was present in the original sentence unless there was something illogical or ambiguous about that information. Use this issue only if necessary, though, as it is possible that four answers are so incorrect that the fifth has to be chosen even if it loses a detail that was present in the original.

A
B
C
~~D~~
~~E~~

Eliminate answer (E). Answer (D) now has two strikes against it: this issue and the issue discussed in the Parallelism section. Eliminate answer (D).

The Correct Answer

Correct answer (C) fixes the original parallelism and modifier errors by replacing *which brightened* with *brightening*. This creates a more flexible "comma -ing" modifier, which refers not to the closest noun but to the entire action discussed in the main clause: *a cloud triggered a storm*, and this entire action then caused the *brightening* of the lights and the *knocking out* of the satellite.

#88 Ozone

(A)	Structure
(B)	**CORRECT**
(C)	Structure
(D)	Structure
(E)	Structure

First Glance

The underline is fairly short; compare the answers before reading the original sentence. The opening splits between *ozone is formed* (main clause) and *ozone, formed* (modifier).

Issues

(1) Structure

 The original sentence contains one independent clause, *ozone is formed*, followed by a modifier starting with the word *from*. Later in the sentence, a second verb, *react*, pops up. What subject goes with that second verb?

 Logically, *react* might go with *hydrocarbons and oxides*. This sentence would result: *ozone is formed from hydrocarbons and oxides react*. *React* is a main verb and needs a main subject to match, but *hydrocarbons and oxides* are part of a prepositional phrase. Prepositional phrases don't contain verbs. A noun in a prepositional phrase isn't eligible to be the subject of a verb. In this structure, no main subject exists for the main verb. Eliminate answer (A).

Answer (E) also uses *from* and further compounds the issue by changing the first independent clause to a modifier: *ozone, formed in X from Y, react with Z*. The verb *react* can't go with ozone (*the hydrocarbons and oxides react* to form *ozone*, not the other way around), so the sentence is a fragment; it contains no main verb. Answer (D) also removes the original independent clause and turns the sentence into a fragment. Eliminate answers (D) and (E).

Answer (C) introduces the word *and* in between the original independent clause and the rest of the sentence. The portion after the word *and* needs to be an independent clause as well, but it is not. Consider this incorrect example, which mimics the error in answer (C): Hamburgers are made at the restaurant, and when customers eat them. A correct version might say: Hamburgers are made at the restaurant, and customers eat them. Eliminate answer (C).

A
B
C̶
D̶
E̶

The Correct Answer

Correct answer (B) fixes the original problem by changing the preposition *from* to the conjunction *when*: *ozone is formed when hydrocarbons and oxides react.* The verb *react* now has a subject.

#89 Mohenjo-Daro

> (A) **CORRECT**
> (B) Verb (*had flourished*)
> (C) Verb (*had flourished*); Pronoun (*those*);
>   Idiom (*at the same time as*)
> (D) Verb (*flourishing*); Pronoun (*those*)
> (E) Verb (*flourishing*); Pronoun (*those*)

First Glance

The underline is fairly short; glance more carefully at the answers before reading the original sentence. The changes at the beginning of each choice indicate a verb issue.

Issues

(1) Verb: *had flourished; flourishing*

 A vertical scan of the answers reveals three different forms at the beginning: *that flourished, that had flourished,* and *flourishing.*

 That flourished (simple past) and *that had flourished* (past perfect) are both regular verb forms. Past perfect is used to distinguish between two past events or time frames, one of which occurred earlier in time than the other. In this case, the various civilizations *flourished at the same time,* so there is no reason to use past perfect. Answer (C) does use the simple past *flourished* but later uses *had* [*flourished*] for the other civilizations. The various civilizations *flourished at the same time,* so they should not be described using different verb tenses. Eliminate answers (B) and (C).

In answers (D) and (E), *flourishing* is a modifier and describes the time frame of the main verb in the sentence. Consider this example: She slipped on the ice, breaking her ankle. The breaking occurred in the past because the main verb "slipped" is in past tense. In the given sentence, the main verb, *threaten,* is in the present tense, illogically implying that *ancient civilizations* are still *flourishing* in the present. Eliminate answers (D) and (E).

(2) Pronoun: *those*

 Answers (C), (D), and (E) replace the noun *civilizations* with the pronoun *those.*

 The pronoun *those* needs to refer to a noun, but the plural noun *civilizations* has been removed from the sentence. Only the singular *civilization* remains, but the plural *those* can't refer to the singular *civilization.* Eliminate answers (C), (D), and (E).

(3) Idiom: *at the same time as*

 Four answers contain the idiom *at the same time as*; answer (C), though, omits the word *as.*

 The word *as* is a necessary component of the idiom *at the same time as*; it can't be omitted. Eliminate answer (C).

A
B
C̶
D̶
E̶

A
B
C̶
D
E

The Correct Answer

Correct answer (A) appropriately uses the simple past to describe two actions that took place at the same time.

#90 Cost Cutting

(A) Pronoun (*it*)
(B) Pronoun (*it*); Verb (*had increased*)
(C) CORRECT
(D) Modifier (*with*)
(E) Modifier (*with*)

First Glance

The underline starts with a "comma *which*" structure. Watch out for Modifier issues.

Issues

(1) Pronoun: *it*

 The original sentence says that *it fell over the last two years*. What *fell*?

 Logically, the *profits fell*. The word *profits*, though, is plural, while the pronoun *it* is singular. Bad match! Answer (B) repeats this error. Eliminate answers (A) and (B).

(2) Verb: *had increased*

 A vertical scan of the answers reveals a difference in verb tenses: *increased*, *had increased*, and *have increased*.

 Two things happened in the past, with one thing happening before the other. Answer (B) uses past perfect for both the *first 3 months of this year* and the *last two years*. Only the longer-ago event should use the past perfect; eliminate answer (B).

It's acceptable to use the simple past, as in answer (A), or the present perfect, as in answer (C). Answer (A) is a bit clunky because it uses the simple past for two events that took place at different times in the past. Don't cross answer (A) off just for this, but be skeptical; it's probably not correct.

(3) Modifier: *with*

 The first word of the answers varies. Answers (A), (B), and (C) start with *which,* while answers (D) and (E) use *with*.

 "Comma *which*" is a noun modifier, so this clause is talking about the main noun before the comma: *profits*. Does that make sense? Yes—*the profits have increased 5 percent*.

"Comma *with*" is an adverbial modifier, which refers to the entire clause, not just the noun before the comma. What was *with a 5 percent increase*? The core of a clause is the subject, verb, and object (if there is an object), so the *results are evident, with a 5 percent increase*. Huh? That doesn't make sense. Here's a correct example: The dog barked happily at the moon, with joy exuding from every fiber of his being. The joy isn't exuding from the moon. The joy is exuding from the happily barking dog.

Eliminate answers (D) and (E) because the "comma *with*" modifier is not clearly referring to the preceding noun, *profits*.

The Correct Answer

Correct answer (C) removes the incorrect pronoun *it*, modifies the logical noun *profits*, and uses an appropriate verb tense.

#91 Italian Vintners

(A)	Structure / Verb (*are*)
(B)	Structure / Verb (*have*)
(C)	**CORRECT**
(D)	Structure / Verb (*have*)
(E)	Structure / Verb (*have*); Verb (*had been*)

First Glance

The underline is on the shorter side; glance at the answers before beginning. Judging by the changes in the answers, verbs seem to be an issue.

Issues

(1) Structure / Verb: *are; have*

 The original sentence tries to use a structure that provides an unstated but assumed repetition of a word: *The wines have been priced to sell, and they are* (selling). When such a structure is used, the word that is understood to be repeated needs to be in the same form in which it already appeared in the sentence: *The wines have been priced to sell, and they are* (sell).

 It's incorrect to say *they are sell*, so answer (A) is wrong. Answers (B), (D), and (E) make a similar error: *they have* (sell). Only answer (C) offers a correct structure: *The wines are priced to sell, and they do* (sell). Eliminate answers (A), (B), (D), and (E).

(2) Verb: *had been*

 Answer (A) begins with the present perfect *have been*. Answers (B), (C), and (D) switch the tense to present tense *are*, while answer (E) uses the past perfect *had been*.

 In the non-underlined portion, the *vintners have cut prices*; the present perfect tense is used. *Pricing* something *to sell* generally means to cut the price, so *pricing the wines to sell* cannot logically take place before the *vintners cut the prices*; these two actions are the same. Eliminate answer (E).

The Correct Answer

Correct answer (C) provides the proper structure for repeating a word in an unstated way: The *wines are priced to sell, and they do* (sell). The repeated word, *sell*, can be picked up as is and inserted as part of the final clause.

#92 Thelonious Monk

(A)   Meaning / Parallelism (*both X and Y*)
(B)   Meaning / Parallelism (*both X and Y*)
(C)   Structure
(D)   CORRECT
(E)   Meaning / Parallelism (*both X and Y*)

First Glance

The underline contains two commas and the answer choices show a significant difference at the beginning. Systemic issues such as Structure, Meaning, Modifiers, and Parallelism are likely to be tested.

Issues

(1) Meaning / Parallelism: *both X and Y*

 The original sentence appears to contain the parallel structure *both X and Y: a body of work both rooted in the tradition of Willie Smith and Duke Ellington*. In this case, the *X* portion is *rooted in …* and the *Y* portion is *Duke Ellington*.

 Rooted can't be parallel to *Duke Ellington*. Either the two people need to be made parallel or two actions need to be made parallel. Eliminate answer (A).

Scan the end of the remaining answers. Answers (B) and (E) also use the word *both: rooted both in the tradition of Willie Smith and Duke Ellington*. As in the first answer choice, *in the tradition* cannot be parallel to *Duke Ellington*. Eliminate answers (B) and (E).

The two remaining answers remove the word *both*; there are not actually two *traditions* or two things *rooted in* something. The only place where the word *both* might make sense is in conjunction with the two people: *both Smith and Ellington*. That portion of the sentence isn't underlined, though, so the word *both* actually should be removed.

(2) Structure

 A comparison of the two remaining answers, (C) and (D), reveals a structural difference:

>   (C) *Thelonious Monk, who produced*
>   (D) *Thelonious Monk produced*

 Answer (D) contains a subject and main verb. Answer (C), though, changes the main verb *produced* into a modifier (*who produced*). Following this modifier, answer (C) contains a subordinate clause: *Monk, who produced X, yet in many ways he stood apart*. The sentence never provides a main verb, so it is a sentence fragment; eliminate answer (C).

The Correct Answer

Correct answer (D) fixes the original meaning / parallelism error by removing the word *both* entirely.

#93 Language Dialects

(A) CORRECT (B) Pronoun (*them*); Meaning (*with*) (C) Pronoun (*it*) (D) Pronoun (*them*); Idiom (*between X or Y*) (E) Pronoun (*them*); Meaning (*with*);   Idiom (*between X or Y*)

First Glance

The underline starts with the word *and*; the split in the answers is between the word *and* and the word *or*. Parallelism or Idiom issues will be tested.

Issues

(1) Pronoun: *them; it*

 A vertical scan of the answers reveals a split between *within it* and *within them*. What is the relevant noun for this pronoun?

 The original sentence states: *distinguishing between a language and the sublanguages or dialects within it*. The pronoun *it* is referring back to the singular *language*. The plural pronoun *them*, then, cannot be correct. Eliminate answers (B), (D), and (E).

Although the first *it* in answer (C) correctly refers to *a language*, the second *it*, in *those who have tried counting it*, logically refers to the word *languages*. You don't count one language; you try to count all of the languages. The singular pronoun *it* cannot correctly refer to the plural *languages*. Eliminate answer (C).

(2) Meaning: *with*

 A vertical scan of the answers shows a difference between *but those* and *with those*. Are both acceptable?

 The sentence is trying to convey a contrast: While it's true that it is difficult to count the number of languages, some people have nevertheless tried to do so. The contrast word *but*, then, is appropriate. What about the preposition *with*? The word *with* fails to convey the intended contrast. Eliminate answers (B) and (E).

A
B̶
C̶
D̶
E̶

A
B̶
C
D
E̶

(3) Idiom: *between X or Y*

 A vertical scan of the answers reveals yet another split: some choices begin with *and* while others begin with *or*. These two words have very different meanings; which should be used?

 The word is part of a construction with the word *between*, earlier in the sentence. The correct idiom is *between X and Y*. Eliminate answers (D) and (E).

The Correct Answer

Correct answer (A) uses the singular pronoun *it* to refer to the singular noun *language* and the proper idiom *between X and Y*. Further, answer (A) conveys a clear contrast between the idea that it is difficult to count the number of languages and the fact that some people have nevertheless tried to do so.

#94 Heating-Oil Prices

> (A) **CORRECT**
> (B) Comparison (*higher over*; *more than*)
> (C) Comparison (*more than*);
>   Parallelism (*X higher than Y*)
> (D) Comparison (*higher over*); Meaning (*what*)
> (E) Comparison (*more than*);
>   Parallelism (*X higher than Y*)

First Glance

The sentence is almost completely underlined; keep an eye out for Structure, Meaning, Modifier, and Parallelism issues.

Issues

(1) Comparison: *higher over; more than*

A vertical comparison of the answers reveals a split between *higher this year than last* and *higher this year over last*.

Higher than is the proper form for a comparison; *higher over* is not. Eliminate answers (B) and (D).

Check the rest of the sentence for similar comparison issues. Answer (A) says *$5 a barrel more for crude oil than*, while answers (B), (C), and (E) say *$5 a barrel for crude oil more than*. Both versions correctly use *more than* but the placement of *more* is incorrect in answers (B), (C), and (E). The price per barrel is more. There is not more oil itself. Eliminate answers (B), (C), and (E).

(2) Parallelism: *X higher than Y*

You might spot this either when examining the comparison issue discussed above or when comparing the answers vertically. For the first comparison, some answers use the form *higher this year than last*, while others say *higher this year than last year's*.

This year and *last year* are the *X* and *Y* of the comparison: *X higher than Y.* As such, parallelism is required. It's acceptable not to repeat the word twice; in the construction *higher this year than last,* it is understood that the *Y* portion refers to *last year.* It is not correct, however, to pair *this year* and *last year's.* Eliminate answers (C) and (E).

(3) Meaning: *what*

Warning: This one's nitpicky. For the second comparison, answer (D) says *$5 a barrel more for crude oil now than what they were last year.*

The word *what*, which is intended to refer to the price, is redundant. The heart of the comparison, *$5 more*, describes the gap between the old and new prices and, therefore, already encompasses both. There is no need to refer to the price again in the second half of the comparison. Eliminate answer (D).

The Correct Answer

Correct answer (A) uses the proper comparison forms *higher this year than last* and *$5 a barrel more than.* It also employs parallelism between *this year* and *last* (year).

#95 Primate Intelligence

(A)	Idiom (*between X with Y*); Verb (*lay*)
(B)	Idiom (*between X with Y*)
(C)	**CORRECT**
(D)	Idiom (*between X from Y*); Idiom (*not X as Y*)
(E)	Idiom (*between X to Y*); Verb (*lay*)

First Glance

Nothing distinctive jumps out at first glance. Be ready for anything!

Issues

(1) Idiom: *between X with Y; between X from Y; between X to Y*

The original sentence uses the construction *distinctions between X (our intelligence) with Y (that of other primates).* The proper idiom is *between X and Y.*

Answers (A) and (B) both use the incorrect idiom. Answer (C) switches to the correct idiom. Answers (D) and (E) change the structure, but both *between X from Y* and *between X to Y* are incorrect as well. Eliminate answers (A), (B), (D), and (E).

(2) Verb: *lay*

The original sentence says that the *distinction may lay*. Other answer choices replace the word *lay* with *lie*. Which is it?

Use *to lay* with a direct object: Sarah lays her book on the table. The action is being performed on the book, the direct object. Use *to lie* when the subject performs the action. Sarah lies down on her bed. Sarah, the subject, is the one performing the action.

In this problem, the *distinction* is not laying something; there is no direct object after this verb. Rather, the *distinction* itself *lies* in a certain thing. Eliminate answers (A) and (E) for using *lay*.

(2) Idiom: *not X as Y*

Several different idiom forms in the answers try to explain that the distinction is not one thing but another:

(A) *not so much* in a skill	*but* in our ability	
(B) *not so much* in a skill	*but instead* in our ability	
(C) *not so much* in a skill	*as* in our ability	
(D) *not* in a skill	*as* in our ability	
(E) *not* in a skill	*but* in our ability	

The three *not so much* variations are all acceptable idioms, as is the *not X but Y* form in answer (E). However, the *not X as Y* form in answer (D) is incorrect; eliminate this answer.

The Correct Answer

Correct answer (C) uses the proper idioms *between X and Y* and *not so much X as Y*. It also correctly uses the verb *lie*, because the *distinctions lie* in a certain thing.

#96 Clovis Points

(A)	**CORRECT**
(B)	Meaning; Meaning (*of*)
(C)	Verb (*have been*)
(D)	Structure
(E)	Meaning; Verb (*have been*)

First Glance

The entire sentence is underlined. Keep an eye out for Structure, Meaning, Modifier, and Parallelism issues.

Issues

Note: You may not find a starting point in the original sentence (ultimately, this is unsurprising, because answer (A) turns out to be the correct answer!). It's also difficult to compare answers because the entire sentence is underlined. If you have no ideas after reading the original, read answer choice (B) instead.

(1) Meaning

 The core of the original sentence discusses a contrast: *although Clovis points have been found throughout North America, they are named for the particular location where they were first discovered.* Answer (B)'s core, though, makes a contrast between the discovery location and the description of *Clovis points*: *Although named for the New Mexico site, Clovis points are spear points.*

 This contrast is illogical. Answer (E) makes the same error: *while Clovis points are spear points, they have been found all over North America.* Eliminate answers (B) and (E).

A
B̶
C
D
E̶

(2) Meaning: *of*

 Answer (A) and answer (B) contain a slight difference in their descriptions of *Clovis points*: *spear points (with / of) longitudinal grooves chipped onto their faces.* Are both versions acceptable?

 It's acceptable to say *spear points with grooves* but *not spear points of grooves*, because the meaning of the second version is illogical. *With grooves* indicates that the spear points consist of cores of material into which grooves have been chipped. *Of grooves* indicates that the *spear points* consist fundamentally or principally of *grooves*; that is, the *spear points* are themselves *grooves*. Eliminate answer (B).

A
B̶
C
D
E

(3) Verb: *have been*

 Answers (A), (B), and (D) all use the past tense *were discovered*. Answers (C) and (E) use the present perfect *have been found / discovered*. Are both tenses acceptable?

 The discovery took place in 1932 and was a one-time event: the *points* were *found* and that was that. As a result, it's inappropriate to use the present perfect tense; eliminate answers (C) and (E).

A
B
C̶
D
E̶

(4) Structure

 The subject of answer (D) is *Clovis points*. What is the main verb of the sentence?

 There isn't one. The *even though* portion is a subordinate clause, as is the *but were found* portion. Answer (D) is a sentence fragment. Further, the sentence introduces both sides of the comparison with contrast words (*even though* and *but*). It's only necessary to use one contrast word; using two is considered redundant. Eliminate answer (D).

A
B
C
D̶
E

The Correct Answer

Correct answer (A) makes a logical contrast between the fact that the *Clovis points* were found in many locations but named for only one particular location. The sentence also uses appropriate verb tenses.

#97 Population Bottleneck

(A) Structure (*that*)

(B) CORRECT

(C) Structure (*some time*); Parallelism (*X and Y*)

(D) Structure (*that*); Structure (*some time*); Parallelism (*X and Y*)

(E) Structure (*that*); Meaning (*so as to*)

First Glance

The underline starts immediately after an em dash. An em dash is typically used to elaborate on something said just before the em dash. Meaning or Structure issues are likely.

Issues

(1) Structure: *that*

In this sentence, the em dash indicates a rephrasing of something written earlier in the sentence; the em dash, then, means "in other words." The sentence structure needs to follow parallelism rules: *Anthropologists believe that X is true—in other words, that Y is true* (a rewording of or an elaboration on *X*). In the original sentence, the *Y* portion is missing the word *that*.

Answers (A), (D), and (E) all lack the word *that* at the beginning of the clause after the em dash. Answer (E) does contain the word *that* later in the clause, but parallelism requires *that* to be at the beginning. Eliminate answers (A), (D), and (E).

(2) Structure: *some time*

A vertical comparison of the answers reveals a split between *at some time in the past* and *some time in the past*.

The prepositional phrase *at some time* refers to some particular (but unspecified) moment in time; this construction is a modifier. If the preposition *at* is not placed before *some time*, then *time* is a noun, not a modifier, but the sentence structure requires a modifier here. The adverb *sometime* could be used, or the prepositional phrase *at some time*. Here are two correct examples:

> At some time in the past, she worked for the rodeo.
> Sometime in the past, she worked for the rodeo.

Eliminate answers (C) and (D) for incorrectly changing a modifier into a noun.

(3) Parallelism: *X and Y*

The original sentence offers a parallel *X and Y* structure:

(A) *greatly reducing* **their numbers**	*and* **our variation**
(B) *greatly reduced* **their numbers**	*and* **our variation**
(C) *their numbers* **were reduced**	*and* **our variation**
(D) *their numbers* **were reduced**	*and* **our variation**
(E) *reduce* **their numbers**	*and* **our variation**

Answers (A), (B), and (E) all contain proper parallelism between the nouns *numbers* and *variation*. Further, the verb just preceding the *X and Y* structure (*reducing*, *reduced*, or *reduce*) applies to both numbers and variation.

Answers (C) and (D), though, break parallelism. The *X* portion is a clause (*numbers were reduced*) and the *Y* portion is a noun (*variation*). It's not acceptable to make a clause parallel to a noun; eliminate answers (C) and (D).

(4) Meaning: *so as to*

The phrase *so as to* means "in order to." This phrase is used in answer (E): *ancestors suffered an event so as to reduce their numbers.*

The *ancestors* did not *suffer the event* on purpose in order to achieve some specific outcome. Rather, something terrible happened that resulted in a significant loss of life and other long-term consequences. Eliminate answer (E).

The Correct Answer

Correct answer (B) begins with the appropriate parallelism marker, *that*, and conveys a clear meaning: a terrible event occurred that caused two related outcomes, one immediate and one longer-term.

#98 Franz Kroetz

(A)	Comparison (*X more than Y*)
(B)	Comparison (*X more than Y*)
(C)	Comparison (*X more than Y*)
(D)	**CORRECT**
(E)	Comparison (*more as*)

First Glance

The underline is very short; glance at the answers to look for major differences before reading the original sentence.

Issues

(1) Comparison: *X more than Y*

 The sentence contains the comparison marker *X more than Y*. Check the *X* and *Y* portions for parallelism.

 In the original sentence, the *X* portion is *works* and the *Y* portion is *dramatist*. It is illogical to compare the *works* of one person to other people. Compare works to works or people to people; don't mix the two. Eliminate answers (A), (B), and (C), which all contain this error.

(2) Comparison: *more as*

 The original sentence contains the comparison marker *X more than Y*. Note that the word *more* is not underlined but the word *than* is. Among the answers, four offer the word *than*, but answer (E) changes *than* to *as*.

 The phrase *more as* is incorrect. Something can be *more than* something else or something can be *as much as* something else, but the two comparison idioms cannot be mixed. Eliminate answer (E).

The Correct Answer

Correct answer (D) fixes the original parallelism error by inserting the pronoun *those*, which refers back to the first part of the comparison, *works*. The sentence properly compares the *works* of one dramatist to the *works* of other dramatists.

Note that the correct answer inserts the word *other*. Some test-takers might use this as an excuse to eliminate the correct answer, believing that it changes the meaning of the sentence. It does change the meaning, though in an acceptable way. Kroetz is himself a dramatist; in the original sentence, his works are illogically included in both the first group and the second group in the comparison. He should not be included in the second group; *his works are produced more often than* the works of the *other* people who are producing similar works.

#99 Stars at Tremendous Speeds

(A) Meaning / Modifier (*at tremendous speeds*); Structure
(B) CORRECT
(C) Structure
(D) Comparison (*as*)
(E) Meaning / Modifier (*at tremendous speeds*)

First Glance

The underline starts immediately; a glance at the beginning of the answers reveals substantial changes. How should the sentence start?

MANHATTAN
PREP

Issues

(1) Meaning / Modifier: *at tremendous speeds*

 The original sentence says that *the stars, some of them at tremendous speeds, are in motion*. The *stars* themselves don't occur *at tremendous speeds*; rather, the *motion* occurs *at tremendous speeds*. The modifier should be pointing to the action (*motion*), not the noun (*stars*).

 Answers (B), (C), and (D) all clearly tie the motion to the speeds: *in motion, some of them at tremendous speeds*. Like answer (A), answer (E) muddles the meaning of this modifier: *the planets, some of which at tremendous speeds are in motion*.

Furthermore, in answer (E), the *some of which* modifier points to the preceding noun, *planets*, not the *stars*. This answer, then, says that *the planets are in motion*. It's already common knowledge that *planets* are *in motion*; the point of the original sentence was to highlight that the *stars* are also *in motion* even though they seem to be fixed in the sky. Eliminate answers (A) and (E).

~~A~~
B
C
D
~~E~~

(2) Structure

 The original sentence consists of an independent clause (*the stars are in motion as the planets are*) followed by a comma and a coordinating conjunction (*yet*), setting up the expectation for another independent clause.

 Chop out the portion after the coordinating conjunction (*being so far that X*) and read it on its own; that portion is not a complete sentence. The word *being* could function as a subject—as in the sentence *Being far away from loved ones can cause homesickness*—but no verb completes the thought. Eliminate answers (A) and (C) because they are sentence fragments.

Answer (C)'s issue is even more severe. *Although like* is momentarily confusing (because one indicates contrast and the other similarity) and the use of both *although* and *yet* is redundant; only one contrast word is needed. Eliminate answer (C).

~~A~~
B
~~C~~
D
E

(3) Comparison: *as*

 Some of the answers contain the comparison marker *like*; others use the marker *as*. *Like* is used to compare two nouns directly; *as* is used to compare clauses.

 Answer (A) correctly uses *as* to compare two clauses. Answers (B), (C), and (E) correctly use *like* to compare two nouns. Answer (D), however, uses *as* to compare two nouns. Eliminate (D).

A
B
C
~~D~~
E

The Correct Answer

Correct answer (B) consists of two independent clauses connected by a comma and a coordinating conjunction. The sentence makes clear that the *motion* occurs *at tremendous speeds*.

#100 Heavy Commitment

(A) Pronoun (*it*)
(B) Pronoun (*ones*) ; Meaning
(C) Pronoun (*it*)
(D) Pronoun (*them*); Parallelism (*X or Y*)
(E) CORRECT

First Glance

The entire sentence is underlined. Keep an eye out for Structure, Meaning, Modifier, and Parallelism issues.

Issues

(1) Pronoun: *it; them; ones*

The original sentence uses the pronoun *it* (twice!). Check the antecedents for the pronouns found throughout the answers.

In answer (A), the first *it* refers to the *course of action*. The second *it*, though, is a dummy pronoun; it doesn't refer to any particular noun in the sentence. While a dummy pronoun is acceptable in general, the two instances of *it* don't refer to the same thing. This is considered ambiguous. Likewise, in answer (D), the first instance of *them* refers to the *executives*; the second refers to the *signs*. Eliminate answers (A) and (D) for ambiguity.

Answer (B) changes *them* to *ones*. The pronoun *ones* does still refer to *signs*, but it refers to different signs. For example: Ava likes most cats, but she finds the ones owned by her next-door neighbor annoying.

The *ones* are still cats, but they are not the same cats mentioned in the first half of the sentence. The original sentence talks about the same signs, so the meaning in answer (B) is illogical.

Further, in (B), the modifier following *ones* (*likely when they do appear*) now applies only to the second set of signs, in the same way that the modifier in Ava's sentence (*owned by her next-door neighbor*) applies only to the second set of cats. Eliminate answer (B).

In answer (C), the pronoun *it* seems to refer to the closest preceding singular noun, *trouble*. The *trouble* has *worked well in the past*? That's illogical. Because the pronoun *it* is acting as a subject, the next logical place to check is the subject of the preceding clause: *an executive*. *An executive*, though, can't be an *it*. The logical noun, *course of action*, is so buried in the early part of the sentence that you may actually have to re-read the sentence in order to find the right noun. Another ambiguous pronoun! Eliminate answer (C).

(2) Meaning

The original sentence conveys a certain meaning: when someone commits heavily to a certain course of action, that person might then overlook signs that this course of action isn't a good idea after all. Check the sentence core:

(A) *Heavy commitment makes it likely to miss*
(B) *An executive makes missing signs likely*
(C) *An executive is likely to miss signs*
(D) *Being heavily committed makes them likely to miss signs*
(E) *Being heavily committed is likely to make an executive miss signs*

Answers (A), (C), (D), and (E) all contain logical meanings. Answer (B), though, is problematic. The *executive* doesn't *make* this phenomenon *likely* to happen; rather, *heavy commitment to a course of action makes it likely* that the *executive* will miss something. Eliminate answer (B).

(3) Parallelism: *X or Y*

The sentence contains the parallelism marker *or*. Check for the correct *X or Y* parallel structure.

In answer (D), the sentence says *makes them likely to miss signs or misinterpreting them*. The *X* form is in the infinitive; the *Y* form is a participle. Eliminate answer (D) for lack of parallelism.

The Correct Answer

Correct answer (E) conveys an unambiguous meaning (the act of *being heavily committed* makes *an executive* likely *to miss* certain *signs*) and does not contain any ambiguous pronouns.

Note: The correct answer ends up using the oft-maligned word *being*. Don't cross off an answer simply because it contains the word *being*!

#101 Anasazi

(A)	**CORRECT**
(B)	Meaning
(C)	Pronoun (*they*)
(D)	Modifier (*less*)
(E)	Modifier (*less*)

First Glance

The underline is short; glance through the answers before reading the full sentence. The answers begin with different Modifier structures; also keep an eye out for Meaning or Structure issues.

Issues

(1) Meaning

 The *Anasazi* moved to a place where they had greater *access to water*. This portion of the sentence changes substantially among the answers; do they all convey an appropriate meaning?

 In answer (B), is the *access* less limited? Or is the *water* less limited? It's illogical to say that the water itself was less limited—rather, the amount of water or the access to water was less limited. Eliminate answer (B).

A
~~B~~
C
D

E

(2) Pronoun: *they*

 Answer (C) contains the pronoun *they*. Who had less limited water access?

 Logically, it's equally possible to say that *they* refers to the *Anasazi* (after the Anasazi moved, they would have more access to water) or to the *other clans* (if those clans had more access to water, the Anasazi would want to move near them). Eliminate answer (C) for pronoun ambiguity.

A
B
~~C~~
D
E

(3) Modifier: *less*

 A scan of the answers reveals a split between *limited* and *limitations*.

 The word *limitations* is countable (one limitation, two limitations, three limitations), so the appropriate modifier is *fewer*. Answers (D) and (E) both say *less limitations* but should say *fewer limitations*. Eliminate answers (D) and (E).

A
B
C
~~D~~
~~E~~

The Correct Answer

Correct answer (A) conveys a logical meaning without any of the errors found in the other choices.

#102 Yellow Jackets

(A) Meaning / Modifier (*where they consist*)
(B) CORRECT
(C) Meaning / Modifier
(D) Parallelism (*X and Y*)
(E) Parallelism (*X and Y*)

First Glance

The answer choices appear to vary a great deal, likely signaling Structure, Modifier, Meaning, or Parallelism issues.

Issues

(1) Meaning / Modifier: *where they consist*

In the original sentence, the modifier *society where they consist* has two problems. First, *where* should introduce information about an actual location, but *society* is not a location. Second, the pronoun *they* must refer to the plural noun *wasps*, but it isn't logical to say that the individual *wasps consist* mostly *of females*. Rather, the *society* consists mostly of females.

Answer (A) is wrong for both reasons listed above. Answers (B), (D), and (E) all contain the correct meaning. Answer (C) separates out *almost all females* by a comma; without any further linkage, these words don't clearly describe *society*. Eliminate answers (A) and (C).

(2) Parallelism: *X and Y*

The original sentence contains an *X and Y* parallel structure. This structure is underlined; check the parallelism in the other choices.

Answers (A), (B), and (C) offer a parallel *X and Y* structure. Answers (D) and (E) change the structure:

> (D) *their society is* cooperative, organized, *and* it is entirely
> (E) *society that is* cooperative, organized, *and* it consists of

In both answers (D) and (E), the first two items are adjectives and the third item starts with a subject and verb. Eliminate answers (D) and (E) for breaking parallelism.

The Correct Answer

An "-ing" modifier that is not separated out from the sentence by a comma is typically a noun modifier, referring to the noun right before it. Correct answer (B) has this structure, properly indicating that the *society* as a whole consists mostly *of females*. Note that this answer sets a trap: it sounds odd to say *social wasps, wasps that live*. It is acceptable, though, to repeat the word *wasps* after the comma.

#103 El Niño

(A)	Structure; Meaning
(B)	Structure; Modifier (*where*); Verb (*combining; accumulating*)
(C)	Structure; Meaning
(D)	**CORRECT**
(E)	Modifier (*where*); Meaning; Verb (*combining*)

First Glance

The beginning of the underline changes from *a phenomenon* to *is a phenomenon*. Look for Structure or Modifier issues.

Issues

(1) Structure

 The subject of the original sentence is *El Niño*. What's the verb?

 There are various verb forms, but none can function as the main verb in the sentence. The verb *combine* is a part of the *in which* modifier, and *has accumulated* is part of the *that* modifier. *To flow* is in the infinitive; a main verb can't be in the infinitive. Answers (B) and (C) also do not contain a main verb. Eliminate answers (A), (B), and (C).

(2) Meaning
Modifier: *where*

 The original sentence contains the text *changes combine allowing water to flow*. There are two possibilities for the participle *allowing* directly following the verb *combine*:

     1. The participle could be a noun acting as the direct object of the verb: I like swimming.
     2. The participle could be part of a present progressive tense: She is driving to the store.

 Neither of the two possible structures fits *allowing* in this sentence, so answer (A) is wrong. The other answers change the structure:

     (B) *phenomenon where changes* **are combining to allow**
     (C) *phenomenon in which changes* **combine and which allows**
     (D) *phenomenon in which changes* **combine to allow**
     (E) *phenomenon where changes* **are combining and allow**

The *to allow* structure in answers (B) and (D) is acceptable. In answers (C) and (E), *combine* and *allow* are now parallel and "separate but equal"; in other words, the second action no longer happens as a result of the first. This loss of meaning is not acceptable. Eliminate answers (A), (C), and (E).

This comparison of the answers highlights another split: *in which* versus *where*. As a general rule, *where* should be used to modify a location; a *phenomenon*, though, is an event or circumstance, not a location. In this case, *in which* is the appropriate modifier structure. Eliminate answers (B) and (E).

(3) Verb: *combining; accumulating*

 Some answers use the simple present *combine*; others use the present progressive *are combining*. Similarly, some answers use *has* or *is accumulated* and some use *accumulating*.

MANHATTAN
PREP

The sentence describes a *phenomenon* that occurs periodically (note the word *periodic* in the sentence), not something that occurs constantly or continuously. The *phenomenon* may not be occurring right now. The present progressive, then, is inappropriate. Eliminate answers (B) and (E).

The Correct Answer

Correct answer (D) fixes the initial structure error by including a main verb: *El Niño is a phenomenon*. It also correctly changes the *combine allowing* portion to *combine to allow*.

#104 Beatrix Potter

(A)	Modifier / Pronoun (*them*)
(B)	Modifier / Pronoun (*them*)
(C)	**CORRECT**
(D)	Meaning
(E)	Modifier / Pronoun (*them*)

First Glance

The underline contains three—count 'em, three!—commas, and Beatrix Potter moves around quite a bit in the answers. Look for Modifier, Meaning, Structure, or Parallelism issues.

Issues

(1) Modifier / Pronoun: *them*

 The initial sentence contains two modifiers in a row, placed between the subject and the verb: *in her book illustrations, coordinating them with her narratives*. In various answers, these modifiers move around and sometimes change form. What refers to what?

 The modifier *in her book illustrations* refers to something that takes place within the illustrations. The pronoun in the next modifier, *carefully coordinating them*, refers back to the *book illustrations*. It's impossible for this coordination to take place within the actual illustrations themselves. Consider this example:

> In her book, she coordinated it with her blog.

That sentence says: In her book, she coordinated her book with her blog. This is illogical! The coordination took place between the two separate items, not within the book.

In the same way, Beatrix Potter coordinated her illustrations and her narratives, but this coordination did not take place literally within the illustrations themselves; rather, she coordinated between the two. Answers (A), (B), and (E) all contain this error; eliminate them.

(2) Meaning

The placement of the modifiers in answers (C) and (D) is completely different:

> (C) *In her illustrations, which she coordinated with her narratives, Potter*
> (D) *Coordinated with her narratives, Potter, in her book illustrations*

Answer (D) says: *coordinated with her narratives, Beatrix Potter*. This choice says that *Beatrix Potter* herself is *coordinated* with her narratives, not that *she coordinated* the illustrations with the narratives. Eliminate answer (D).

The Correct Answer

Correct answer (C) fixes the initial ambiguity with the modifiers and also properly places the modifiers relative to the other parts of the sentence. The *which* modifier refers to the *book illustrations* modifier, and *in her illustrations* refers to Potter.

#105 Marconi

(A)	Structure; Pronoun (*it*)
(B)	Modifier (*which*)
(C)	**CORRECT**
(D)	Modifier (*which*); Idiom (*conceive X to be Y*)
(E)	Meaning ; Idiom (*conceive X to be Y*)

First Glance

The long underline contains a semicolon, while only some of the other answers do. Systemic issues, such as Structure and Meaning, are more likely to be tested.

Issues

(1) Structure
  Pronoun: *it*

The original sentence contains the structure: *Marconi's conception of the radio was as X.* The other four answers all say that *Marconi conceived* something.

The original sentence structure is an example of something called a nominalized noun: a verb (*to conceive*) has been turned into the noun form, and that noun is then paired with a verb that does not actually offer any action (*was*). While this structure is technically possible, it is not preferred. Because the remaining four answers all offer regular constructions (*Marconi conceived*), the correct answer is probably not (A).

In addition, the pronoun *it* doesn't refer to *radio* as clearly as it should. In fact, the parallel positions of *conception* and *it* as subjects of the clauses before and after the semicolon, respectively, would suggest that *Marconi's conception is a tool for communicating*. This ambiguity is a second negative consequence of the nominalized noun. Together, these provide enough reason to eliminate answer (A).

(2) Modifier: *which*
Meaning

 Answers (B) and (D) change the semicolon into a noun modifier beginning with *which*. Answer (E) changes the structure even more substantially.

 It might be possible to write a correct sentence that uses a noun modifier for the second portion, but in this case, the *which* modifier appears to refer to the noun *telephone* in both answers (B) and (D). Logically, the second half of the sentence should refer to the *radio*, not the *telephone*. Eliminate answers (B) and (D).

In answer (E), the second half of the sentence needs some kind of clear transition: a semicolon, a conjunction, even potentially a modifier structure. Answer (E), though, is unclear. What does *other than what it is* refer to? What is the meaning of the sequence *other than what it is, precisely the opposite*? This ambiguity is bad; eliminate answer (E).

(3) Idiom: *conceive X to be Y*

 The answers contain a split between *conceived as* in answers (A), (B), and (C) and *conceived to be* in answers (D) and (E).

 The correct idiom is to *conceive X as Y*, not to *conceive X to be Y*. Eliminate answers (D) and (E).

The Correct Answer

Correct answer (C) fixes the issue in the original sentence by changing the noun *conception* to the verb *conceived*.

Note that the test writers set a trap in answer (C) via this sequence: *a tool for private conversation that could substitute for the telephone*. Under most circumstances, an essential *that* modifier needs to be placed immediately adjacent to the noun it modifies, *tool*, not another noun (*conversation*). It is acceptable, though, for the short descriptive phrase *for private conversation* to intervene because this description of the noun *tool* is necessary in order to understand the full meaning of the sentence.

#106 Proton-Induced X-Ray Emission

(A) CORRECT
(B) Modifier (*having the ability*)
(C) Modifier (*called*)
(D) Modifier (*called*)
(E) Modifier (*called*)

First Glance

This long sentence is almost completely underlined. Keep an eye out for Structure, Modifier, Parallelism, or Meaning issues.

Sentence Structure

The original sentence is complex enough that it may be worth the time to deconstruct the sentence:

Original Sentence (correct):

Originally developed
for detecting air pollutants,

A technique . . .   is finding uses   in medicine, archaeology,
                                                                            and criminology.

called proton-induced
x-ray emission ← which can quickly analyze
                              the chemical elements in
                              almost any substance
                              without destroying it

There are so many modifiers hanging off of the core sentence that this problem is almost certainly testing modifiers.

Issues

(1) Modifier: *called*

  Once you suspect that modifiers are being tested, examine the sentence structure and answer choices with this in mind.

What was *originally developed for* something? The technique.
What is *called proton-induced* … ? The technique.
What *can quickly analyze* … ? Wow—once again, the technique!

  Of the three modifiers referring to *technique*, only *called proton-induced X-ray emission* is an essential modifier and so should not be separated from *technique* by words or punctuation marks.

Answer (A) correctly places the *called* modifier immediately adjacent to *technique* without any intervening punctuation. Scan the other answers for the placement of the *called* modifier:

    (B) *a technique called* …
    (C) *a technique* … *pollutants, called* …
    (D) *a technique* … *pollutants, called* …
    (E) *a technique* … *substance, called* …

Answers (C), (D), and (E) all separate *technique* from its essential modifier. In answers (C) and (D), it appears that the *air pollutants* are *called proton-induced X-ray emission*. In answer (E), it appears that the *substance* is called this name. Eliminate all three answers.

(2) Modifier: *having the ability*

After examining the essential modifier, look at the nonessential ones. The nonessential modifier *originally developed for detecting air pollutants* should be placed as close as possible to *technique*.

Answers (A), (C), (D), and (E) all place *originally developed* as close as possible to *technique*. Answer (B), however, differs:

    (B) *originally developed for detecting air pollutants, having the ability to analyze,*

The second part (*having*) appears to refer to the first part (*originally*), but nothing in the first part has the ability to analyze anything; rather, the *technique* (which appears much later in the sentence) has the ability to do so. Eliminate answer (B) for bad modifier placement.

The Correct Answer

Although answer (A) does not place the *which* modifier immediately adjacent to *technique*, this answer is correct. The sentence contains three separate modifiers that refer to the same noun, *technique*. A single word can have only two sides on which modifiers can be placed (before and after), so one of the three modifiers cannot be placed immediately next to *technique*. Further, the essential modifier (*called*) must be placed right next to technique. As a result, the *which* modifier is placed further from technique; it modifies the entire phrase *a technique called proton-induced X-ray emission*.

#107 Nuclear Plants

(A) Subject–Verb (*makes*); Meaning / Pronoun (*it*)

(B) CORRECT

(C) Subject–Verb (*makes*);
Comparison (*the same to do X as to do Y*)

(D) Comparison (*the same to do X as to do Y*);
Meaning / Pronoun (*they*)

(E) Comparison (*the same to do X as to do Y*);
Meaning / Pronoun (*they*)

First Glance

Yuck—the entire sentence is underlined. Be prepared for anything, especially Structure, Modifier, Meaning, or Parallelism issues.

Issues

(1) Subject–Verb: *makes*

 In the original sentence, the plural noun *costs* is the subject of the modifying clause *that makes it more expensive*. The verb *makes*, however, is singular.

 Check the remaining answers for the same subject–verb mismatch. Answer (C) repeats the original error: *costs … makes*. The other answers don't maintain this error. Eliminate answers (A) and (C).

(2) Comparison: *the same to do X as to do Y*

 The five answer choices contain small differences in the comparison structure:

(A) *it costs about the same to run* **nuclear plants** *as* **other types** *of plants*

(B) *the cost of running* **nuclear plants** *is about the same as* **for other types** *of plants*

(C) *it costs about the same to run* **nuclear plants** *as* **for other types** *of plants*

(D) *it costs about the same to run* **nuclear plants** *as* **for other types** *of plants*

(E) *the cost of running* **nuclear plants** *is about the same as* **other types** *of plants*

 Each sentence requires the reader to carry some words of the comparison to both the *X* and the *Y* components. Answer (A) is properly parallel and maintains an appropriate meaning: *It costs the same to run X as [to run] Y.* Likewise, in answer (B), *the cost of running X is the same as [the cost] for [running] Y.*

Answers (C), (D), and (E), however, are problematic. Answers (C) and (D) indicate that *it costs the same to run X as [to run] for Y.* To run *for* plants? That's a big difference in meaning (and an illogical one). Answer (E) says that *the cost of running X is the same as the cost running Y;* the preposition (either *of* or *for*) is missing from the second part. Eliminate answers (C), (D), and (E).

(3) Meaning / Pronoun: *it; they*

The original sentence uses the pronoun *it* three times. Are all three instances clear, and do they refer to the same noun?

In the first instance, *it* is used as a dummy pronoun, as in the sentence "It is raining outside." This is an acceptable usage of *it*. Each additional instance of the word *it* in the sentence is also a dummy pronoun, but each refers to somewhat different abstract ideas. Such ambiguity is not preferred. Don't choose answer (A) unless all of the other answers contain clear errors.

Answers (D) and (E) also introduce some ambiguity related to a pronoun. Both introduce *nuclear plants* versus *other power plants* and then use the word *they*. It's not clear until finishing the sentence that the pronoun *they* is intended to refer to the *nuclear plants* and not to the *other power plants*. Again, don't choose answer (D) or (E) unless all of the other answers contain clear errors.

A ?
B
C
D ?
E ?

The Correct Answer

Correct answer (B) offers a proper subject–verb pairing and a structure that accurately compares the two sets of costs. Furthermore, answer (B) doesn't contain even slight pronoun ambiguity.

#108 Authoritative Parents

| (A) **CORRECT** |
| (B) Structure |
| (C) Meaning / Comparison (*X rather than Y*); Parallelism (*X, Y, and Z*) |
| (D) Parallelism (*X, Y, and Z*); Pronoun (*they*) |
| (E) Meaning / Comparison (*X rather than Y*); Parallelism (*X, Y, and Z*) |

First Glance

The entire sentence is underlined! Anything can happen, but pay particular attention to Structure, Meaning, Modifier, and Parallelism issues.

Issues

(1) Structure

It turns out that (A) is the correct answer on this problem, so you may not spot a starting point when reading the original sentence. Read answer (B) next and, because the whole sentence is underlined, try to strip the sentence down to the core structure:

(B) *Parents who are more likely to have children that are X, Y, and Z.*

A
B
C
D
E

Answer (B) has a subject (*parents*), but no main verb. The first instance of the verb *are* is part of the modifier *who are more likely*, and the second instance is part of the modifier *that are self-confident*. Eliminate answer (B) because it is a sentence fragment.

(2) Meaning / Comparison: *X rather than Y*

 The original sentence makes a comparison between *authoritative* and *permissive parents*. Check the comparison in other answer choices.

 Answers (A), (B), and (D) compare the two types of parents. What's going on in answer (C)?

> Is it this?
> (C) *Children of* authoritative parents   *rather than* permissive parents
> Or this?
> (C) Children *of authoritative parents*   *rather than* permissive parents

The sentence is ambiguous: It could compare the two types of *parents*, but it could also compare the *children* of one type of parent to the *permissive parents*.

The wording in answer (E) definitely compares permissive parents to the children of other parents:

> (E) *Rather than* **permissive parents,** *the children of authoritative parents*

Eliminate answer (C) for ambiguity and answer (E) for an illogical comparison.

(3) Parallelism: *X, Y, and Z*

 Check the answers for parallelism in the *X, Y, and Z* list:

> (A) *self-confident, high in self-esteem, and independent*
> (B) *self-confident, high in self-esteem, and independent*
> (C) *to be self-confident, have high self-esteem, and to be independent*
> (D) *to have self-confidence, a high self-esteem, and be independent*
> (E) *to have self-confidence, a high self-esteem, and to be independent*

 Answers (C), (D), and (E) all break parallelism. Answer (C) needs a *to* either before all three items or before only the first one. Answers (D) and (E) use verbs for the first and third items but not for the second. Eliminate answers (C), (D), and (E).

(4) Pronoun: *they*

 The pronoun *they* is plural; the noun *adolescent* is singular.

 The sentence does previously mention *children*, so the plural pronoun *they* is acceptable in that sense. However, the plural *children* would agree better with the plural *adolescents* than it does with the singular *adolescent*. Eliminate answer (D).

MANHATTAN
PREP

The Correct Answer

Correct answer (A) makes a logical and unambiguous comparison and presents a parallel list of three items.

#109 Bona Dea

(A) CORRECT	
(B) Idiom / Parallelism (*either X or Y*)	
(C) Idiom / Parallelism (*either X or Y*)	
(D) Idiom / Parallelism (*either X or Y*)	
(E) Idiom (*aid to*);	

First Glance

The relatively short underline may make it worthwhile to glance at the answers before reading the original sentence. Notice any obvious differences?

Issues

(1) Idiom / Parallelism: *either X or Y*

 The original sentence contains the (correct) idiom *either X or Y*. The word *either* is not underlined, but the second half, *or*, is. Check the answers for both idiom structure and parallelism.

 Answers (B) and (C) both change the word *or* to *and*. *Either X and Y* is incorrect; in this parallel structure, the word *either* can be paired only with the word *or*. Eliminate answers (B) and (C).

Answers (A), (C), and (E) correctly pair *asking* with *thanking*. Answers (B) and (D) incorrectly use the structure *to thank*, which is not parallel to *asking*. Eliminate answers (B) and (D).

(2) Idiom: *aid to*

 The sentence contains the idiom *aid X*. The correct structure is to *aid in* doing something.

 Answers (D) and (E) change the idiom to *aid to* do something. It's unacceptable to use an infinitive here; this particular idiom requires the preposition *in* after the word *aid*. Eliminate answers (D) and (E).

The Correct Answer

Answer (A) correctly uses the idioms *aid in doing X* and *either X or Y*.

#110 Published in Harlem

(A)	Modifier (*published in Harlem*); Meaning
(B)	Modifier (*published in Harlem*); Meaning
(C)	**CORRECT**
(D)	Meaning
(E)	Meaning

First Glance

The whole sentence is underlined, and commas offset big chunks of the sentence. The problem is most likely testing Structure, Modifier, Parallelism, or Meaning issues.

Structure

Published in Harlem,   of The Messenger

the owner and editor . . .   were two young journalists, Chandler Owen and A. Philip Randolph

, who would later make his reputation as a labor leader

Issues

(1) Modifier: *published in Harlem*

 The original sentence starts with an opening modifier followed by the subject: *Published in Harlem, the owner and editor.* The people themselves were fed into a printing press? Ouch! The paper (*The Messenger*) was published, not the people.

 Answers (A) and (B) incorrectly say that the people were published in Harlem. Answers (C), (D), and (E) handle the modifier correctly, although the distance between *Messenger* and *published* is less than ideal in answer (D). Eliminate answers (A) and (B).

A̶ B̶ C D E

(2) Meaning

 This sequence appears fine until the pronoun *his*:

> (A) *Chandler Owen and A. Philip Randolph, who would later make his reputation as a labor leader*

Wait, who made his reputation—was it Owen or Randolph? Or maybe it was both of them?

 The pronoun *his* is singular, but the two people are connected by the word *and*, so the *who* modifier afterwards should apply to both of them. Most people would guess that the *who* modifier applies to Randolph because he is mentioned second, but the meaning is ambiguous. The correct answer could fix this issue in one of two ways: by referring clearly to just one person or by changing the modifier to refer to both men (for example, *their reputations as labor leaders*).

Answers (A), (B), (D), and (E) all contain this same error. Answer (C) separates the two men, placing Randolph first with the *who* modifier immediately afterwards; Owen isn't mentioned until later. Now, the *who made his reputation* modifier unambiguously applies only to Randolph.

The Correct Answer

Correct answer (C) makes clear that *The Messenger* was published in Harlem, not the people. Further, answer (C) states unambiguously that Randolph was the one to make his reputation as a labor leader.

#111 Mutual Fund

(A) **CORRECT**	
(B)	Meaning (*and*); Meaning (*it*)
(C)	Meaning (*and*); Pronoun (*they*)
(D)	Pronoun (*they*)
(E)	Pronoun (*they*)

First Glance

The underline contains a comma; because the answers are short, glance down at the differences surrounding the comma. There's a split between "comma -ing" and a participle modifier (*holding*) and *and*. Also, one answer has a semicolon. Look for Structure, Meaning, and Modifier issues.

Sentence Structure

The original sentence consists of a sentence core followed by a "comma -ing" modifier:

First Read: Original Sentence	**Thoughts**
A mutual fund	Noun … is this the subject?
having billions of dollars in assets	Modifier, describing the *mutual fund*
will typically invest	Bingo. This is the verb and *mutual fund* is the subject.
that money	*That* is referring back to the *money* mentioned in the first modifier.
in hundreds of <u>companies,</u>	The underline starts here.
<u>*rarely holding*</u>	A "comma -ing" modifier refers to the main clause (subject and verb).
<u>*more than one percent*</u> *of the shares of any particular corporation*	Does this "comma -ing" modifier actually modify the main clause? Yes, this is a follow-up to the fact that the mutual fund invests in tons of companies.
	Hmm. The modifier sounds a little funny—but I can't actually find anything wrong with the sentence. I'll need to go look at the other answer choices next.

Issues

(1) Meaning: *and*

 Compare the beginnings of each answer vertically. Answers (B) and (C) insert the conjunction *and*, turning the "comma -ing" modifier into an independent clause.

 In the original sentence, the fact that the mutual fund invests in so many different companies results in the fact that the fund holds only a very small share of each company. When answers (B) and (C) insert the word *and*, they change what used to be a modifier into a separate clause. Two independent clauses should be read as two independent pieces of information unless some word exists to create a cause-effect relationship.

For example: Yesterday, Xiying visited the shoe store and she bought some milk. Those are two separate pieces of information (she probably didn't buy milk at the shoe store!); the only connection is that she did both things yesterday.

The sentence should contain a cause-effect relationship. Eliminate answers (B) and (C).

A
B̶
C̶
D
E

(2) Pronoun: *they*
Meaning: *it*

 Continue to compare the answers vertically. Answer (B) introduces a pronoun, *it*; answers (C), (D), and (E) contain the pronoun *they*. Which nouns do these pronouns refer to?

 They is a plural pronoun, but in all three cases, the pronoun is meant to refer to the singular noun *mutual fund*. Eliminate answers (C), (D), and (E).

In answer (B), the pronoun *it* does not refer to the *mutual fund*; rather, *it* is a dummy pronoun, as in the sentence "It is raining outside." Is there anything wrong with that? Yes. The second half of answer (B) never clearly indicates that it is talking about the *mutual fund*. Eliminate answer (B) for faulty meaning.

A
B̶
C̶
D̶
E̶

The Correct Answer

Correct answer (A) uses a participle modifier to convey a cause-effect meaning. It avoids the pronoun issues by not using a pronoun at all.

#112 Flavian Amphitheater

(A)	Structure
(B)	Verb (*begun*)
(C)	**CORRECT**
(D)	Structure
(E)	Structure

First Glance

The multiple commas just before and within the underline likely signal Modifier, Structure, Meaning, or Parallelism issues.

Issues

(1) Structure

The initial sentence contains a double-verb structure to go with the main noun: *Construction began …* [*construction*] *was completed.* Two verbs mapped to one subject require a conjunction, such as *and*, in between the two verbs: *Construction began … and was completed.*

Answer (A) is incorrect due to the missing conjunction; compare the remaining answers:

(B)	*Construction* **begun**	*and was completed*
(C)	*Construction* **began**	*and was completed*
(D)	*Construction,*	*it was completed*
(E)	*Construction, which* **was begun**	*and was completed*

Answers (B) and (C) do insert the conjunction *and* between the two verbs. (You might spot another issue here. See the Verb issue below!) Answers (D) and (E) both change the structure more significantly.

Answer (D) still contains the main verb *was completed* but inserts a second subject beforehand, *it*. A double-subject structure requires a conjunction between the two subjects; that conjunction is missing here. (Plus, if there are two subjects, they should be different things. It's not correct to say "Tina and she went to the store" when "she" refers to Tina!)

In answer (E), both verbs are part of the new *which* modifier: *which was begun … and [which] was completed.* No main verb exists in the sentence! Eliminate answers (A), (D), and (E).

(2) Verb: *begun*

You might spot this when examining the structure issues discussed above. Answer choice (B) tries to use a double-verb structure: *Construction begun … and was completed.*

Begun is the past participle of the verb *to begin*. A participle can't be a main verb by itself; it has to be combined with another verb form. For example: The construction has begun. Eliminate answer (B).

The Correct Answer

Correct answer (C) repairs the initial structure error by inserting the conjunction *and* between the two parallel main verbs: *Construction began in A.D. 69 and was completed later.*

#113 Vision 20/500

(A) Pronoun (*it*)	
(B) Meaning	
(C) Structure	
(D) CORRECT	
(E) Verb (*would deemed*)	

First Glance

A full-sentence underline! Anything goes, but pay special attention to Structure, Meaning, Modifiers, and Parallelism.

Issues

(1) Pronoun: *it*

There are two instances of the pronoun *it* in the sentence. Check them.

In the first case, *it would be rated* refers to the *vision* (not the *baby*—a baby's *vision* is rated, not the actual *baby*). The second *it* must be referring to the *baby*: *if it* (the baby) *were an adult*. Mismatch! The same pronoun can't refer to two different things in the same sentence. Eliminate answer (A).

Of the other answers, only answer (C) also uses the pronoun *it* and, in that case, the pronoun usage is fine.

(2) Meaning

This subtle issue will likely only be spotted when reading answer choice (B) in full. (There's a good chance answer (B) will be one of your last answers standing.)

> (B) A baby emerges with a sense of vision that would be rated 20/500, or legally blind as an adult.

Legally blind as an adult isn't a full sentence, so it must be a modifier. What is it modifying?

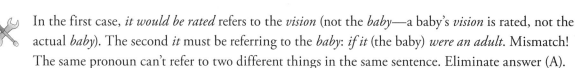

Logically, the sentence is trying to say that an adult with 20/500 vision would be considered legally blind. Consider this example:

> A mouse emerges from its hole with its whiskers quivering frantically, or _____.

Fill in that blank. What kind of information would you expect to see? The sentence sets up the expectation that it's going to tell us something else about the whiskers quivering frantically, perhaps something like:

A mouse emerges from its hole with its whiskers quivering frantically, or twitching at really high speed.

That information after the comma provides additional information about the last thing that was said before the comma. In answer choice (B), though, it doesn't make sense to say that the rating, or even the *sense of vision*, is *legally blind as an adult*. Eliminate answer (B).

(3) Structure

Answers (C) and (D) contain a semicolon; test the structure.

In answer (C), the part before the semicolon, *As a baby … about 20/500*, is a complete sentence. The part after the semicolon, *qualifying it to be legally blind if an adult*, is not a complete sentence. Eliminate answer (C).

In answer (D), both the part before and the part after the semicolon are complete sentences.

(4) Verb: *would deemed*

This issue is a tough one to spot. The *which* modifier reads: *sense of vision, which would deemed legally blind for an adult*.

What is this portion of the sentence referring to? A comma followed by *which* indicates a noun modifier, so *which would deemed* is referring to the *sense of vision*.

A person can deem something: The CEO deemed (or considered) it necessary to institute layoffs. A *sense of vision*, however, cannot *deem* (active voice) anything. Rather, the sentence would have to say that a *sense of vision would be deemed* (passive voice) *legally blind*. Eliminate answer (E).

The Correct Answer

Correct answer (D) fixes the original pronoun error by removing all instances of the pronoun *it*. It does also change the structure somewhat (by inserting a semicolon), but the change is made correctly.

#114 Starfish

(A)   Pronoun (*it*); Parallelism (*if X then Y*); Meaning
(B)   CORRECT
(C)   Meaning
(D)   Pronoun (*they*); Parallelism (*if X then Y*)
(E)   Parallelism (*if X, then Y*)

First Glance

The word *if* shows up right before the underline; this word is often part of the idiom *if X (then) Y*. Further, the Parallelism marker *and* appears at the end of the underline.

Issues

(1) Pronouns: *it; they*
Parallelism: *if X then Y*

The original sentence contains this piece: *If one arm is lost it quickly replaces it*. Check the pronouns.

(A) *if one arm is lost …*   *(then) it quickly replaces it*
(B) *if one arm is lost …*   *(then) it is quickly replaced*
(C) *if they lose one arm …*   *(then) they quickly replace it*
(D) *if they lose one arm …*   *(then) they are quickly replaced*
(E) *if they lose one arm …*   *(then) it is quickly replaced*

If one sentence uses the same pronoun to refer to two different things, the sentence is considered ambiguous—and therefore wrong. In answer (A), the first *it* refers to *starfish*; the second refers to *one arm*.

Notice, too, that the noun *starfish* could be singular or plural. Which is it in this sentence? Check out the verb: *starfish have*. He have? Or they have? *They have* is correct, so starfish is plural. The pronoun *it* is singular, another reason to eliminate (A). Check the remaining answers for both pronoun ambiguity and singular versus plural.

Answer (D) also contains the double pronoun error. The first instance of the plural pronoun *they* refers to the *starfish*, while the second refers to *one arm* (which is also a number mismatch—*one arm* is singular). Eliminate answers (A) and (D).

This examination also highlights the parallelism required for the idiom *if X (then) Y*. (Note: The word "then" is optional; this problem doesn't use it.) When *X* and *Y* are in the form of clauses, the entire clauses should be parallel. A subject pronoun in the second clause should refer to the subject of the first clause. Eliminate answers (A), (D), and (E) for failing to do so.

(2) Meaning

 The original sentence indicates that *starfish* can regenerate an arm, though they sometimes *overcompensate* and grow extra arms:

(A), (C): *by overcompensating and growing an extra one*
(B), (D), (E): *with the animal overcompensating and growing an extra one*

 In answers (A) and (C), the preposition *by* means that the starfish replaces the arm *by overcompensating*. The meaning is illogical; the first arm grown is not an overcompensation; rather, the first one is the intended replacement arm. Only the *extra* arms represent overcompensation—and the extras, by definition, are not the replacement arm. The other choices use the preposition *with* instead of *by*, avoiding the meaning error. Eliminate answers (A) and (C).

The Correct Answer

Correct answer (B) employs a properly parallel structure with clear pronoun usage: *If one arm is lost it is quickly replaced*. This choice also correctly uses *with* to introduce the extra information that the animal sometimes accidentally grows extra arms.

#115 Maritime Code

(A) Pronoun (*they*)
(B) CORRECT
(C) Structure / Modifier (*stimulating*);
     Meaning (*sea areas under provisions*)
(D) Pronoun (*this*);
     Meaning (*sea areas under provisions*)
(E) Structure / Modifier (*which*);
     Meaning (*sea areas under provisions*)

First Glance

Nearly the entire sentence is underlined, increasing the chances that Structure, Meaning, Modifier, or Parallelism issues will be tested.

Issues

(1) Pronoun: *they; this*

 The original sentence begins with an opening modifier followed by a main clause: *Because there are provisions, they have stimulated*. To which noun does the pronoun *they* refer?

(A) *Because **there** are provisions ... areas, **they** have stimulated disputes.*
(B) *Because **the code** provides that ... areas, **it** has stimulated disputes.*
(C) *Even tiny islets can be ... code, already stimulating disputes.*
(D) *Because **tiny islets** can be ... code, **this** has stimulated disputes.*
(E) *Because tiny islets can be ... code, which is already stimulating disputes.*

Answers (A), (B), and (D) all use an opening modifier followed by a main clause. In this structure, when a pronoun is the subject of the main clause, the expectation is that the pronoun refers to the opening modifier—ideally, the main noun of that modifier.

In answer (A), the main noun *there* can't be the antecedent for *they*. The rest of the modifier contains multiple possibilities: the *provisions*, the *islets*, the *claims*. Ambiguity is bad; eliminate answer (A).

The subject pronoun *it* in answer (B) does logically refer to *code*, the main noun in the opening modifier. Answer (B) is okay.

Answer (D) changes the subject pronoun of the main clause to *this*. When the pronoun *this* is the subject of a sentence, it cannot refer to a noun or situation in the same clause or to a modifier attached to that clause. An example of correct usage:

She is allergic to many foods; this makes it difficult for her to eat at restaurants.

The example above is correct because *this* refers to a situation described in a different independent clause. In answer (D), however, the word *this* refers to the situation described in the attached modifier. Eliminate answer (D).

Note that answers (C) and (E) change the structure significantly; examine this issue next.

A̶
B
C̶
D̶
E

(2) Structure / Modifier: *which; stimulating*
   Meaning: *sea areas under provisions*

As noted above, answers (C) and (E) change the structure.

The portions after the comma in answers (C) and (E) have transformed from main clauses into modifiers:

   (C) *Even tiny islets can be the basis for claims, already stimulating disputes.*
   (E) *Because tiny islets can be the basis for claims, which is already stimulating disputes.*

A sentence isn't a sentence without a main clause somewhere! Answer (C) does have an independent clause before the comma, but answer (E) does not. Eliminate answer (E) because it is a sentence fragment.

Answer (C) inserts a participle modifier, *stimulating*. This modifier should refer to *islets can be the basis*, but logic dictates that the *code* is *stimulating disputes*, not the *islets*. Eliminate answer (C).

Finally, answers (C), (D), and (E) create an illogical meaning with the structure *sea areas under provisions of the new code*. The *provisions* are not literally *under*, or even a part of, the *sea areas*. Eliminate answers (C), (D), and (E).

A
B
C̶
D̶
E̶

The Correct Answer

Correct answer (B) fixes the initial pronoun error by changing the subject of the opening modifier to match the pronoun used as the subject of the main clause: *Because the code provides* something, *it* (the code) *has stimulated disputes.*

#116 Building and Loan

(A) Structure / Parallelism (*X and then Y*)
(B) Structure / Parallelism (*X and then Y*)
(C) CORRECT
(D) Structure / Meaning
(E) Structure / Meaning

First Glance

The underline is short; consider examining the answers before reading the sentence. The structure of *taking turns drawing* changes substantially. Four answers use the word *and*—is Parallelism an issue?

Issues

(1) Structure / Parallelism: *X and then Y*

 In the original sentence, the *members made payments, then taking turns drawing.* Some sort of sequence of events exists, but it's a bit difficult to understand. The First Glance revealed that the other four answers all change the word *then* to *and*; would this make the sentence easier to understand?

 Yes! First the members made payments, *and* then *took turns* doing something else. Answer (A) doesn't make this parallel relationship clear because it's missing the conjunction *and*.

Furthermore, the implied parallelism means the *members made payments* and the members then *took turns* doing something, but answer (A) says the *members made, then [the members] taking turns. Taking* isn't the right form of the verb; it should be *took*. Answer (B) does insert the parallelism marker *and* but continues to use the incorrect participle form *taking*. Eliminate answers (A) and (B).

(2) Structure / Meaning

 Because structure has already been tested once, with the missing *and* in answer (A), examine the remaining answers with this in mind. Answers (C), (D), and (E) are all parallel, but what happens with the remaining portion of the construction?

    (C) *members made payments and* **took turns drawing** *on the funds.*
    (D) *members made payments and* **took turns, they drew** *on the funds.*
    (E) *members made payments and* **drew, taking turns** *on the funds.*

 Answer (C) ends on one complete thought: *took turns drawing.* Answer (D) splits out the last portion as its own independent clause: *they drew on the funds.* It is incorrect to connect an independent clause to another portion of the sentence without some kind of conjunction or a semicolon. Eliminate answer (D).

Answer (E) splits up the actions. It's no longer clear what the members are *drawing*, nor do you know what they're *taking turns* doing. Although you may know the intended meaning based upon the original sentence, this choice does not actually indicate what the members took turns doing. Eliminate answer (E).

The Correct Answer

Correct answer (C) fixes the initial structure problem by inserting the parallel marker *and*. It also changes the incorrect verb form *taking* to the correct form *took*.

#117 Gall's Hypothesis

(A) Idiom (*hypothesis of*)
(B) Idiom (*hypothesis of*)
(C) CORRECT
(D) Modifier / Meaning
(E) Modifier / Meaning

First Glance

The vast majority of the sentence is underlined, increasing the chances that Structure, Meaning, Modifier, or Parallelism issues will be tested.

Issues

(1) Idiom: *hypothesis of*

 The original sentence introduces the description of a *hypothesis* with the words *of there being different functions* (in different locations).

 If the description of the *hypothesis* includes a verb, then the proper idiom is *hypothesis that* + clause. For example:

> The restaurant manager has a *hypothesis that* people will tip better when the weather is good.

Answers (A) and (B) both use the construction *hypothesis of*; eliminate them.

Answers (D) and (E) change the construction by placing a *which* modifier directly after *hypothesis*. Such a construction might work; see the Modifier discussion for more.

(2) Modifier / Meaning

 You'd spot this one either when noticing the original idiom error or when comparing the beginning of each answer choice. Is it acceptable to use a *which* modifier at this location?

Which modifiers are nonessential and are typically separated from the rest of the sentence by commas. It's possible, in rare circumstances, to use *which* as an essential modifier without commas, but the word *that* is preferred when introducing such a construction.

Answers (D) and (E) don't use commas, so both would have to be interpreted as essential modifiers. The meaning of answer (E), then, changes: the sentence is referring to the one hypothesis (of all of Gall's hypotheses) that is widely accepted today; the original sentence never indicates that only one of Gall's hypotheses is widely accepted today. Eliminate answer (E).

Compare answer (D) to answer (C):

  (C) *Gall's hypothesis* **that functions are localized** *is accepted.*
  (D) *Gall's hypothesis* **which is that there are functions localized** *is accepted.*

The test writers prefer to use *that* to introduce an essential modifier. Eliminate answer (D).

The Correct Answer

Correct answer (C) fixes the initial idiom error by replacing the word *of* with the word *that*. Further, the word *that* is an appropriate choice because this portion of the sentence is an essential modifier.

#118 Mauritius

(A) Structure; Idiom (*excepting for*)
(B) Structure
(C) CORRECT
(D) Idiom (*excepting for*)
(E) Structure

First Glance

The underline is extremely short; examine the differences among the answers before reading the original sentence. A scan of the answers reveals various forms of *excepting* as well as an interesting split: two of the answers begin with a conjunction (*but*). Structure may be an issue.

Issues

(1) Structure

 The original sentence is a run-on sentence or comma splice; it consists of two independent clauses connected only by a comma:

  (A) *Mauritius was a colony, the English language was never spoken.*

 It's necessary to insert a coordinating conjunction or a semicolon between two independent clauses. For example:

  The elevator got stuck, but the people didn't panic.

Answers (A), (B), and (E) all lack a coordinating conjunction; eliminate them.

(2) Idiom: *excepting for*

 In the original sentence, the idiom *excepting for* is incorrect.

There are multiple ways in which to fix the idiom. Of the options given in the answers, *except in* and *with the exception of* are both acceptable. Eliminate answers (A) and (D).

The Correct Answer

Correct answer (C) inserts the necessary coordinating conjunction (*but*) and also fixes the idiom by changing the form to *except in*.

Note: When the answer choices are this short, try not to spend more than one minute on the question; there will only be one or two issues, and you either know them or you don't.

#119 George Sand

(A)	Idiom (*consider X Y*); Pronoun (*these*)
(B)	Idiom (*consider X Y*); Pronoun (*these*)
(C)	Idiom (*consider X Y*); Parallelism (*X and Y*)
(D)	Idiom (*consider X Y*)
(E)	**CORRECT**

First Glance

Notice that the first word of the underline changes significantly in the answer choices; there may be Structure, Meaning, or Idiom issues.

Issues

(1) Idiom: *consider X Y*

 The answer choices present you with a wide range of choices for words that follow *consider*. Which ones are idiomatically legal?

 If you want to say that someone believes a certain thing to be true, the proper structure is *consider X Y*, as in: She considers Anya funny

The *Y* portion of this structure should not be introduced with *to be* or *as* or any other expression. Answers (A), (B), (C), and (D) all insert unnecessary words between the *X* (*the rural poor*) and *Y* (*legitimate subjects*). Eliminate all four.

(2) Pronoun: *these*

The pronoun *these* is a demonstrative pronoun. A simple example of usage might be: She likes these apples. In that example, the pronoun refers to the noun *apple*. What does *these* refer to in this sentence?

In the original sentence, *these* refers to *legitimate subjects*, a noun within the same clause. When *these* is used as a subject, though, it is not allowed to refer to another noun within the same clause. Answer (B) repeats the error; answers (C), (D), and (E) all replace *these* with the object pronoun *them*, an acceptable usage. Eliminate answers (A) and (B).

(3) Parallelism: *X and Y*

The word *and* indicates parallelism: *to consider and portray*. *Consider* is not underlined, so *portray* must match that form. Either *portray* or *to portray* would be acceptable.

Answer (C) changes *portray* to *portraying*. This isn't parallel to the non-underlined construction *to consider*; eliminate answer (C).

Note: It is actually acceptable not to repeat the word *to* before *portray,* but when the two parts of the parallel structure are far apart, it's preferable to repeat the full infinitive structure for both.

The Correct Answer

Correct answer (E) fixes the initial idiom error by removing the extraneous words included in the other choices; it also corrects the initial pronoun error by replacing *these* with *them*.

#120 WWF

(A)	Verb (*to be*); Idiom (*in burning*)
(B)	Idiom (*that*)
(C)	**CORRECT**
(D)	Meaning
(E)	Verb (*to be*); Meaning

First Glance

Two commas appear: just before the underline and right at the end. Check for Modifier and Meaning issues.

Issues

(1) Verb: *to be*

The underline in the original sentence begins *a phenomenon most scientists agree to be caused*.

If the scientists agree in the present, then the cause is in either the present or the past. It cannot be in the future, as the construction *to be* implies. An acceptable alternative would be *a phenomenon most agree is caused*. Eliminate answers (A) and (E).

(2) Idiom: *in burning*

 The original sentence says *caused … in burning fossil fuels.*

 In burning is an incorrect idiom. Possible correct alternatives for this sentence include *when burning* or *while burning*, indicating that the cause occurs when or while human beings take a certain action. Eliminate answer (A).

(3) Idiom: *that*

 You would probably only notice this difference when comparing answers directly:

> (B) *a phenomenon most scientists agree **that** is caused*
> (C) *a phenomenon **that** most scientists agree is caused*

 The modifier beginning *a phenomenon* has a complex structure. The simpler version would be:

> *a phenomenon that is caused by* (something)

The author wants to introduce further support by indicating that most scientists agree with this assessment. In this type of construction, the *scientists agree* portion should be placed between *that* and *is*: *that most scientists agree is*. Answer (C) does this correctly. Eliminate answer (B).

(4) Meaning

 Answers (D) and (E) change up the meaning:

> (D) *which scientists agree on as a phenomenon caused by human beings who burn fuels*
> (E) *which scientists agree to be a phenomenon caused by fuels burned by human beings*

 Consider these examples:

> Bjorn and Jim agree on this topic.
> Bjorn and Jim agree on as a topic.

The second is confusing. They agree that the topic exists? They are in agreement about something to do with the topic? Answer (D) says that *scientists agree on* global warming *as a phenomenon*, but really they *agree* about the *cause* of the *phenomenon*; that meaning is lost in this answer.

Further, the direct cause is not the people themselves, nor is it the existence of the *fuels*. The cause is the *burning* of the *fuels*. This meaning is obscured in both answers (D) and (E); eliminate them.

The Correct Answer

Correct answer (C) fixes the original verb error by replacing *to be* with the present tense *is*. The authors likely used the awkward but correct construction *human beings' burning of fossil fuels* in order to tempt people to cross off the correct answer.

#121 Split Apart Continents

(A) Parallelism (*splitting*)
(B) CORRECT
(C) Meaning / Parallelism
(D) Meaning / Parallelism
(E) Meaning / Parallelism

First Glance

The very short underline makes it worthwhile to study the differences in the answers before reading the sentence. The word *continents* moves about and the form of the other portion (*splitting / split*) changes substantially.

Issues

(1) Parallelism: *splitting*

The initial sentence could be read in one of two ways:

> *Impacts may have caused (W) reversals, (X) the onset, (Y) splitting, and (Z) eruptions.*
> *Impacts may have caused (J) reversals, (K) the onset, (modifier) splitting continents, and (L) eruptions.*

Is the *splitting* portion the third item in a list of four? Or is it a modifier providing extra information about *the onset of ice ages*?

Ambiguity in general is bad, so the initial sentence can't be correct. As a general rule, the test writers don't like to make action nouns (such as *reversals*, *onset*, and *eruptions*) parallel to simple gerunds (such as *splitting*) because this pairing can result in the ambiguity outlined above. Eliminate answer (A).

Note: Answer (B) also contains *splitting*, but includes the article *the* in front. *The splitting* is a complex gerund and it is acceptable to make a complex gerund parallel to an action noun.

A
B
C
D
E

(2) Meaning / Parallelism

Answers (A) and (B) focus on the action of *splitting* something. Answers (C), (D), and (E) focus on a description of the noun *continents*. Are both acceptable in the context of the sentence?

The non-underlined portions list nouns that were *caused* by the *impacts*: *reversals* of something, the *onset* of something else, and *volcanic eruptions*. Would these impacts have caused the action of *splitting*? Or would these impacts have caused the *continents* themselves?

It's possible that the impacts might have caused the formation of the continents or something similar, but it's illogical to say that the *impacts caused the continents*. Caused them to exist? In that case, the sentence would need to say something such as "impacts created the continents." Eliminate answers (C), (D), and (E).

The beginning of answer (C) could also be interpreted as a verb, *split*. If that were the case, however, then the list would not be parallel, as the other three items are all nouns. Either way, answer (C) is incorrect.

The Correct Answer

Correct answer (B) fixes the initial ambiguity by changing the simple gerund *splitting* to the complex gerund *the splitting*. Further, *the splitting* is an action noun, properly parallel to the other action nouns in the list.

#122 Handwriting Analysis

(A) Meaning / Modifier (*from*)
(B) Meaning / Modifier (*from*); Idiom (*claims it*); Idiom (*ability of*)
(C) Idiom (*claims the ability*); Idiom (*ability of*)
(D) CORRECT
(E) Idiom (*claims being able*)

First Glance

The answers change quite a bit at the beginning; keep an eye out for Structure, Meaning, and Idiom issues.

Issues

(1) Meaning / Modifier: *from*

What, exactly, is *from a one-page writing sample?* The original sentence seems to indicate that the firm claims something from the sample.

It's certainly possible to claim something from an essay or some other written document, but this interpretation doesn't match the full sentence. Rather, *from a one-page writing sample* explains how the firm is able to assess personality traits. This modifier should be placed closer to *assess*, as it is in

answers (C), (D), and (E). Eliminate answers (A) and (B) for conveying the illogical meaning that the claim is contained in the writing sample itself.

(2) Idiom: *claims it; claims the ability; claims being able*

 The answers offer several variations of this idiom:

> (A) *A firm* claims *from a sample* that it can assess
> (B) *A firm* claims *from a sample* it has the ability
> (C) *A firm* claims the ability
> (D) *A firm* claims to be able
> (E) *A firm* claims being able

 The word *claims*, when followed by an action or event, can be used correctly in two primary ways:

> Claim that: She *claims that* her handwriting is beautiful.
> Claim + infinitive: She *claims to* write beautifully.

Answers (A) and (D) both use an acceptable idiom. Answers (B), (C), and (E) do not; eliminate them.

A
B̶
C̶
D
E̶

(3) Idiom: *ability of*

 Several answer choices introduce the phrase *the ability of assessing*.

 The ability of doing something is an incorrect idiom. Eliminate answers (B) and (C) for using this construction.

A
B̶
C̶
D
E

The Correct Answer

Correct answer (D) fixes the initial meaning error by placing the *from* modifier later in the sentence and also separating that modifier out using commas. This choice clearly indicates that the firm *claims to be able to assess* something based upon *the writing sample*.

#123 Wine Sales

(A) CORRECT
(B) Meaning / Modifier (*red wine*)
(C) Meaning / Parallelism; Meaning (*in a 1991 report*)
(D) Meaning / Modifier (*red wine*)
(E) Meaning / Parallelism; Meaning (*in a 1991 report*)

First Glance

A long underline with multiple commas points to potential Modifier, Meaning, and Parallelism issues.

Structure

The initial sentence is a beast, making it worth the time to break out the sentence structure:

Original Sentence Core

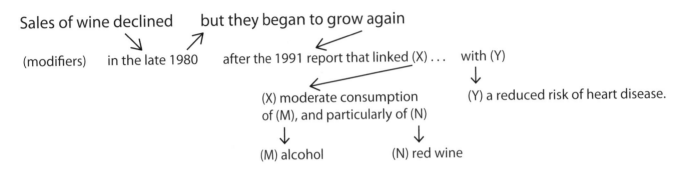

There are two different parallel structures interwoven into the second half:

> First: *linked (X) consumption with (Y) risk*
> Second: *consumption of (M) alcohol and of (N) wine*

Although the sentence seems very convoluted, the parallelism is actually 100% correct.

Issues

(1) Meaning / Modifier: *red wine*

 Answer (B) says *a moderate alcohol consumption, particularly red wine*. What is *red wine* describing? Answer (D) has a similar structure.

 In answer (B), *red wine* is describing the main noun before it—*consumption*. *Red wine* is not an example of *consumption*, a type of *consumption*, or in any way a description of *consumption*; the meaning is illogical. Rather, *red wine* is a type of *alcohol*. Answer (D) repeats this error; eliminate both (B) and (D).

A
~~B~~
C
~~D~~
E

(2) Meaning / Parallelism

 Answers (C) and (E) both use the parallel marker *and*:

> (C) *moderate alcohol consumption, and particularly of red wine*
> (E) *consumption in a report and in particular red wine*

 In answer (C), *of red wine* doesn't have a parallel "of + noun" match. Logically, the noun *wine* should match with *alcohol*, but *alcohol* is an adjective in this sentence. Answer (E) also doesn't have a parallel match. The structure *in a 1991 report*, appearing just before *and in particular red wine*,

A
B
~~C~~
D
~~E~~

appears to try to make those two items parallel, but it's illogical to make *report* and *wine* parallel. Eliminate answers (C) and (E).

(3) Meaning: *in a 1991 report*

When time markers, such as *in a 1991 report*, move around, there is likely a Meaning issue.

The *1991 report linked* two items (*modest consumption* and *a reduced risk*). This time marker has to point to the linking action and not another action. In answers (A), (B), and (D), the time marker is very close to the *linked* action. Answers (C) and (E), however, have issues.

> (C) *in a 1991 report, moderate consumption … caused them to begin to grow.*

The time marker is attached to the main clause; the *consumption caused* something *to grow in the report* itself.

> (E) *a reduced risk linked to modest consumption in a 1991 report …*

Again, although you might know logically what the sentence is trying to say, answer (E) actually says that the *consumption* occurred *in the 1991 report*. Eliminate answers (C) and (E) for conveying illogical meanings.

The Correct Answer

Correct answer (A), while convoluted, is grammatically correct and uses proper parallelism to convey a logical and unambiguous meaning.

#124 Lotte Jacobi

(A)	Comparison (*less successful*); Structure
(B)	Comparison (*less successful*)
(C)	**CORRECT**
(D)	Comparison (*less successful*)
(E)	Structure; Verb (*had been*)

First Glance

The underline appears at the very beginning; if an early error pops out, you may choose to jump to the answers before reading the full sentence. If so, return to the full sentence if you get stuck.

Issues

(1) Comparison: *less successful*

The initial sentence contains a comparison marker: *less successful*.

There are two problems with *she was less successful compared to Germany*. First, the correct idiom is *less successful than* but the *than* is missing in this case. Second, it's illogical to compare a person or a person's success to Germany. Scan the other answers for either of these errors:

(B) *less successful*	*as compared to Germany*
(C) *less successful*	*than she had been in Germany*
(D) *she was less successful*	*when compared to Germany*
(E) *she had been less successful*	*than in Germany*

~~A~~
~~B~~
C
~~D~~
E

Answers (A), (B), and (D) all lack the word *than* in the construction *less successful than*. Eliminate all three.

(2) Structure

The original connects two independent clauses with a comma:

> *She was less successful, Lotte Jacobi earned a small group.*

~~A~~
B
C
D
~~E~~

Two independent sentences must be connected either by some kind of conjunction (such as "and") or by a semicolon. Neither is the case here, so this is a run-on sentence. Answer (E) repeats this structure; eliminate both answers (A) and (E).

(3) Verbs: *had been*

The verb tenses change throughout the answers. What is the sequence of events?

Lotte Jacobi is *native* to *Germany* and *emigrated* to *New York*. Therefore, she was in Germany first and later went to New York.

Answers (A) and (B) both say that she was *less successful after she had emigrated to New York*. First, she emigrated; then, she had less success. It's acceptable to use past perfect to refer to emigration, the earlier of the two events. Answer (C) says that she was *less successful after she emigrated than she had been in Germany*. This is also acceptable, as she was in Germany first.

A
B
C
D
~~E~~

In contrast, answer (E) says that *she had been less successful after* (*going to New York*) *than in Germany*. Her success in New York occurred later, so it cannot take past perfect in this construction. Eliminate answer (E).

The Correct Answer

Correct answer (C) fixes the original error by using the correct construction *less successful than*; further, it appropriately compares her success in New York with her success in Germany.

#125 Double the Apples

(A) Verb (*has*)
(B) CORRECT
(C) Verb (*has*); Modifier (*much*)
(D) Meaning
(E) Meaning

First Glance

The answer choices contain a large amount of variation for such a short underline, increasing the chances that Structure, Meaning, or Modifier issues will be tested.

Issues

(1) Verb: *has*

 The initial sentence makes a comparison between something happening *today* and something that happened *in 1910*. The 1910 portion uses a present tense verb, *has*.

 Answers (A) and (C) incorrectly use the present tense verb *has* to refer to an action that took place more than 100 years ago. The remaining answers all properly use past tense verbs to discuss the past time frame. Eliminate answers (A) and (C).

(2) Modifier: *much*
Meaning

 The form of the comparison changes substantially:

> The same acreage produces:
> (A) *double* the apples
> (B) *twice as many* apples
> (C) *as much as twice* the apples
> (D) *two times as many* apples
> (E) *a doubling of* the apples

 The sentence is trying to compare the number of apples produced in 1910 to the number of apples produced today (via the same amount of acreage). The original wording (*double*) isn't great, but it's not outright incorrect either. Answer (B) is also acceptable. Answer (C) uses the comparison marker *as much as*, but the number of apples is countable. *Much* is used for uncountable quantities: there is much water, but there are many apples. Eliminate answer (C).

Answer (E) says, in effect, that the *acreage produces a doubling of the* actual *apples that* this acreage *produced in 1910*. The actual apples from 1910 no longer exist; rather, the *number* of apples *produced* doubled. Eliminate answer (E).

The first portion of answer (D), *two times as many*, is acceptable, but examine the rest of the structure. The wording *as there were in 1910* refers to the number of apples in existence in general in 1910, not the number produced on a certain amount of acreage. It would be pretty amazing if a limited amount of acreage today could produce twice as many apples as existed everywhere in the world in 1910! Eliminate answer (D).

The Correct Answer

Correct answer (B) fixes the original verb tense error by replacing *has* with *did*. It also uses the unambiguous comparison structure *twice as many apples as*.

#126 Lie Detectors

(A) CORRECT
(B) Subject–Verb (*creates*); Meaning (*in turn*)
(C) Meaning (*creating*)
(D) Meaning (*to create*)
(E) Meaning (*in turn*); Meaning (*who creates*)

First Glance

The underline starts with the word *that* and other answers start with *creating*, *to create*, and *who creates*. Meaning or Modifier issues will likely be tested.

Issues

(1) Subject–Verb: *creates*

Answers (A) and (B) are almost identical. Answer (A) uses the plural *create* while answer (B) uses the singular *creates*.

What is the subject? *Lying produces reactions,* and those *reactions create physiological responses.* The subject *reactions* is plural, so the sentence requires the plural verb *create*. Eliminate answer (B); no other choices repeat this error.

Note: In answer (E), the singular verb *creates* is matched with the singular subject *individual*.

A
~~B~~
C
D
E

(2) Meaning: *in turn*

Answers (A) and (B) also differ in one other way: the placement of the phrase *in turn*. What is this information describing?

The phrase *in turn* illustrates a series of events: *X* causes *Y* and *Y*, in turn, causes *Z*. *In turn*, then, is best placed to show that the second event causes the third one: *Lying (X) produces reactions (Y)* and those *reactions, in turn, create responses (Z)*. Answer (B) moves *in turn* to the end of the sentence, after *responses*, creating an ambiguity: the original meaning could hold, or it could be the case that the *responses* then do something *in turn*. Eliminate answers (B) and (E).

A
~~B~~
C
D
~~E~~

(3) Meaning: *creating; to create; who creates*

The beginning of each answer choice varies:

(A) *reactions in an individual* **that create** *responses*
(B) *reactions in an individual* **that creates** *responses*
(C) *reactions in an individual* **creating** *responses*
(D) *reactions in an individual* **to create** *responses*
(E) *reactions in an individual* **who creates** *responses*

A noun followed by the word *that* typically signals a noun modifier. In this case, the construction is tricky. The closest noun, *individual*, is a modifier of the main noun, *reactions*. The *that* modifier, then, refers to the main noun *reactions*, not to the modifier *individual*. Answers (A) and (B) are acceptable.

Answer (C) changes the first word to *creating*. A participle that is not separated out from the main clause by a comma describes the noun to which it is directly attached. Consider this alternate sentence:

An earthquake will result in instability for a person hopping on one foot.

The instability isn't hopping on one foot; the person is.

In answers (C) and (E), both modifiers refer to the *individual*, not the *responses*. In this construction, the reactions occur only in individuals who have been creating unconscious physiological responses for some other reason. This meaning is nonsensical; rather, the reaction to lying then creates the unconscious responses. Eliminate answers (C) and (E). (Note: This issue is very subtle; most people miss it.)

Answer (D) uses the infinitive *to create*. An infinitive verb used during a discussion of causation implies that one thing was done on purpose in order to cause another thing to happen. It is illogical to suggest that *lying produces emotional reactions* on purpose in order to *create unconscious physiological responses*. Eliminate answer (D).

The Correct Answer

Correct answer (A) employs an appropriate modifier signal (*that*) to refer to the main noun *reactions*. Further, the phrase *in turn* is suitably placed near the follow-on action that occurred as part of a sequence.

#127 Joan of Arc

(A) Parallelism (*X and Y*)
(B) Idiom (*in claiming*)
(C) Idiom (*persuading that*)
(D) CORRECT
(E) Idiom (*persuading that*)

First Glance

The word *and* appears immediately before the underline; check the sentence for Parallelism issues.

Issues

(1) Parallelism: *X and Y*

The *and* just before the underline is a key clue: *X and Y* need to be parallel. Check the *Y* portion in the answer choices.

The original sentence says *Joan of Arc turned the tide and she persuaded*. The pronoun *she* refers to *Joan of Arc*; it is sufficient to say *Joan of Arc turned the tide and persuaded*. Eliminate answer (A).

Although the sentence also contains the verb *claimed*, that verb is in a noun modifier (*a young Frenchwoman who claimed to be divinely inspired*) and so does not need to be in a parallel structure with *turned* and *persuaded*.

The sentence contains a trap here regarding *persuaded* versus *persuading*; see the next issue for more.

(2) Idiom: *persuading that*

When scanning the answers for the first issue (parallelism), note that answers (C) and (E) change *persuaded* to *persuading*.

Interestingly, changing from the -ed to the -ing form of the word might not automatically disqualify answers (C) and (E). Why? Take a look at this:

*Joan of Arc ... turned the tide by **liberating** X and **persuading** Y.*

Answers (C) and (E) both have this same structure: *Persuading* could be paired with *liberating*! Up until the word *persuading*, in fact, both choices are fine. *Persuading that* an action happen, though, is an incorrect idiom. You could persuade someone that something should happen, but you can't persuade the action or event itself. Eliminate answers (C) and (E).

(3) Idiom: *in claiming*

If you followed the same order of examining the issues, then you'd have narrowed the answers down to answers (B) and (D). Whenever you're down to two answers, compare the two directly:

> (B) *persuaded Charles* **in claiming** *his throne*
> (D) *persuaded Charles* **to claim** *his throne*

This one's an idiom. You can *persuade X to do Y*. (The *to do* represents the infinitive form of whatever verb the sentence uses.) You can't *persuade X in doing Y*. In this case, the sentence is using the verb *claim*; the infinitive is *to claim*. Eliminate answer (B).

The Correct Answer

Correct answer (D) fixes the original redundancy by removing the word *she* and does not introduce any new errors.

#128 The Elephant

(A)	Parallelism (*X and Y*)
(B)	Verb (*has suggested*)
(C)	Verb (*had descended*); Structure
(D)	Verb (*had descended*)
(E)	**CORRECT**

First Glance

The underline is relatively long, signaling possible Meaning, Structure, Parallelism, or Modifier issues.

Issues

(1) Parallelism: *X and Y*

In the original sentence, the word *and* signals a parallelism or structure issue of some type: *X and Y*.

The conjunction *and* could serve as the connection between two independent clauses, but *its trunk evolving* is not independent. Alternately, *and* could signal a dependent portion that is parallel to some other part of the sentence. However, nothing earlier in the sentence is parallel to *its trunk evolving*.

Scan the remaining answers in the same location. Answers (B) and (C) both remove the *and*. Answers (D) and (E) both use the form *X and Y*, where the *X* and *Y* portions are parallel. Eliminate answer (A).

(2) Verb: *has suggested; had descended*

 A comparison of the beginning of each answer reveals several changes to the initial verb *suggests*: *has suggested, suggesting,* or *to suggest.*

 A switch from the construction *evidence that suggests* to the construction *evidence that has suggested* changes the meaning. *Suggests* implies that the suggestion will continue to be true. *Has suggested* indicates only that it was once true. The other variations (*suggesting, to suggest*) all acceptably convey the same meaning as the original construction. Eliminate answer (B).

Because one verb form had an error, check for other verb issues. The verb *is descended* changes to *descended* or *had descended* in various choices. Both the simple past *descended* and the present *is descended* are acceptable. However, correct usage of the past perfect *had descended* requires a separate event or time marker at a more recent time in the past. The only other verb in the same clause of the sentence is *evolved*. This evolution was a part of the transition from aquatic animal to elephant; it did not occur afterwards. Eliminate answers (C) and (D).

(3) Structure

 Answer (C) changes the *and* connector to the preposition *with*, followed by a complete sentence (*its trunk originally evolved as a kind of snorkel*).

 Two complete sentences must be connected by some kind of conjunction, such as *and*, or by a semicolon; the preposition *with* is not acceptable. This would be the equivalent of writing "The elephant is gray with its trunk is long" (incorrect) as opposed to "The elephant is gray, and its trunk is long." Eliminate answer (C).

The Correct Answer

Correct answer (E) contains proper parallelism between the *X* and *Y* elements: *that the elephant is descended … and that its trunk evolved.*

#129 Cajuns

(A)	Subject–Verb (*has*)
(B)	Subject–Verb (*is*); Verb (*is*)
(C)	**CORRECT**
(D)	Meaning
(E)	Verb (*are*); Meaning

First Glance

The multiple commas signal a list. The portion before the semicolon is not underlined, so it is probably only needed for reference. Make sure that the portion after the semicolon is a complete sentence.

Issues

(1) Subject–Verb: *has; is*

 The underline contains the verb *has been added*; what subject goes with this verb?

 The original sentence contains an unusual inverted sentence structure. Normally, the subject comes before the verb. In this case, however, the subject *words* appears after the verb: *words has been added*. While inverted sentences can be correct in general, they still have to follow subject–verb agreement rules; a plural subject can't be paired with a singular verb. Answer (B) repeats this error: *words is added*. Eliminate answers (A) and (B).

(2) Verb: *is; are*

 A comparison of the answers reveals a mix of verb tenses: present perfect (*has been, have been*) and present (*is, are*).

 The development of the *Cajun dialect* began in the past. Any discussion of that development, then, should use either past or present perfect. Simple present tense refers only to today; it can't apply to the past. Eliminate answers (B) and (E).

(3) Meaning

 A comparison of the beginning of each choice exposes a challenging split:

(A) *to which has been added English words*
(B) *added to which is English words*
(C) *to which English words have been added*
(D) *with English words having been added*
(E) *and, in addition, English words are added*

The pronoun *which* and the preposition *with* both signal modifiers. The word *and* indicates parallelism.

Let's take the *and* case first. When two independent clauses are connected by the word *and*, those two clauses are considered separate things: Lucia is tall, and Bjorn likes cats. The two halves are not required to refer to each other at all.

(E) *Their language is French and words are added.*

Those *words are added* to… what? The sentence doesn't actually say. Further, *in addition* is redundant when the phrase immediately follows the word *and*. Eliminate answer (E).

What about *which* versus *with*? This gets tricky. *To which* is required to refer to the main noun immediately beforehand (*French* in this case); however, the preposition *with* is more flexible. Look at these two sentences:

I'll have my pie with ice cream.

I'll have the pie with the apples.

The first one is talking about having something along with the pie: Can you please add ice cream on the side? The second is talking about a specific characteristic inherent in the pie: No, I don't want the cherry pie. I want the one with the apples.

If *with* is used, is the sentence trying to indicate that the English, Spanish, and Italian words exist alongside of the French? Or that those words have been incorporated into the 17th-century French? Logically, it should be the latter, but technically the meaning is ambiguous. Eliminate answer (D).

The Correct Answer

Correct answer (C) repairs the initial subject–verb agreement error while maintaining the noun modifier construction that most clearly signifies the logical meaning: The words were added to the 17th-century French language.

#130 Energy France

(A) Meaning (*while*); Pronoun (*it*)
(B) Comparison (*X compared to Y*); Meaning (*33 percent*)
(C) CORRECT
(D) Meaning (*the energy*)
(E) Pronoun (*it*); Meaning (*the energy*)

First Glance

The underline starts just after a comma, increasing the likelihood that the question is testing a Modifier or some form of Parallelism issue.

Issues

(1) Meaning: *while*

While is the first word underlined, so there must be at least one difference in the answers. The word *while* has two primary meanings: *simultaneously with* or *although*. Which is it in this case?

The meaning of *while* is ambiguous in answer (A). It would make the most sense for the sentence to indicate a contrast: It's one way in France and another way in Germany. It's possible, though, that the sentence is trying to indicate that something is a certain percentage in France while at the same time it's something else in Germany. Eliminate answer (A).

(2) Pronoun: *it*
Meaning: *33 percent*

The underline contains one of the Deadly Five pronouns (*it, its, they, their, them*):

    (A) *it is just over 33 percent*
    (B) *which uses just over 33 percent*
    (C) *nuclear power accounts for just over 33 percent*
    (D) *just over 33 percent comes from nuclear power*
    (E) *where it is just over 33 percent*

Answers (A) and (E) use the pronoun *it*. It would be illogical for the pronoun to refer to *75 percent* or to *the energy produced in France*. What about just *the energy*? In this case, the sentence would read *the energy is just over 33 percent*. The sentence isn't clear.

Logically, the sentence is trying to compare something about the energy produced in France to something about the energy produced in Germany, but the original sentence doesn't say that. Answers (A) and (E) both contain the ambiguous *it*. Answer (B) removes the pronoun *it* but still doesn't explain *33 percent* of what. Eliminate all three.

(3) Comparison: *X compared to Y*

When examining the initial meaning issue, you may have noticed that the remaining answer choices change the initial word *while* to various contrast words.

The structure *X compared to Y* indicates a comparison. In answer (B), *X* is *percent of the energy* and *Y* is *Germany*—bad comparison! The remaining answer choices also indicate a comparison, but none repeats this faulty structure. Eliminate answer (B).

(4) Meaning: *the energy*

This one is very hard to spot. When the article *the* is used in front of a word, it's referring to one specific example of that thing.

Arya likes the apple.	→	She likes one specific apple.
Arya likes the apple whereas Jon despises the apple.	→	The two are passing judgment on one particular apple.

Answers (D) and (E) contain two instances of *the energy*; are both referring to the same energy?

In the first half of the sentence, *the energy* mentioned is specifically *the energy produced in France*. Answers (D) and (E) both refer to *the energy* in the second half of the sentence, but you don't want to talk about the French energy again. The sentence is attempting to contrast the energy produced in France with the energy produced in Germany.

The second half is talking about different energy, not the same energy mentioned in the first half. Eliminate answers (D) and (E).

The Correct Answer

Correct answer (C) replaces *while* with *whereas*, unambiguously indicating a contrast and clearly delineating that contrast: *75 percent of the energy produced in France* versus *33 percent of the energy produced in Germany.*

#131 Psychopath

(A) Pronoun (*someone*)
(B) Meaning
(C) Pronoun (*they*); Meaning
(D) CORRECT
(E) Meaning

First Glance

The underline is very short; look at the answers before reading the original sentence. *It* versus *they* indicates a singular versus plural issue.

Issues

(1) Pronoun: *someone; they*

 The original sentence contains two pronouns in the underline: *it* and *someone*. Are both used correctly?

 The pronoun *it* refers back to *the term "psychopath,"* a logical referent. *It* also refers to the following pronoun, *someone*: *It is someone.* Can *the term "psychopath"* be a person? No; the second pronoun doesn't make sense. Eliminate answer (A).

Further, answer (C) changes the pronoun to *they*. The plural *they* doesn't agree in number with the singular word *term*. Eliminate answer (C).

(2) Meaning

 Several of the answer choices change the initial pronoun *someone* to various forms of a noun: *person* or *people*.

 Although answers (B) and (C) do change the pronoun to a noun (*person* and *people*, respectively), the original problem still exists; the *term* cannot be called a *person* or *people*. Eliminate answers (B) and (C).

Answer (E) does correct part of the problem by inserting the language *in reference to*, making clear that *the term* itself is not actually a *person*. This answer, however, uses the plural *people*. *The term "psychopath"* is singular and cannot refer to multiple *people* at once. Eliminate answer (E).

Note: Answer (E) would also need to include some kind of main verb after *is*. For example: *The term "psychopath" is used when referring to X.*

The Correct Answer

Correct answer (D) fixes the original pronoun error by changing the verb to *refers*: A *term* can refer to *someone*.

#132 Heirloom Tomatoes

(A)	Structure
(B)	**CORRECT**
(C)	Structure
(D)	Structure
(E)	Structure

First Glance

The underline is long, with multiple commas, and the sentence even includes em dashes. Look for Structure, Meaning, Modifier, or Parallelism issues.

Sentence Structure

The sentence is incredibly complex. Here's how a 99th percentile test-taker would strip it down to its core:

First Read: Original Sentence	Thoughts
Although	This is an opening modifier.
appearing less appetizing than most of their round and red supermarket cousins,	The modifier is talking about some kind of food. Other than that, I can ignore this for now.
heirloom tomatoes,	Okay, the modifier is referring to tomatoes. That's fine. This is also the subject of the sentence.
grown from seeds saved during the previous year	Another modifier. Interesting. Where's the verb?
—they are often green and striped, or have plenty of bumps and bruises—	Wow, another modifier? I want that verb! Oh, and I can ignore anything within the hyphens; none of it is underlined and the hyphens separate out this piece from the rest of the sentence.
heirlooms are	Hmm. There's a verb here… but there's also a subject. I already had a subject earlier! What's going on?
more flavorful and thus in increasing demand.	This is fine as the end of the sentence. I need to go back and look at *heirloom tomatoes* again….
	Yep. Heirloom tomatoes is NOT a modifier, and it follows the comma after the opening modifier, so it has to be a subject. And then there's a second subject later… without an *and* or any other connecting word in between.

Issues

(1) Structure

 According to the 99th percentile tester above, the core of the sentence is *heirloom tomatoes heirlooms are.*

 The core of this sentence would be equivalent to "Bob Anne are in town," as opposed to "Bob and Anne are in town." In other words, there are two subjects without any kind of connecting word in between—illegal move! Eliminate answer (A).

Scan the other answers to see whether any repeat this error.

> (B) *Although W, grown from X, appear Y,* **heirlooms are** *Z …*
> (C) *Although W,* **heirloom tomatoes,** *grown from X,* **heirlooms are** *Z …*
> (D) *Grown from X,* **heirloom tomatoes appear** *Y,* **heirlooms are** *Z …*
> (E) **Heirloom tomatoes,** *grown from X, although W,* **heirlooms are** *Z …*

Answers (C) and (E) repeat the original error: *heirloom tomatoes heirlooms are.* Eliminate answers (C) and (E).

While answer (D) does not repeat the exact error, it does introduce a different structural error. The core here is *heirloom tomatoes appear Y heirlooms are Z.* This is the equivalent of saying "Bob appears happy Bob is tall." This is a run-on sentence. Eliminate answer (D).

The Correct Answer

Correct answer (B) changes the sentence structure by placing *heirloom tomatoes* in the subordinate clause, leaving the later *heirlooms* as the sole subject of the sentence:

Although heirloom tomatoes, grown from seeds, appear less appetizing—they are often green—heirlooms are more flavorful and thus in increasing demand.

#133 Shrimpers

(A) Subject–Verb (*protect*)	**First Glance**
(B) CORRECT	
(C) Subject–Verb (*protect*)	The first word of the answers changes from *requiring* to
(D) Subject–Verb (*are*); Meaning (*to require*)	*that require* to *to require.* Watch for Modifier, Meaning, and
(E) Meaning (*to require*)	Structure issues.

Issues

(1) Subject–Verb: *protect; are*

 If you have trained yourself to find the sentence core when reading, then you may notice the subject–verb mismatch in the original sentence. Alternately, a comparison of the ends of each answer reveals a split between a singular option (*is protecting*) and two plural options (*protect* and *are protecting*).

 The singular subject *compliance* doesn't match the plural verb *protect* in the original sentence. Eliminate answers (A), (C), and (D), all of which try to match plural verbs to the singular subject.

(2) Meaning: *to require*

 A vertical scan of the beginning of each answer choice reveals a split between *requiring*, *that require*, and *to require*.

 Officially, the error here rests on meaning, but the particular reasoning can almost be considered an idiom. A law *requiring X* means simply that the law requires something to be done, but doesn't comment on why or for what purpose. A law *to require X* implies that the purpose for the law is specifically to make X happen. In this sentence, it's nonsensical to say that the purpose for which the law was passed was to use the devices; rather, the law was passed in order to protect the turtles. Eliminate answers (D) and (E).

The Correct Answer

Correct answer (B) fixes the subject–verb agreement error by replacing the plural *protect* with the singular *is protecting*.

#134 Shift-Work

(A) Structure / Parallelism
(B) Structure / Parallelism
(C) CORRECT
(D) Structure / Parallelism
(E) Parallelism (*reduced W, X, and Y*)

First Glance

There is a comma just before the underline and a comma followed by the word *and* in the underline. Is there a list? Parallelism or Modifier issues might come into play.

Issues

(1) Structure / Parallelism
Parallelism: *reduced W, X, and Y*

 The original sentence appears to offer a list of four things: *Studies have reduced (W) sickness, (X) sleeping, (Y) fatigue, and (Z) have raised efficiency.* The fourth item on the list (a verb) is not parallel to the first three (nouns). Also note that the verb leading into the list is *reduced*. How can the studies *reduce* something and *raise* it at the same time?

 The exact nature of the lack of parallelism reveals an important clue towards the fix: the structure of the sentence is faulty. Three things were reduced: sickness, sleeping, and fatigue. A fourth thing was raised: efficiency. The correct answer should separate this fourth thing from the other three.

Answers (A), (B), and (D) all incorrectly maintain the four-item list structure; eliminate them.

Answers (C) and (E) partially fix the initial structural problem by adding the word *and* before the third item in the list, but the structure of the rest of the sentence changes:

> (C) *have reduced (W), (X), and fatigue while raising efficiency*
> (E) *have reduced (W), (X), and fatigue was lowered while raising efficiency*

The addition of the verb *was lowered* in answer (E) changes the nature of the third item on the list. It is no longer just a noun, *fatigue*, but a clause, *fatigue was lowered*. Parallelism is broken. Eliminate answer (E).

The Correct Answer

Correct answer (C) fixes the initial parallelism error by breaking the sentence into two parts: a three-item list followed by a fourth separate piece of information. That last piece of information is properly introduced with the contrast word *while*.

Note: The structure of incorrect answer (D) is particularly tricky. Items *W*, *Y*, and *Z* in this four-item list could all be considered parallel, but non-underlined item *X* breaks the parallelism:

> *Studies have (W) reduced sickness, (X) sleeping on the job, (Y) lowered fatigue, and (Z) raised efficiency.*

MANHATTAN
PREP

#135 Friedrich Müller

(A)   Meaning; Parallelism
(B)   CORRECT
(C)   Idiom (*apprenticeship of*)
(D)   Meaning; Idiom (*apprenticeship of*);
      Verb / Parallelism
(E)   Idiom (*apprenticeship of*); Verb / Parallelism

First Glance

The underline isn't particularly long and appears towards the beginning of the sentence. If you spot an early error, you may choose to look at the answers before finishing the entire original sentence. Look for Meaning, Parallelism, or Idiom issues.

Issues

(1) Meaning

The sentence begins with the opening modifier *Spanning more than 50 years*. Whatever spanned that time frame should be the subject following the comma.

A person can't literally span 50 years; a person's lifetime could span 50 years, or a person's *career*, but not the person himself. Answers (A) and (D) both make this mistake; eliminate them.

(2) Idiom: *apprenticeship of*

A scan of the end of each answer choice reveals a split: *apprenticeship as* versus *apprenticeship of*.

Is it an *apprenticeship as a scholar*? Or an *apprenticeship of a scholar*? In this case, the information immediately following the idiom is the type of apprenticeship. This structure requires the idiom *apprenticeship as a scholar*. Eliminate answers (C), (D), and (E).

(3) Verb / Parallelism

A vertical comparison exposes a difference in the main verb tense, as well as a parallel verb later in the non-underlined portion:

(A) *Müller began* his career   *and culminated* in
(B), (C): *Müller's career began*   *and culminated* in
(D) *Müller had begun* his career   *and culminated* in
(E) *The career of Müller has begun*   *and culminated* in

First, *Müller* himself did not *culminate* in anything; his *career* did. Eliminate answers (A) and (D).

Further, in answer (D), parallelism would allow the *had* portion of *had begun* to apply to *culminated: had begun and (had) culminated*. This is illogical; the two events took place at different times in the past.

Finally, if *Müller's career* has already *culminated* in something, then the beginning of that career (which must have happened earlier!) cannot be described with the present perfect *has begun*. Eliminate answer (E).

The Correct Answer

Correct answer (B) fixes the original meaning error by making clear that *Müller's career*, not the man himself, spanned 50 years *and culminated* in something. This choice also correctly uses the simple past tense *began* and the idiom *apprenticeship as*.

#136 Tiny Tubes

(A) CORRECT
(B) Comparison (*whereas X, Y*)
(C) Comparison (*unlike X, Y*)
(D) Comparison (*unlike X, Y*)
(E) Parallelism (*unlike X, Y*)

First Glance

Most of the sentence is underlined. Keep an eye out for Structure, Meaning, Parallelism, or Modifier issues.

Issues

(1) Comparison: *whereas X, Y; unlike X, Y*
   Parallelism: *unlike X, Y*

The word *whereas* is a comparison marker. Scan the answers:

(A) *whereas in mammals the tubes,*	*in birds the tubes*
(B) *whereas the tubes,*	*birds*
(C) *unlike mammals,*	*birds' tubes*
(D) *unlike mammals,*	*the tubes*
(E) *unlike the tubes,*	*in birds the tubes*

In answers (B), (C), and (D), the *X* and *Y* portions of the comparison are not parallel. A sentence can compare *tubes* to *tubes* or *birds* to *mammals*, but not a type of animal to a *tube*. Eliminate (B), (C), and (D).

Answer (E) is a bit tricky. It is comparing *tubes* to *tubes* (that is, it is technically parallel), but notice the difference between the placement of the *X* element and the *Y* element in the two remaining answers, (A) and (E).

Answer (A) follows very strict parallelism: *in mammals, the tubes* are a certain way and *in birds, the tubes* are a certain (different) way. In answer (E), notice that *in mammals* has moved elsewhere in the sentence:

> (E) *unlike the tiny tubes, which in mammals are* (something), *in birds the tubes form* (something else).

Whose *tiny tubes* are the subject of the first half of the comparison? Presumably, the *mammals*, but the *mammals* are only mentioned as an afterthought. The structure of answer (A) doesn't contain this ambiguity. Eliminate (E).

The Correct Answer

Correct answer (A) provides a logical and parallel comparison between the *tiny tubes* found *in mammals* and the *tubes* found *in birds*.

#137 Composers

(A)	Meaning (*goes into decline*); Meaning (*again*)
(B)	Meaning (*again*); Structure / Parallelism
(C)	**CORRECT**
(D)	Meaning (*again*); Structure / Parallelism
(E)	Structure / Parallelism

First Glance

The sentence contains a comma just before the underline and a "comma and" structure in the underline. Watch for Parallelism, Structure, Meaning, and Modifier issues.

Issues

(1) Meaning: *goes into decline*

Pay attention to meaning when reading these sentences. The original sentence contains a list of three things:

> *a composer who* (X) *receives popular acclaim,* (Y) *goes into decline after death, and* (Z) *never regains popularity again.*

It's illogical to say that the person himself *goes into decline* after dying. The other answers introduce the word *reputation* into the sentence; someone's *reputation* can decline after that person dies. Eliminate answer (A).

(2) Meaning: *again*

Now that you've spotted one meaning issue, watch for others! The third item on the list says that the composer *never regains popularity again*.

To *regain* means to gain something back again—the meaning of *again* is already included in the word *regain*. Answers (A), (B), and (D) all pair *regain* with the redundant *again*; eliminate them.

(3) Structure / Parallelism

Compare the list structure in each choice:

     (A) *composer who* **receives** *acclaim,* **goes** *into decline,* **and** *never* **regains**
     (B) *composer who* **receives** *acclaim,* **whose reputation declines and** *never* **regains**
     (C) *composer who* **receives** *acclaim,* **but whose reputation declines and** *never* **regains**
     (D) *composer* **who receives** *acclaim,* **who declines** *in reputation* **and who** *never* **regained**
     (E) *composer who* **receives** *acclaim,* **then has declined and** *never* **regained**

Answer (A) is technically parallel (though the meaning is illogical). The remaining four answers share one very tiny but crucial difference from (A): there is no longer a comma before the parallel marker *and*. What does this mean?

The sentence is no longer attempting to provide a list of three parallel items. Parallelism must still exist, but only the portions about *declining* and *regaining* need to be made parallel. This parallelism shift also requires a structural shift to separate what used to be the first item in the list from the two later items.

For example, in answer (C), the conjunction *but* is introduced, followed by a new subject, *reputation*. Consider this example:

> The company gained market share, but its competitor was even more successful and took over the number one spot.

This sentence first says something about the company and then says two things about the competitor. Likewise, in answer (C), the sentence first says something about the *composer* and then says two things about the *composer's reputation*.

Answers (B) and (D) are missing the necessary conjunction (*but*, or similar) to launch its new subject, *reputation*. Eliminate answers (B) and (D).

Answers (D) and (E) have verb tense problems. It is acceptable to have different verb tenses in a parallel structure as long as the meaning of the sentence dictates a different tense. It's illogical, though, to say that the reputation *declines* (present) or *has declined* (present perfect) and then say that the reputation *never regained popularity,* when this final action should take place at the same time as or later than the *decline* action. Eliminate answers (D) and (E).

The Correct Answer

Correct answer (C) fixes the original Meaning errors by making clear that a composer's *reputation* declines after death and by eliminating the redundant *again*. The three verb tenses (*receives, declines, regains*) make logical sense.

#138 Malaria and Dengue

(A)	Idiom (*such X like Y*); Parallelism (*either X or Y*)
(B)	Idiom (*such X like Y*); Parallelism (*either X or Y*)
(C)	Parallelism (*either X or Y*)
(D)	Parallelism (*either X or Y*)
(E)	**CORRECT**

First Glance

The underline starts with the word *like*; other choices start with the word *as*. The sentence may contain a Comparison or be testing an Idiom issue.

Issues

(1) Idiom: *such X like Y*

 The original sentence uses *such like* to introduce some examples. Cleverly, the writers have separated the words *such* and *like* by sticking *mosquito-borne diseases* in between, making it harder to spot the full idiom.

 The word *such* isn't underlined, so the correct answer needs to start with *as*. Eliminate answers (A) and (B).

Although uncommon in everyday speech, it is okay to separate the *such* and the *as*, but the words in between need to be the category of thing under discussion. The sentence wants to give examples of *mosquito-borne diseases*, so it's acceptable to say *such mosquito-borne diseases as X and Y*.

(2) Parallelism: *either X or Y*

 In the idiom *either X or Y*, the X and Y portions have to be parallel:

(A) *focused either* **on the vaccination** …	*or* **on exterminating**
(B) *focused either* **on vaccinating** …	*or* **on the extermination**
(C) *focused on either* **vaccinating** …	*or* **on exterminating**
(D) *focused on either* **vaccinating** …	*or* **on extermination**
(E) *focused on either* **vaccinating** …	*or* **exterminating**

The sentence uses the idiom *focused on*. If the word *on* is part of the X portion, as in answer (A), then it has to be repeated as part of the Y portion; answers (A) and (B) do this. If the word *on* comes before *either*, however, then *on* should not be part of either the X or the Y portions. Answer (E) shows this version correctly, but answers (C) and (D) both incorrectly repeat *on* as part of the Y element. Eliminate answers (C) and (D).

Next, the *X* and *Y* elements in all five answer choices are nouns, which seems to be good. There are different kinds of nouns, though: regular nouns, such as *extermination*, and *-ing* words called gerunds, such as *vaccinating*. Gerunds can be written in one of two ways: simple (such as *running* in the sentence "Running is fun") and complex (such as *the running* in the sentence "The running of the bulls is a tradition in Spain.") The GMAT test writers don't like to make regular nouns parallel to simple gerunds—though it is okay to pair regular nouns and complex gerunds. Eliminate answers (A), (B), and (D) for pairing regular nouns with simple gerunds.

The Correct Answer

Correct answer (E) uses the proper idiom *such X as Y* to introduce examples and also corrects the parallelism error by pairing the simple gerunds *vaccinating* and *exterminating*.

#139 Halley's Comet

(A)	Comparison (*did*)
(B)	Comparison (*had*); Verb (*had*)
(C)	**CORRECT**
(D)	Comparison (*did*)
(E)	Comparison (*its return*)

First Glance

With such a short underline, look through the answers before reading the sentence. Verbs are changing and words are moving around. There aren't any great clues, even though there aren't many words here—this is going to be a tough one.

Sentence Structure

This sentence structure is unbelievably hard. The beginning is unusual. Pieces seem to be jumbled together. Here's how a 99th percentile test-taker might read this:

First Read: Original Sentence	Thoughts
In no other historical sighting	This is kind of a weird opener. I'm not sure yet what's going on.
did Halley's Comet cause	Weirder. Okay, *did cause* is a verb; I know that much. What's the subject?
such a worldwide sensation as	Oh, I see. *Halley's Comet caused a worldwide sensation.* The subject is *Halley's Comet.* Ah, and the word *as* can indicate a comparison! Let's see….
did its return in 1910–1911.	So there were multiple sightings of this comet, but this one particular sighting in 1910–1911 caused the biggest worldwide sensation. They seem to want to make a comparison between this one particular sighting and all of the others. Okay, maybe I have a starting point. Is the comparison logical? Is it parallel?

Issues

(1) Comparison: *did; had*

The structure *no X caused such a worldwide sensation as Y* indicates a comparison. One sighting (*Y*) caused much more excitement than all of the others (*X*).

The sentence should compare the *other historical sightings* with the one sighting *in 1910–1911*. Answer (A), though, uses the word *did* to introduce the *Y* portion of the comparison. *Did* already appears elsewhere in the sentence: *did Halley's Comet cause.* Parallelism seems to dictate a comparison between the comet itself and one instance of the comet's return (in 1910–1911), but this is illogical. Answer (D) makes this same error. Finally, answer (B) also introduces the *Y* portion of the comparison with a verb (*had*); the same issue exists even though the specific verb has changed. Eliminate answers (A), (B), and (D).

(2) Verb: *had*

Answer (B) changes the verb from *did* to *had.*

Comparisons should be parallel. In this case, the non-underlined portion says *did cause* and the *cause* portion is not repeated later. The word *cause* would therefore have to be able to be repeated with *had* as well as *did.* It's incorrect to say *had cause.* (Note: The sentence shouldn't have a verb form here at all; see the comparison issue discussed above.) Eliminate answer (B).

(3) Comparison: *its return*

After dealing with the first issue (an illogical comparison), you'll have only two answers left:

      (C) *in its return of 1910–1911*
      (E) *its return in 1910–1911*

The *X* portion of the comparison is *in no other historical sighting*; this structure is a prepositional phrase. Ideally, then, the *Y* portion of the comparison should also be in the form of a prepositional phrase. The word *in* appears in both answers, but in different places. Logically, the *Y* portion should be the *return* of the comet, not simply the year in which it returned. The word *in* should be before *its return.* Eliminate answer (E).

The Correct Answer

Correct answer (C) fixes the initial comparison error by removing the verb form that implied a comparison of Halley's Comet to a single instance of the comet's return. Further, the construction *in its return* is properly parallel to *in no other sighting.*

#140 Rock Samples

(A) Subject–Verb (*has; is*); Idiom (*dated to be*)
(B) Subject–Verb (*has*); Structure
(C) Idiom (*dated to be*)
(D) Idiom (*dated as being*); Structure
(E) **CORRECT**

First Glance

The underline starts with the verb *has*; other answers start with *have*, so look for subject–verb issues.

Issues

(1) Subject–Verb: *has; is*

 In the original sentence, the subject is the plural *rock samples* and the verb is the singular *has been dated*. Mismatch!

 A plural subject needs a plural verb; eliminate answers (A) and (B), which both use the singular *has*. It turns out that the sentence also contains a second verb that goes with the same plural subject: *is*. Only answer (A) contains this error. The remaining answers use either the plural *are* or eliminate the verb entirely. (Remember that split for later.)

A̶ B̶ C D E

(2) Idiom: *dated to be; dated as being*

 If you know the correct idiom, you might spot the error in the original sentence. If you don't, a vertical scan reveals that the answers offer three different options: *dated to be*, *dated at*, or *dated as being*.

 The correct idiom for estimating the age of something is *dated at* a certain age. Eliminate answers (A), (C), and (D).

A̶ B C̶ D̶ E

(3) Structure

 Tackle the *are* versus nothing split mentioned in the subject–verb discussion above. (Remember that you already eliminated answer (A) for using *is*.)

(B), (D): *Rock samples* **have been dated**	*and thus* **evidence**
(C), (E): *Rock samples* **have been dated**	*and thus* **are evidence**

 The *and* creates a parallel construction. Answers (B) and (D) are missing the needed verb *are* and are therefore sentence fragments; eliminate them.

A B̶ C D̶ E

The Correct Answer

Correct answer (E) changes both verbs to the plural form to match the plural subject *rock samples*. Further, this choice uses the correct idiom, *dated at* a certain age.

Appendix *of* A

The Official Guide Companion
for Sentence Correction

Grammar

In This Chapter...

Meaning on the GMAT

Grammar Overview

Meaning on the GMAT

Everything you write, and every rule you use, is ultimately in service of one thing: conveying a logical and clear meaning. In fact, many grammar rules are really all about meaning. Is there anything wrong with this sentence?

Tomorrow, she bought some milk.

Technically, no grammar rule is violated in that sentence, but something is wrong! The past tense verb *bought* doesn't make any sense because the word *tomorrow* implies something that will happen in the future. You know that sentence is wrong because the meaning is illogical, not because some rule is wrong.

The GMAT contains many (much more complex) examples of meaning issues. You'll learn how to spot and handle these but here's the overall meaning rule: Correct sentences must be logical and clear. Anything illogical or ambiguous is wrong.

Sentence Structure

There are just a few important things to know about the Structure of sentences.

First, every single correct GMAT Sentence Correction (SC) sentence has one thing in common: it contains at least one independent clause. Here's a simple example (a lot simpler than you'll see on the GMAT!):

The executive worked.	This is the bare minimum needed to make an independent clause: a subject and a verb.

The executive analyzed the competition.
Subject   Verb   Object

This independent clause contains a subject, a verb, and an object.

A more complex sentence might include a compound subject or compound verb:

The executive and his team analyzed the competition.
Subject 1   Subject 2   Verb   Object

The executive analyzed the competition and produced a report.
Subject   Verb 1   Object 1   Verb 2   Object 2

Although some of those sentence are more complex then others, each one consists of just one independent clause. These are the simplest kinds of sentences.

More complex sentences can involve two or more independent clauses.

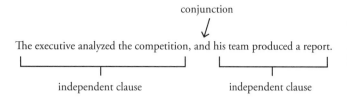

This sentence combines two independent clauses by placing a comma and a coordinating conjunction in between.

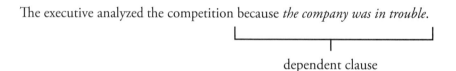

This sentence combines the same two independent clauses by placing a semicolon in between.

The executive analyzed the competition, his team produced a report.

This is a run-on sentence! It is not acceptable to connect two independent clauses using only a comma. This is an error.

Complex sentences can contain subordinate or dependent clauses, which contain verbs but cannot stand alone as sentences.

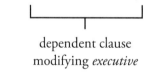

Special conjunctions such as *because* or *although* often introduce dependent clauses, which, as their name implies, depend on independent clauses.

Some dependent clauses act as modifiers to nouns:

The executive who won the lottery analyzed the competition.

dependent clause
modifying *executive*

Relative pronouns such as *who*, *which*, *that*, and *whose* often follow nouns to introduce these kinds of clauses.

That can also follow verbs. In these cases, that introduces another kind of dependent clause—one that doesn't modify a noun but in fact acts like a noun itself.

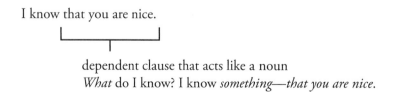

In this manner, *that* provides a way to embed a full thought (*you are nice*) within a larger sentence: I know [that you are nice].

Here's another example:

The executive demanded that his team produce a report.
Subject   Verb   THAT   Subject   Verb   Object

This sentence consists of an independent clause followed by a subordinate clause, but you don't need to know the grammar terms. You really need to know two things:

1. Subject–Verb-THAT-Subject–Verb-Object is a very common complex sentence structure; start looking for it in GMAT sentences.

2. The whole thing is considered part of the sentence core. Even though the second part of the sentence is a subordinate clause, it is essential to the meaning of the sentence. *The executive demanded*, by itself, doesn't mean anything. The executive must have *demanded something*.

Because *that* can introduce more than one kind of clause, it's a tricky word.

As soon as you hear or read the word *that*, you know that a more complex structure is coming and you're prepared to absorb all of the words before you try to understand the meaning. There are many examples of this structure throughout the official questions; you'll read all about them as you use this book.

Grammar Overview

The Five Grammar Terms You Need to Know

We try to keep fancy terms to a minimum in this book, but there's no way to discuss grammar without using at least a few actual grammar terms. Here are the five terms you absolutely need to know:

1. Clause

A **clause** is a set of words that contains a subject and a working verb. This is a clause:

　She was offered the job.

Independent clause is the official term for a complete, stand-alone sentence. Independent clauses have, at the very least, a subject and a verb. Every correct sentence must have at least one independent clause.

A **dependent clause** also contains a verb but cannot stand alone as a sentence.

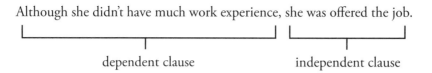

Although she didn't have much work experience, she was offered the job.

dependent clause   independent clause

More complex sentences will still consist of at least one independent clause but will also include something else: another independent clause, a dependent clause, or other modifiers.

Without an independent clause, you have a **sentence fragment**. This is a fragment:

Although she didn't have much work experience.

2. Modifier

A **modifier** provides additional information in a sentence, beyond the core the subject and verb). The simplest example is an adjective: the happy child. The word *happy*, an adjective, is a modifier.

Modifiers can also be more complex:

The large dog, which has black fur, is a Labrador.

The modifier *which has black fur* is called a **nonessential modifier**. If you remove it from the sentence, the core of the sentence still makes sense: the large dog is a Labrador.

Compare that to this sentence:

The job that she started last week is much harder than her previous job.

In this sentence, *that she started last week* is called an **essential modifier**. Why is this one essential? Look what happens when you remove it from the sentence:

The job is much harder than her previous job.

The *job*? Which *job*? The meaning of the sentence is no longer clear. This is the hallmark of an essential modifier: the modifier is necessary in order to understand the meaning of the sentence.

Two modifier forms are very common in GMAT sentences: the "comma *which*" modifier and the "comma -ing" modifier. A "comma *which*" modifier is a noun modifier and typically refers to the closest main noun before the modifier starts. You saw an example of this in the Labrador sentence above.

A "comma -ing" modifier is an adverbial modifier and refers to the entire main clause to which it is attached. Here's an example:

Aun slipped on the ice, twisting his ankle.

The modifier *twisting his ankle* does not apply to the *ice*. Nor does it apply only to the subject, Aun. Rather, the action *twisting his ankle* resulted from the entire clause: Aun slipped.

You can find a full discussion in the Modifiers chapter of our *Sentence Correction GMAT Strategy Guide*.

3. Sentence Core

The **core** of a sentence consists of any independent clauses along with some essential modifiers. This is the bare minimum needed in order to have a coherent sentence.

Any extra information modifiers are stripped out of the sentence core. See the section on Sentence Structure in this chapter for more.

4. Conjunction

Conjunctions are words that help to stick parts of sentences together. Here's an example:

He worked hard, **and** a raise was his reward.

Coordinating conjunctions, such as *and*, can glue two independent clauses together. Both *he worked hard* and *a raise was his reward* are independent clauses. The most common coordinating conjunctions are the FANBOYS: for, and, nor, but, or, yet, so.

Modifiers can be connected to independent clauses by **subordinating conjunctions**. You saw an example of this before:

Although she didn't have much work experience, she was offered the job.

The word *although* is a subordinating conjunction. Other examples include because, while, though, unless, before, after, and if.

5. Marker

This one's not actually a grammar term. Throughout the book, we talk about certain kinds of **markers**. For example, the word *unlike* is a comparison marker; when you see *unlike*, you should think about comparisons.

Let's say you read an explanation and think, "Hmm, I didn't know that that word was a marker for that kind of grammar issue." If this happens, immediately write that marker down! Keep a list, make flashcards, record it however you prefer—but do record (and study) the fact that this particular marker should have made you think about a certain grammar issue.

That's all to start. (Yes, technically, we snuck more than five terms into that list. The terms are all related, though.)

If you run across other unfamiliar terms, you can look them up in the glossary at the end of this section or in our *Sentence Correction GMAT Strategy Guide*.

Appendix B of
The Official Guide Companion for Sentence Correction

Glossary

Glossary

The following is a list of grammatical terms used in this guide.

Absolute Phrase

A phrase that consists of a noun and a noun modifier and that modifies a whole clause or sentence. An absolute phrase cannot stand alone as a sentence, but it often expresses an additional thought. An absolute phrase is separated from the main clause by a comma; it may come before or after that main clause. See Modifier.

> *Examples:*
> The car fell into the lake, <u>the cold water filling the compartment.</u>
> <u>His arm in pain</u>, Guillermo strode out of the building.

Action Noun

A noun that expresses an action. Action nouns are often derived from verbs. In general, action nouns should be made parallel only to other action nouns or to complex gerunds.

> *Examples:*
> verb + -TION: construction, pollution, redemption
> verb + -AL: arrival, reversal
> verb + -MENT: development, punishment
> Same as verb: change, rise

Active Voice

The form of a verb in which the subject is doing the action expressed by the verb.

> *Examples:*
> The driver <u>swerved</u>.
> The tires <u>exploded</u>.
> They <u>broke</u> the lamp.

Additive Phrase

Modifier phrases that add nouns onto another noun. However, additive phrases cannot change the number of the noun they modify.

> *Examples:*
> <u>along with</u> me; <u>in addition to</u> the memo; <u>as well as</u> a dog; <u>accompanied by</u> her; <u>together with</u> the others; <u>including</u> them

Adjective

A word that modifies a noun.

> *Examples:*
> <u>wonderful</u> food; <u>green</u> eyes; <u>forest</u> fire; the <u>changing</u> seasons

Adverb

A word that modifies a verb, an adjective, another adverb, or even a whole clause. Most adverbs end in -*ly*, but not all.

Examples:
The stone fell <u>slowly</u>.
A <u>swiftly</u> frozen lake appears cloudy.
We ran <u>very</u> quickly.

Antecedent

The noun that a pronoun refers to.

Example:
The <u>rowers</u> lifted the <u>boat</u> and flipped <u>it</u> over <u>their</u> heads.
(*Rowers* is the antecedent of *their*. *Boat* is the antecedent of *it*.)

Appositive

A noun or noun phrase that is placed next to another noun to identify it. Often separated from the rest of the sentence by commas.

Example:
The coach, <u>an old classmate of mine</u>, was not pleased.
(*An old classmate of mine* is an appositive phrase to the noun *coach*.)

Article

The words *a*, *an*, or *the*. An article must be followed by a noun (perhaps with modifiers in between). Articles can be considered special adjectives.

Bare Form

The dictionary form of a verb (what you would look up in a dictionary). A bare form has no endings added on, such as -*s*, -*ed*, or -*ing*. The bare form is the infinitive without the *to* in front.

Examples:
assess, bark, command, decide, eavesdrop, furnish, gather

Bossy Verb

A verb that tells someone to do something. Bossy verbs take the command subjunctive or an infinitive (or either construction), depending on the verb.

Examples:
I <u>told</u> him to run. He <u>requested</u> that the bus wait another minute.
(The verb *to tell* (*told*) takes the infinitive. *Request* takes the command subjunctive.)

Case

The grammatical role that a noun or pronoun plays in a sentence.

Examples:

Subject case (subject role): I, you, she, he, it, we, they

Object case (object role): me, you, her, him, it, us, them

Possessive case (ownership role): my/mine, your(s), her(s), his, its, our(s), their(s)

Nouns show the possessive case by adding *'s* or *s'*.

Clause

A group of words that contains a subject and a working verb.

Examples:

Main or independent:

> This is nice.
>
> Yesterday I ate a pizza in haste.

Subordinate or dependent:

> Yesterday I ate a pizza that I did not like.
>
> When I think about that pizza, I feel ill.

Collective Noun

A noun that looks singular (it does not end in *-s*) but that refers to a group of people or things. Almost always considered singular on the GMAT.

Examples:

The army is recruiting again.

This team was beaten.

Command Subjunctive

Subjunctive form used with certain bossy verbs and similar constructions. Same in form as a direct command. See Subjunctive Mood.

Example:

The draft board required that he register for selective service.

Comparative Form

Form of adjectives and adverbs used to compare two things or people. Regular comparative forms are either the base word plus *-er* (if the base is short, e.g., *greener*) or the base word preceded by *more* (*more intelligent*). Irregulars are listed below:

Adjective or Adverb	Comparative
good/well	better
bad/badly	worse
much, many	more
little	less
far	farther, further

Comparisons

Structures by which we compare things or people in sentences. Usually marked with signal words such as *like*, *unlike*, *as*, or *than*. Comparisons can be between two things or people (comparative) or among three or more things or people (superlative).

Complex Gerund

A gerund is an *-ing* form of a verb that functions as a noun; a complex gerund includes an article or something similar to indicate that the *-ing* word is definitely functioning as a noun. In general, complex gerunds can be put in parallel with action nouns. Simple gerunds should not be. See Simple Gerund.

Examples:
The running of the bulls is a tradition in Spain.
The volcanic eruption resulted in the melting of the iceberg.

Concrete Noun

A noun that does not represent an action. Concrete nouns refer to things, people, places, and even time periods or certain events. Generally, concrete nouns are not logically parallel to action nouns.

Examples:
volcano, hole, proton, senator, area, month, Halloween

Conditional Tense

A verb tense formed by combining the helping verb *would* with the base form of the verb. See Tense.

Examples:
Future as seen from the past:
He said that he would write.
Hypothetical result of unlikely condition:
If she liked pizza, she would like this restaurant.

Conjunction

A word that joins two parts of a sentence together. Coordinating and correlative conjunctions give the two parts equal weight. Subordinating conjunctions put one part in a logically junior role; in relation to the other part.

Examples:

Coordinating: and, but, or   (Less common: for, nor, so, yet)

Correlative: either … or …; neither … nor …; not … but …; not only … but also …

Subordinating: after, although, because, before, if, since, when, etc.

Conjunctive Adverb

A transition word or phrase that is used after a semicolon to help connect two main clauses. Conjunctive adverbs are not true conjunctions.

Examples:

therefore, thus, consequently, however, nevertheless, furthermore, etc.

The general was stuck in traffic; therefore, the ceremony started late.

Connecting Punctuation

The comma (,), the semicolon (;), the colon (:), and the dash (—). Used to link parts of the sentence.

Connecting Words

Conjunctions, conjunctive adverbs, and relative pronouns. Used to link parts of a sentence.

Countable Noun

A noun that can be counted in English. For instance, you can say *one hat, two hats, three hats*. Countable nouns can be made singular or plural.

Examples:

hat/hats, month/months, thought/thoughts, person/people

Dangling Modifier

A noun modifier that does not properly modify or describe any noun in the sentence. In fact, the noun that should be modified has been omitted from the sentence. Likewise, a verb modifier that requires a subject but lacks one in the sentence is considered dangling. Dangling modifiers are always incorrect. See Modifier.

Example:

Walking along the river bank, the new tower can be seen.

(The modifier *walking along the river bank* has no subject. The sentence could be rewritten thus: *Walking along the river bank, one can see the new tower.*)

Demonstrative Pronoun

The pronouns *this, that, these,* and *those.* Demonstrative pronouns can be used as adjectives *(these plants, that company).* They can also be used in place of nouns, but they must be modified in some way, according to the GMAT. See <u>Pronoun</u>.

Example:

The strategy taken by Livonia is preferable to <u>that</u> taken by Khazaria.

(The demonstrative pronoun *that* properly stands for the noun *strategy.* The pronoun *that* is modified by the phrase *taken by Khazaria.*)

Dependent Clause

A clause that cannot stand alone without a main or independent clause. A dependent clause is led by a subordinator. Also known as a Subordinate Clause. See <u>Clause</u>.

Direct Object

The noun that is acted upon by a verb in the active voice. Can be a pronoun, a noun phrase, or a noun clause.

Examples:

I broke <u>the lamp</u>.

Who let <u>the big dogs</u> out?

I believe <u>that you are right</u>.

Essential Modifier

A modifier that provides necessary information. Use an essential modifier to identify the particular noun out of many possibilities or to create a permanent description of the noun. Do not use commas to separate an essential modifier from the modified noun. See <u>Modifier</u>.

Example:

I want to sell the car <u>that my sister drove to the city</u>.

Fragment

A group of words that does not work as a stand-alone sentence, either because it is begun by a subordinator or because it lacks a subject or a verb.

Examples:

Although he bought a pretzel.

The device developed by scientists.

Future Tense

The form of a verb that expresses action in the future. Also known as Simple Future. See <u>Tense</u>.

Examples:

The driver <u>will swerve</u>.

The tires <u>will be punctured</u>.

They <u>will break</u> the lamp.

Gerund

An *-ing* form of a verb used as a noun.

>*Examples*:
>Skiing is fun.
>She enjoys snowboarding.
>She often thinks about sledding.

Gerund Phrase

A phrase centered on an *-ing* form of a verb used as a noun.

>*Examples:*
>Simple: Skiing difficult trails is fun.
>Complex: We discussed the grooming of the horses.

Helping Verb

A verb used with another verb. Helping verbs create various grammatical structures or provide additional shades of meaning.

>*Examples:*
>Primary: be, do, have
>   I am running. He did not run. She has run.
>Modal: can, could, may, might, must, shall, should, will, would
>   We must go to the bank. He should take his medicine.

Hypothetical Subjunctive

Subjunctive form that indicates unlikely or unreal conditions. This form is used in some cases after the words *if, as if,* or *as though*, or with the verb *to wish*. The Hypothetical Subjunctive is equivalent to the Simple Past tense of every verb, except the verb *to be*: the Hypothetical Subjunctive of *be* is *were* for every subject. See Subjunctive Mood.

>*Example:*
>If he were in better shape, he would win the race.

Idiom

An expression that has a unique form. Idioms do not follow general rules; rather, they must simply be memorized.

If–Then Statement

A sentence that contains both a condition (marked by an *if*) and a result (possibly marked by a *then*). Either the condition or the result may come first. The verbs in if–then statements follow particular patterns of tense and mood.

>*Examples*:
>If he were in better shape, he would win the race.
>They get sick if they eat dairy products.
>If she swims, then she will win.

Imperative Mood

The form of a verb that expresses direct commands. Identical to the bare form of the verb as well as to the Command Subjunctive. See <u>Mood</u>.

Example:
<u>Go</u> to the store and <u>buy</u> me an ice cream cone.

Indefinite Pronoun

A pronoun that does not refer to a specific noun. Most indefinite pronouns are singular:

anyone, anybody, anything	no one, nobody, nothing
each, every (as pronouns)	someone, somebody, something
everyone, everybody, everything	whatever, whoever
either, neither *(may require a plural verb if paired with or/nor)*	

A few indefinite pronouns are always plural:
both, few, many, several

The SANAM pronouns can be either singular or plural, depending on the noun in the *of*-phrase that follows the pronoun.
some, any, none, all, more/most

Independent Clause

A clause that can stand alone as a grammatical sentence. Contains its own subject and verb. Also known as a <u>Main Clause</u>.

Indicative Mood

The form of a verb that expresses facts or beliefs. Most verbs in most English sentences are in the indicative mood. See <u>Mood</u>.

Examples:
I <u>went</u> to the store and <u>bought</u> an ice cream cone.
I <u>will do</u> so again.

Indirect Object

The noun that expresses the recipient or the beneficiary of some action. Can be a pronoun, a noun phrase, or a noun clause.

Examples:
I gave <u>him</u> the lamp.
She found <u>the man</u> a good book.

Infinitive

The bare form of the verb plus the marker *to*. Used as a noun or as a modifier within a sentence.

> *Examples*:
> I prefer <u>to read</u> novels.
> She drove many miles <u>to see</u> her uncle.

-ing Form

The bare form of the verb plus the ending *-ing*. When used as a noun, the *-ing* form is called a gerund. When used as a modifier or as part of the progressive tense, the *-ing* form is called a present participle.

> Present Participle (part of verb): I am <u>eating</u> an apple.
> Gerund (noun): <u>Eating</u> an apple is good for you.
> Present Participle (noun modifier): The man <u>eating</u> an apple is my friend.
> Present Participle (verb modifier): I sat on the porch, <u>eating</u> an apple.

Intransitive Verb

A verb that does not take a direct object. Intransitive verbs cannot be put in the passive voice.

> *Examples*:
> The driver <u>swerved</u>. I <u>went</u> to the library.
> (Intransitive verb *-ing* forms followed by nouns are usually adjectives: *The <u>swerving driver</u> wound up on the sidewalk.*)

Linking Verb

A verb that expresses what a subject is, rather than what it does. The most important linking verb is *to be*.

Main Clause

A clause that can stand alone as a grammatical sentence. A main clause contains its own subject and verb, and is not introduced by a subordinator. Also known as an <u>Independent Clause</u>.

> *Examples:*
> <u>I prefer to read novels</u>.
> While eating lunch, <u>she finished reading the report</u>.

Middleman

Words that the GMAT inserts between the subject and the verb to hide the subject. Middlemen are usually modifiers of various types.

Misplaced Modifier

A noun modifier that is not positioned next to the noun it needs to describe in the sentence. Misplaced modifiers are incorrect. See Modifier.

Example:
I collapsed onto the sofa, underline exhausted by a long day of work.
(The modifier *exhausted by a long day of work* refers to the nearest noun, *sofa*, but a sofa can't be exhausted. The modifier needs to be placed as close as possible to the noun it modifies: *Exhausted by a long day of work, I collapsed on the sofa*.)

Modal Helping Verb

See Helping Verb.

Modifier

Words, phrases or clauses that describe other parts of the sentence. Noun modifiers modify nouns. Adverbial modifiers modify anything other than nouns (verbs, clauses, adjectives, etc.).

Mood

The form of the verb that indicates the attitude of the speaker toward the action.

Examples:
Indicative: I drive fast cars. We drove to Las Vegas.
Imperative: Drive three blocks and turn left.
Command Subjunctive: I suggested that he drive three blocks.
Hypothetical Subjunctive: If he drove three blocks, he would see us.

Nonessential Modifier

A modifier that provides extra information. If this modifier were removed from the sentence, the core meaning of the sentence would still make sense. Use commas to separate a nonessential modifier from the modified noun. See Modifier.

Example:
I want to sell this beat-up old car, which my sister drove to the city.

Noun

A word that means a thing or a person. Nouns can be the subject of a verb, the direct or indirect object of a verb, or the object of a preposition. Nouns can be modified by an adjective or another noun modifier.

Noun Clause

A subordinate clause (with its own subject and verb) that acts as a noun in the sentence. That is, it is the subject of a verb, the object of a verb, or the object of a preposition. Led by relative pronouns *which, what, when, why, whether,* or *that*.

Examples:
I care about what he thinks.
Whether I stay or go is unimportant.
I believe that you are right.

Noun Modifier

A word, phrase, or clause that describes a noun.

Examples:
Adjective: <u>This big</u> window needs replacing.
Past Participle: <u>Broken in the storm</u>, this window needs replacing.
Present Participle: The window <u>rattling against the sill</u> needs replacing.
Prepositional Phrase: The window <u>on the right</u> needs replacing.
Appositive: This window, <u>an original installation</u>, needs replacing.
Infinitive: The window <u>to replace</u> is on the second floor.
Relative Clause: The window <u>that needs replacing</u> has a missing pane.

Noun Phrase

A phrase that acts as a noun in the sentence. A noun phrase typically consists of a noun and its modifiers.

Example:
<u>A new government survey of taxpayers</u> is planned.
(The subject of the sentence is the noun phrase consisting of the noun *survey* and its modifiers: *a, new, government, of taxpayers.*)

Noun-Adjective

A noun that is placed in front of another noun and that functions as an adjective.

Example:
A <u>government</u> survey; The <u>stone</u> wall
(*A government survey* is a type of survey; a *stone wall* is a type of wall.)

Object Case

The form of a pronoun used as the object of a verb or of a preposition. Nouns do not change form in the object case. See <u>Case</u>.

Parallel Element

A part of a sentence made parallel to another part or parts of the sentence through the use of parallel markers.

Example:
We will invite both <u>his friends</u> and <u>her family</u>.

Parallel Marker

The words that link or contrast parts of a sentence, forcing them to be parallel.

Example:
We will invite both his friends <u>and</u> her family.

Parallelism Category

A type of word, phrase, or clause. Something in one parallelism category can be made parallel to something else of the same type, but it should not be made parallel to anything in another category.

Examples:

Concrete Nouns: I like to eat <u>peanut butter</u> and <u>ice cream.</u>

Action Nouns and Complex Gerunds: I like to watch <u>the release of the doves</u> and <u>the changing of the guard</u>.

Simple Gerunds: I like <u>eating ice cream</u> and <u>watching birds</u>.

Working Verbs: I <u>like</u> ice cream but <u>hate</u> sorbet.

Infinitives: I like <u>to eat</u> ice cream and <u>to watch</u> birds.

Adjectives and Participles: I like ice cream, either <u>frozen</u> or <u>warm</u>.

Clauses: She knows <u>that I like ice cream</u> and <u>that I hate sorbet</u>.

Parts of Speech

The basic kinds of words. A word's part of speech is determined both by what the word means and by what role or roles the word can play in a sentence.

Examples:

Noun: peanut, lake, vacuum, considerations, opportunity

Verb: swim, proceed, execute, went, should

Adjective: wonderful, blue, the, helpful

Adverb: slowly, very, graciously

Preposition: of, for, by, with, through, during, in, on

Conjunction: and, but, or, although because

Participle

One of two kinds of words derived from verbs. Present participles typically end in *-ing* and can be used as a verb, a noun, a noun modifier, or a verb modifier. Present participles typically indicate ongoing action (though not necessarily in the present). Past participles typically end in *-ed* and can be used as a verb or a noun modifier. Past participles tend to indicate a completed action relative to the given time frame in the sentence.

Examples:

Present Participle: hiking, growing, doing

She will be <u>hiking</u> next week. <u>Studying</u> for the GMAT is fun. He slipped on the ice, <u>injuring</u> his ankle.

Past Participle: hiked, grown, done

The tires will be <u>punctured</u>. The tires were <u>punctured</u>. <u>Punctured</u> by a nail, the tire slowly deflated.

Passive Voice

The form of a verb in which the subject is receiving the action expressed by the verb.

Examples:

The driver <u>was thrown</u> from the car.

The crystal vases <u>have been broken</u> by the thieves.

Past Participle

The participle used in perfect tenses and passive voice. A past participle may also be used as an adjective. Past participles tend to indicate completed action, although not necessarily in the past (relative to now).

Examples:

The tires will be <u>punctured</u>. They have <u>broken</u> the lamp. A <u>frozen</u> lake.

(Regular past participles are formed by adding *-d* or *-ed* to the base form of the verb. Many irregular past participles are listed below, together with irregular past-tense forms. Sometimes the past-tense form and the past participle are identical. Non-native English speakers should study this list. Native English speakers already know these forms intuitively.)

Base Form	Past Tense	Past Participle	Base Form	Past Tense	Past Participle
be	was, were	been	lose	lost	lost
become	became	become	make	made	made
begin	began	begun	pay	paid	paid
break	broke	broken	put	put	put
bring	brought	brought	rise	risen	risen
build	built	built	say	said	said
buy	bought	bought	see	saw	seen
catch	caught	caught	seek	sought	sought
choose	chose	chosen	sell	sold	sold
come	came	come	send	sent	sent
cost	cost	cost	set	set	set
cut	cut	cut	show	showed	shown
do	did	done	shrink	shrank	shrunk
draw	drew	drawn	speak	spoke	spoken
drive	drove	driven	spend	spent	spent
eat	ate	eaten	spread	spread	spread
fall	fell	fallen	stand	stood	stood
fight	fought	fought	steal	stole	stolen
find	found	found	strike	struck	struck
forget	forgot	forgotten	sweep	swept	swept
freeze	froze	frozen	take	took	taken
give	gave	given	teach	taught	taught
go	went	gone	tell	told	told
grow	grew	grown	think	thought	thought
hold	held	held	throw	threw	thrown
keep	kept	kept	understand	understood	understood
know	knew	known	win	won	won
lead	led	led	write	wrote	written

Past Perfect Tense

The form of a verb that expresses action that takes place before another past action or time. The past perfect tense is formed with the verb *had* and the past participle.

Examples:

The officer said that the driver <u>had swerved</u>.

By 2005, she <u>had visited</u> India three times.

Past Tense

The form of a verb that expresses action in the past. See <u>Tense</u>.

Examples:

The driver <u>swerved</u>.

The tires <u>were punctured</u>.

They <u>broke</u> the lamp.

(Common irregular past tense forms are listed under the entry for <u>Past Participles</u>.)

Person

Indicates whether the word refers to the speaker or writer (first person), the listener or reader (second person), or someone/something else (third person). Personal pronouns are marked for person. Present tense verbs in the third person singular add an -*s*: *the doctor writes*.

Examples:

First person: I, me, my, we, us, our

Second person: you, your

Third person: she, he, it, its, they, them, their

Phrase

A group of words that has a particular grammatical role in the sentence. The type of phrase is often determined by one main word within the phrase. A phrase can contain other phrases. For instance, a noun phrase can contain a prepositional phrase.

Examples:

Noun phrase: <u>The short **chapter** at the end of the book</u> is important.

Verb phrase: The computer <u>must have been **broken**</u> in the move.

Adjective phrase: The employee <u>most **reluctant** to volunteer</u> was chosen.

Prepositional phrase: The wolf <u>**in** the cage</u> has woken up.

Plural

A category of number that indicates more than one. Nouns, pronouns, and verbs can be made plural. See <u>Singular</u>.

Examples:

<u>Many dogs are</u> barking; <u>they are</u> keeping me awake.

Possessive Case

The form of a pronoun or a noun that owns another noun. In possessive case, nouns add -'s or -s'. See Case.

Preposition

A word that indicates a relationship between the object (usually a noun) and something else in the sentence. In some cases, prepositions can consist of more than one word.

> *Examples:*
> of, in, to, for, with, on, by, at, from, as, into, about, like, after
> between, through, over, against, under, out of, next to, upon

Prepositional, Phrase

A prepositional phrase consists of a preposition and an object (a noun). The preposition indicates a relationship between that object and something else in the sentence.

> *Examples:*
> I would like a drink of water. (*Of* is the preposition; *of water* modifies *drink*.)
> The man in the gray suit is the CEO. (*In* is the preposition; *in the gray suit* modifies *man*)

Present Participle

The participle used in progressive tenses. A present participle may also be used as a noun, a noun modifier, or a verb modifier. Present participles tend to indicate ongoing action, although not necessarily at the present moment. To form a present participle, add -*ing* to the base form of the verb, possibly doubling the last consonant.

> *Examples:*
> The tires were rolling.
> Jump in that swimming pool.
> Hiking is great.

Present Perfect Tense

The form of a verb that expresses action that begins in the past and continues to the present or whose effect continues to the present. The present perfect tense is formed with the verb *has* or *have* and the past participle.

> *Examples:*
> The tires have been punctured. (The tires were punctured in the past, and it is still true in the present that they were punctured.)
> You have broken my lamp! (The lamp was broken in the past, and it is still broken now.)

Present Tense

The form of a verb that expresses action in the present. The simple present (non-progressive) often indicates general truths. See Tense.

Examples:
The driver <u>swerves</u>.
The tires <u>are</u> on the car.
They <u>speak</u> English.

Primary Helping Verb

See <u>Helping Verb</u>.

Progressive Tense

The form of a verb that expresses ongoing action in the past, present, or future. See <u>Tense</u>.

Examples:
The driver <u>is swerving</u>.
The tires <u>were rolling</u>.
They <u>will be running</u>.

Pronoun

A pronoun stands in for another noun elsewhere in the sentence or for an implied noun. The noun is called the antecedent. For example, in the sentence "When Amy fell, she hurt her knee," the pronoun *she* refers to the antecedent *Amy*.

Examples:
When it started to rain, the tourists pulled out <u>their</u> umbrellas. (*Their* refers to *tourists*.)
The term bibliophile refers to <u>someone who</u> loves books. (*Someone* is a pronoun but does not need to have a specific antecedent; *who* refers to *someone*.)

Relative Clause

A subordinate clause headed by a relative pronoun. Relative clauses may act as noun modifiers or, more infrequently, as nouns.

Examples:
The professor <u>who spoke</u> is my mother.
<u>What you see</u> is <u>what you get</u>.

Relative Pronoun

A pronoun that connects a subordinate clause to a sentence. The relative pronoun plays a grammatical role in the subordinate clause (e.g., subject, verb object, or prepositional object). If the relative clause is a noun modifier, the relative pronoun also refers to the modified noun. If the relative clause is a noun clause, then the relative pronoun does not refer to a noun outside the relative clause.

Examples:

The professor <u>who</u> spoke is my mother.

(The relative pronoun *who* is the subject of the clause *who spoke*. *Who* also refers to *professor*, the noun modified by the clause *who spoke*.)

<u>What you see</u> is a disaster waiting to happen.

The relative pronoun *what* is the object of the clause *what you see*. *What* does not refer to a noun outside the clause; rather, the clause *what you see* is the subject of the sentence.

Reporting Verb

A verb, such as *indicate, claim, announce,* or *report,* that in fact reports or otherwise includes a thought or belief. A reporting verb should be followed by *that* on the GMAT.

Example:

The survey <u>indicates</u> that CFOs are feeling pessimistic.

Run-on Sentence

A sentence incorrectly formed out of two main clauses joined without proper punctuation or a proper connecting word, such as a coordinator or subordinator.

Example:

The film was great, I want to see it again.

(This sentence could be fixed with a semicolon as follows: *The film was great; I want to see it again.* Alternately, the two clauses could be joined by a coordinating conjunction: *The film was great and I want to see it again.* Finally, one of the clauses could be made into a subordinate clause: *Because the film was great, I want to see it again.*)

SANAM Pronouns

An indefinite pronoun that can be either singular or plural, depending on the object of the *of*-phrase that follows. The SANAM pronouns are *some, any, none, all, more/most.*

Examples:

<u>Some</u> of the milk <u>has</u> gone bad.

<u>Some</u> of the children <u>are</u> angry.

Sentence

A complete grammatical utterance. Sentences contain a subject and a verb in a main clause. Some sentences contain two main clauses linked by a coordinating conjunction, such as *and*. Other sentences contain subordinate clauses tied to the main clause in some way.

Examples:

My boss is angry.

(This sentence contains one main clause. The subject is *boss*; the verb is *is*.)

He read my blog, and he saw the photos that I posted.

(This sentence contains two main clauses linked by *and*. In the first main clause, the subject is *he*; the verb is *read*. In the second main clause, the subject is *he*; the verb is *saw*. There is also a subordinate clause, *that I posted*, led by the relative pronoun *that*.)

Simple Gerund

A gerund is an *-ing* form of a verb used that functions as a noun. A simple gerund typically does not include an article or something similar (as a complex gerund does).

Examples:

<u>Swimming</u> is fun.

She likes <u>running</u> and <u>hiking</u>.

(In general, simple gerunds should not be put in parallel with action nouns. Complex gerunds can be put in parallel with action nouns. See <u>Complex Gerund</u>.)

Singular

A category of number that indicates one. Nouns, pronouns, and verbs can be made singular. See <u>Plural</u>.

Example:

<u>A</u> <u>dog</u> <u>is</u> barking; <u>it</u> <u>is</u> keeping <u>me</u> awake.

State Verb

A verb that expresses a condition of the subject, rather than an action that the subject performs. State verbs are rarely used in progressive tenses.

Examples:

Her assistant <u>knows</u> Russian.

I <u>love</u> chocolate.

This word <u>means</u> "hello."

Subgroup Modifier

A type of modifier that describes a smaller subset within the group expressed by the modified noun.

Example:

French wines, <u>many of which I have tasted</u>, are superb.

Subject

The noun or pronoun that goes with the verb and that is required in every sentence. The subject performs the action expressed by an active-voice verb; in contrast, the subject receives the action expressed by a passive-voice verb. The subject and the verb must agree in number and in person.

Examples:

The <u>market</u> closed.

<u>She</u> is considering a new job.

<u>They</u> have been seen.

Subjunctive Mood

One of two verb forms indicating desires, suggestions, or unreal or unlikely conditions.

Examples:

Command Subjunctive: She requested that he <u>stop</u> the car.

Hypothetical Subjunctive: If he <u>were</u> in charge, he would help us.

Subordinate Clause

A clause that cannot stand alone without a main or independent clause. A subordinate clause is led by a subordinator. Also known as a dependent clause. See <u>Clause</u>.

Examples:

Her dog, <u>which is brown</u>, is friendly.

<u>Although he barely studied</u>, he scored well on the test.

Subordinator

A word that creates a subordinate clause.

Examples:

Relative Pronoun: which, that, who, whose, whom, what

Subordinating Conjunction: although, because, while, whereas

Superlative Form

Form of adjectives and adverbs used to compare three or more things or people. The reference group may be implied. Regular superlative forms are either the base word plus *-est* (if the base is short, e.g., *greenest*) or the base word preceded by *most* (*most intelligent*). Irregulars are listed below:

Adjective or Adverb	Superlative
good/well	best
bad/badly	worst
much, many	most
little	least
far	farthest, furthest

Tense

The form of the verb that indicates the time of the action (relative to the present time). The completed or ongoing nature of the action may also be indicated.

Examples:

Present: She <u>speaks</u> French.

Past: She <u>spoke</u> French.

Future: She <u>will speak</u> French.

Present Progressive: She <u>is speaking</u> French.

Past Progressive: She <u>was speaking</u> French.

Future Progressive: She <u>will be speaking</u> French.

Present Perfect: She <u>has spoken</u> French.

Past Perfect: She <u>had spoken</u> French.

That **Clause**

A clause that begins with the word *that*.

Examples:

Relative Clause: The suggestion <u>that he made</u> is bad.

(The clause *that he made* modifies *suggestion*. *That* is the object of the clause. In other words, *he made that = the suggestion*.)

Subordinate Clause: He suggested <u>that the world is flat</u>.

(The clause *that the world is flat* is the object of the verb *suggested*.)

Subordinate Clause: The suggestion <u>that the world is flat</u> is bad.

(The clause *that the world is flat* modifies *suggestion*. However, *that* is not the object of the clause, nor is it the subject. Rather, *that* provides a way for the idea in the sentence *the world is flat* to be linked to *the suggestion*.)

Transitive Verb

A verb that takes a direct object. Transitive verbs can usually be put in the passive voice, which turns the object into the subject.

Examples:

The agent <u>observed</u> the driver. The driver <u>was observed</u> by the agent.

(Transitive verb *-ing* forms followed by nouns are usually simple gerund phrases: *The agent was paid for <u>observing the driver.</u>* Some verbs can be either transitive or intransitive. In particular, verbs that indicate changes of state can be either: *The lamp <u>broke</u>. I <u>broke</u> the lamp.* This duality means that some *-ing* forms in isolation can be ambiguous. The phrase *melting snow* could mean "the act of causing snow to melt" or "snow that is melting." Use context to resolve the ambiguity.)

Uncountable Noun

A noun that cannot be counted in English. For instance, you cannot say *one patience, two patiences, three patiences*. Most uncountable nouns exist only in the singular form and cannot be made plural.

> *Examples:*
> patience, furniture, milk, information, rice, chemistry

Verb

The word or words that express the action of the sentence. The verb indicates the time of the action (tense), the attitude of the speaker (mood), and the role of the subject (voice). The verb may also reflect the number and person of the subject. Every sentence must have a verb.

Verb Modifier

A word, phrase, or clause that describes a verb.

> *Examples:*
> Adverb: He walked <u>quickly</u>.
> Prepositional Phrase: He walked <u>toward the building</u>.
> Subordinate Clause: He walked <u>because he was thirsty</u>.
> Present Participle: He walked ahead, <u>swinging</u> his arms.
> Infinitive: He walked <u>to buy</u> a drink.
> Preposition + Simple Gerund: He walked <u>by putting</u> one foot in front of the other.

Verbal

A word or phrase that is derived from a verb and that functions as a different part of speech in the sentence: as a noun, as an adjective (noun modifier), or as an adverb (verb modifier).

> *Examples:*
> Infinitive: He likes <u>to walk</u> to the store.
> Gerund: I enjoy <u>walking</u>.
> Present Participle: She is on a <u>walking</u> tour.
> Past Participle: The facts <u>given</u> in the case are clear.

Voice

The form of the verb that indicates the role of the subject as performer of the action (active voice) or recipient of the action (passive voice).

> *Examples:*
> Active Voice: She <u>threw</u> the ball.
> Passive Voice: The ball <u>was thrown</u> by her.

Warmup

Words that the GMAT inserts at the beginning of the sentence to hide the subject in question. Warmups are either modifiers of various types or "frame sentences" (that is, you really care about the subject of a subordinate clause, not the subject of the main clause).

<u>Working Verb</u>

A verb that could be the main verb of a grammatical sentence. A working verb shows tense, mood, and voice, as well as number and person in some circumstances. The use of this term helps to distinguish working verbs from verbals, which cannot by themselves be the main verb of a sentence.